Teachings from the American Earth

Teachings from the American Earth

Indian Religion and Philosophy

edited by

Dennis Tedlock and Barbara Tedlock

Liveright   New York

Copyright © 1975 by Dennis Tedlock and Barbara Tedlock

Library of Congress Cataloging in Publication Data

Tedlock, Dennis, 1939–   comp.
    Teachings from the American earth.

    Includes bibliographical references.
    CONTENTS: Introduction.—Seeing and curing.—[etc.]
    1. Indians of North America—Religion and mythology
—Addresses, essays, lectures. I. Tedlock, Barbara,
joint comp. II. Title.
E98.R3T42 1975   299′.7   74–34146
ISBN 0–87140–559–7
ISBN 0–87140–097–9 pbk.

This book was designed by Madelaine Caldiero.

Typefaces in this book are Times Roman and Cheltenham Bold Extra Condensed.
It was manufactured by Vail-Ballou Press, Inc.

All Rights Reserved
Published simultaneously in Canada by
George J. McLeod Limited, Toronto

PRINTED IN THE UNITED STATES OF AMERICA

7 8 9 0

Ho'na aalhasshinaawe aawan.
For all our elders.

Contents

PREFACE   *ix*

INTRODUCTION (BY THE EDITORS)   *xi*

Part One: Seeing and Curing

1   The Career of a Medicine-Man
     Isaac Tens, through Marius Barbeau   *3*

2   A Shaman's Journey to the Sea Spirit Takánakapsâluk
     Knud Rasmussen   *13*

3   Hanblecheyapi: Crying for a Vision
     Black Elk, through Joseph Epes Brown   *20*

4   The Salt Pilgrimage
     Ruth Underhill   *42*

5   The Doctrine of the Ghost Dance
     James Mooney   *75*

6   The Peyote Way
     J. S. Slotkin   *96*

7   The Clown's Way
     Barbara Tedlock   *105*

Part Two: Thinking About the World

8   An American Indian Model of the Universe
     Benjamin Lee Whorf   *121*

9   Linguistic Reflection of Wintu Thought
    Dorothy Lee   130

10 Ojibwa Ontology, Behavior, and World View
    A. Irving Hallowell   141

11 The Tewa World View
    Alfonso Ortiz   179

12 The Inner Eye of Shamanism and Totemism
    Robin Ridington and Tonia Ridington   190

13 Oglala Metaphysics
    *Sword, Finger, One-Star, and Tyon, through
    J. R. Walker*   205

14 Monotheism Among American Indians
    Paul Radin   219

15 An American Indian View of Death
    Dennis Tedlock   248

INDEX   272

Preface

One thing unites all the authors represented here: they are either Indians who have tried to make themselves heard, or whites who have tried to hear Indians and were changed by this experience. For us, finding authors of this kind was more important than attempting a systematic coverage of the continent. Our own understanding of American Indian religion and philosophy is still far from complete. We have benefited most from pondering the spoken words of Andrew Peynetsa, Dennis Peynetsa, Alfonso Ortiz, Larry Bird, Essie Parish, Lame Deer, and Beeman Logan.

Introduction

By Dennis Tedlock and Barbara Tedlock

The American Indian has already taught us a great deal, whether we remember it or not. In the far north of this continent, life is still dependent in part on the technology of the Eskimo and Indian, who gave us among other things the parka, snowshoe, toboggan, and kayak. Maize, potatoes, sweet potatoes, and manioc, which today make up more than half the world's tonnage of staple foods, were first domesticated in the New World. Most modern cotton, including that grown in the Old World, is the long-staple cotton of the American Indian. Some 220 American Indian drugs have been or still are official in the *Pharmacopeia of the United States of America* or the *National Formulary*. Even in these practical areas, we have sometimes been slow to learn. As recently as thirty years ago, Indian oral contraceptives were dismissed as mere magic; later, when these same botanical drugs were found to suppress ovulation, they set medical researchers on the road to ''the pill.'' [1]

Although we have accepted a great deal of technology from the American Indian, we have not yet learned his more difficult lessons, lessons about the mind and spirit. Some of these lessons concern the very things we have borrowed, as in the case of that most famous of Indian stimulants, tobacco. For the Indian, tobacco always had a sacramental meaning: the smoke was exhaled east and west, north and south, above and below, and then the smoker blew smoke on himself. In this way he joined the self with the cosmos. When we adopted tobacco we turned it into a personal habit, and we have overused it to the point where it has killed many of us. The final irony is that there should be a righteous public campaign against this sacred gift of America, as if there were something inherently wrong with smoking. Beeman Logan, a Seneca medicine man, suggests that the trouble is with ourselves: tobacco kills us, he says, because we do not respect it.

An easy way of reading Logan's message is to say that the Indian has a different relationship to the natural world than we do. If he can "respect" a plant, he must be "closer" to nature than we are, and we imagine ourselves more like him in our own distant past, before we started to dominate nature. Those of us who are believers in material progress see our task as elevating the Indian to our level by teaching him how to make nature better serve material ends. If, on the other hand, we are suspicious of material progress, we envy the Indian and wish that we could somehow "return to nature," suspecting all the while that there is really no way to recover our own innocence. The trouble with both of these views is that they allow us to picture the living Indian as a fossil from which to learn about the past. If there are any lessons to be had about the present, we think they are ours to teach him, whether we wish to initiate him into the present or to warn him away from it "for his own good."

There is quite another way to approach Logan's message, and that is to defer the question of its meaning and call attention instead to a supposed error in the thought process which produced it. From the point of view of Lucien Lévy-Bruhl, it would be argued that the Indian's characteristic *participation mystique,* his feeling of one-ness with the world, has here blinded him to the difference between himself and the tobacco plant. If he only had a "logical" mind, he could see that a plant is an inanimate object and is neither owed respect nor able to punish. From the more recent point of view of Claude Lévi-Strauss, the supposed error is not in a lack of logic but in an overzealous and premature application of it, which in this case seeks to link facts from the disparate realms of psychology (the attitude of "respect") and biology (tobacco and death) in a single system of cause and effect.

All of the approaches presented so far permit us to sidestep the possibility of learning directly from the Indian. It is true that anthropologists sometimes describe themselves as students of the Indian; they may indeed appear to be his students while they are in the field, but by the time they publish their "results," it is usually clear that the Indian is primarily an *object* of study. If anthropologists would seriously put themselves in the position of being the Indian's students, they would have to take more seriously what he considers to be important. But instead of learning to experience respect for tobacco, for example, they simply wish to find an explanation for why someone like Beeman Logan might respect it, thereby keeping him and his lesson at arm's length. They may listen to him, but they do not hear him.

In order to become the Indian's students, we have to recognize that some of what he has to teach transcends cultural or historical boundaries. Paul Radin took precisely this position with respect to American Indian religion, saying that we would never make any progress in our understanding "until scholars rid themselves, once and for all, of the curious notion that everything possesses an evolutionary history; until they realize that certain ideas and certain concepts are . . . ultimate for man." [2] Mircea Eliade, in his classic study of shamanism, puts the matter this way: "The various types of civilization are, of course, organically connected with certain religious forms; but this in no sense excludes the spontaneity and, in the last analysis, the ahistoricity of religious life." [3] And the Sioux holy man Lame Deer, fully aware of the diversity of external religious forms among American Indians, says, "I think when it comes right down to it, all the Indian religions are somehow part of the same belief, the same mystery." [4]

The realm that Radin, Eliade, and Lame Deer all have in mind is open to all men in all places at all times, but it is also universally hard to talk about in ordinary language. Carlos Castaneda has called it "nonordinary" or "separate" reality, as opposed to "ordinary" reality. The Hopis refer to it as *'a'ne himu,* "Mighty Something." It is open to what Martin Heidegger calls *contemplative* as opposed to *calculative* thought, or thinking that is oriented toward meaning as opposed to thinking that is oriented toward results. One must "release oneself into nearness" rather than propel oneself at a definite target, or, as a Papago relating his vision quest puts it, "I somehow tried to move toward my desire." [5] For the American Indian in general, it is a world composed entirely of persons, as opposed to the everyday world of ego and object. For the Hopi, Tewa, Zuñi, and Wintu it is the realm of soft, unripe, unmanifest essence, as opposed to hard, ripe, manifest form. Its location in space, for the Eskimo, Beaver, Sioux, Hopi, Tewa, and many others, is above and below the horizontal plane of our everyday world, and it is reached through a vertical axis that passes through the seeker. For the Sioux, Hopi, Tewa, and Papago, it is also encountered at the periphery of the horizontal plane. In these upper, lower, and peripheral regions, linear, historical, irreversible time gives way to a time which is far in the "past" when viewed "objectively," but the very present moment when experienced. [6]

Sometimes the entering of this other world just happens. Black Elk, a Sioux, had his first and greatest vision during a childhood illness. Don Talayesva blundered into a Hopi shrine as a boy and was captured by the being who lived there. [7] Isaac Tens, a Gitksan, was out cutting wood one evening when a loud noise carried him into the other world. More commonly, the experience must be sought. In some ways of seeking, the mind is prepared with drugs. In the contemporary Native American Church, the peyote cactus is used as a sacrament, and in various Southwestern and California tribes, it is the Jimsonweed that shows the way to the other world. The Papago use tobacco as a path, following the exhaled smoke with their thoughts.

An Ojibwa shaman in a clear sky with the moon and stars. There are several skies, one above the other, represented here by concentric circles. The lines from the man's head are the power that enables him to enter the skies, power received through his membership in the Midewiwin, or "Grand Medicine Society." Engraving on birch bark, from Bulletin 45 of the Bureau of American Ethnology, p. 72.

Whether or not drugs are used, the body and mind must be purified or emptied. A Sioux, for example, must take a sweat bath before his vision quest, and the Peyotist must bathe and put on clean clothes. Both the Sioux and Papago fast from food and water; the Peyotist is purged of whatever is in him by his sacrament, which may cause him to vomit. The mind must be set upon the sacred task itself and emptied of all else; as Black Elk says, the seeker "must be careful lest distracting thoughts come to him." The Papago on a pilgrimage even ties up his hair so that he will not distract himself or others by having to brush it back from his face in the wind; he must concentrate on the rules of the journey and give no thought to home. In this emptying of the everyday mind, the seeker humbles himself; in the words of Black Elk, he must see himself as "lower than even the smallest ant." This means that he must let go of the self, which belongs to the calculative world of ego and object. He experiences this letting go as death itself; as Lame Deer puts it, "You go up on that hill to die."

The death which opens the way to the other world requires a special setting. The Zuñi priest, when he seeks contact with the rainmakers of the world-encircling ocean, secludes himself in a windowless room, four rooms removed from any outside door. The Eskimo shaman who seeks to travel to the bottom of the sea puts himself behind a curtain in the sleeping place of a darkened house. Participants in the Ghost Dance of the Plains, seeking visions of their lost relatives, moved in a circle on consecrated ground just outside the camp. The members of the Native American Church, though they live in modern houses, set up a tipi for their visions of Jesus, the Peyote Spirit, and the Water Bird. The Sioux, seeking the knowledge of the oneness of all things, goes away to a mountaintop and places himself within a sacred circle. The Papago salt pilgrim travels on foot and horseback all the way to the edge of the world and even beyond, walking into the ocean until four waves have broken behind him.

The experience itself is difficult to translate without destroying its nature, for ordinary language belongs to the world of the self and is concerned with the differentiation of the multitude of objects. Black Elk puts the matter this way: "While I stood there I saw more than I can tell and I understood more than I saw; for I was seeing in a sacred manner the shapes of all things in the spirit, and the shape of all shapes as they must live together like one being." [8] One approach to this problem of inexpressibility is to *approximate* the experience of oneness by using language in a way that draws the speaker and his subject closer together than they would ordinarily be. The nouns that best express a speaker's nearness to his subject are those of blood relationship. The seeker, as Black Elk says, must "know that all things are our relatives," and he must use terms of relationship whether he is talking about a coyote, a willow, a lump of salt, the earth, or the sun. The verbs that draw speaker and subject most strongly together are those of being and becoming. An Ojibwa, describing what happened during a boyhood fast, says that when he discovered that his own body was covered with feathers, he realized that he had *become* an eagle. Black Elk, speaking of a visionary encounter with the Spirit of Earth, says, "I stared at him, for it seemed I knew him somehow; and as I stared, he slowly changed, for he was growing backwards into youth, and when he had become a boy, I knew that he was myself." [9]

The vision itself may provide the seeker with the voice of its own expression, but this will be in chant or song rather than in the plainspoken word. The songs are not merely ordinary descriptions set to music; instead, the words may give brief, enigmatic sketches which evoke a whole vision. Here is the song of a returned Papago salt pilgrim:

> The ocean water hurts my heart.
> Beautiful clouds bring rain upon our fields.

Some of the words may be archaic, or the whole song may seem to be in another language. The syllables of the words may be embedded in other syllables which are meaningless, or the entire song may be in nonsense syllables. Archaic language, foreign language, and these meaningless syllables—or better, abstract syllables—all share an otherness. The singer knows what is meant; may even, as

in the case of Isaac Tens, keep the meaning in his mind while singing aloud the "nonsense." This is a noncalculative use of language, a way of communicating directly the joy and strangeness of
the other world without explaining it away in ordinary language. As
the Kashia Pomo healer Essie Parish puts it, "I speak another language so that the people will understand."

Some visionaries, instead of expressing the enigmatic quality
of the other world by using strange language or nonlanguage, take
ordinary language and break it in half, separating the words from
their meanings and putting them back together again the wrong way
around. Then, whatever they may seem to be saying, they mean
just the opposite. If they say "Turn to the left," they mean, "Turn
to the right." This is the way of the sacred clown of the Plains and
Southwestern tribes.

Another way of talking about the experience of the other world
is to give *names* to its enigmatic qualities, names which will evoke
these qualities when the experiencer speaks them. If a name of this
kind is further understood to be that of a person, a *blood relative* of
the other world, then it simultaneously expresses the strangeness of
that world and the seeker's own nearness to all things when he is in
that world. These are the names of God.

There is *Tirawa* of the Pawnee, who is a mighty power in
human form, yet cannot be seen or heard or felt except through sixteen lesser powers, especially Wind, Cloud, Lightning, and Thunder.[10] There is *Wakan Tanka* of the Sioux, who "is like sixteen different persons; but . . . they are all only the same as one." This
same *Wakan Tanka,* in his person as *Wakinyan Tanka,* the Thunder
Being and the giver of revelation, is shapeless but winged, headless
but beaked; all of his young come from a single egg, and when he
devours them they become his many selves. Then there is
Takánakapsâluk of the Eskimo, who sends all the worst misfortunes to mankind but also sends all the good things of the sea, the
many animals which are her fingers. There is *Yagesatī* of the Beaver, who is both male and female, motionless but the creator of all
motion. *Poshayaank'i* of the Zuñi, who lives in a place of mists, is
"almost like a human, but he looks like fire." *Ma'ura,* the "Earth-

maker'' of the Winnebago, made man in his own image but appears only as a voice and a ray of light.

In the other world, everything is numinous, suffused with sacredness, holiness, light in proportion to the seeker's nearness to the ultimate being. The Sioux call this holiness *wakan,* the Ojibwa and other Algonkian peoples call it *manitu,* and the Iroquois call it *orenda.* Among the Zuñi it is expressed not by a word but by an affix, *te,* which may be attached to the words for ordinary actions, qualities, or objects in order to give them a cosmic dimension.

The vision of this holiness, once ended, is of no value unless something of it can be brought back into the ordinary world and kept alive there. For the Papago pilgrim, it was possible to bring back a token, a strand of seaweed, a shell, or a pebble that he noticed while he was at the edge of the world. The Plains seeker who saw an eagle in his vision might later put an eagle's head in his personal medicine bundle, or paint an eagle on his shield, or his vision might even show him directly the actual design he should paint on his shield or his drum or, in the case of the Ghost Dance, his shirt. If the use of a particular plant was suggested to him in his vision, he might later include this plant in his medicine bundle.[11] The Gitksan shaman Isaac Tens, instead of keeping objects or making paintings, held visual images of Mink, Otter, and Canoe in his mind. Over half the continent and especially in the Columbia Plateau, the seeker hopes to encounter a being of the other world who will become his lifelong guardian.[12] Everywhere the visionary hopes that songs will be sung through him, songs that he will keep with him, repeating them to himself as he lives.

A person who has these gifts from the other world can use them to help him see as he did there, to recognize manifestations of that world in this one. This ability to see what is going on in the world is the source of good fortune, of sudden strength in times of danger or uncertainty, as when a man hunts or goes to war. A person who has had an especially potent vision may be able to make *himself* a manifestation of the holiness of the other world, giving him the ability not only to see but to work a change. This is the shaman, the holy man, who uses this power to cure the sick and may even translate his visions into ceremonies that give a whole

A member of the Midewiwin in the state of being *manitu* (holy). The lines coming down to his ears represent his knowledge of the holy beings of the skies; the lines coming up are his knowledge of the secrets of the earth. Engraving on birch bark, from the 10th Annual Report of the Bureau of American Ethnology, p. 233.

group of people some access to the cosmos, some understanding, as when Black Elk dramatized his great vision in the Horse Dance. Among the Navajo, it was similarly powerful visions that gave rise to the present-day ceremonies called "sings," with their long chants and elaborate sand paintings. Throughout North America, there are secret societies in which holy men share the power of their visions with a group of initiates, sometimes their former patients: the Iroquois Society of the Mystic Animals, the Midewiwin of the Ojibwa, the numerous medicine societies of the Pueblos, and many others.[13]

But it is not enough to share the visions of others. Over much of North America, young Indians are encouraged and even expected to seek their own visionary encounters with the other world. Indeed, the seeking is a prerequisite for adulthood itself. In some tribes, the first attempt may be made as early as age five, and in most it has to be made before adolescence. Among the Beaver, in the Mackenzie Basin, boys and girls go out alone to seek direct contact with the other world through the medium of animals. Ojibwa boys go into the woods to learn "seeing and hearing," to "fill their emptiness." [14] Among the Winnebago of Wisconsin, in a series of quests, both boys and girls went out to seek the blessings of a multiplicity of beings, "the spirits . . . of the earth, those who are pinned through the earth, and those underneath the earth; and . . . all those in the waters, and all those on the sides of the earth." [15] On the Plains, both men and women fasted for visions repeatedly throughout their lives, and similar fasts took place in some of the Pueblos.[16] Among the Kwakiutl of the Northwest Coast, relationships with the beings of the other world were inherited, but even so the inheritor had to go on a fast to establish a personal acquaintance with them. Wherever there were secret societies, the initiate had to have visions of his own in order to rise to the highest ranks.

The American Indian's insistence on direct, personal religious experience remains preserved when he comes into contact with Christianity: he finds it difficult to accept experiences of the other world which are said to have happened two millenia ago and which are attested to only by a book. The Peyotist takes this problem into his own hands; as a Comanche once put it, "The White Man talks *about* Jesus; we talk *to* Jesus." Hearing this, J. S. Slotkin concluded that the Indian, epistemologically speaking, "is an individualist and empiricist; he believes only what he himself has experienced." [17]

An empirical attitude toward the other world is a difficult one to put into action. It requires an emptying of the body and the mind, a humbling of the self before all other beings, "even the smallest ant." It is not as though the Indian were "close to nature" and therefore found such an experience easier to come by than ourselves; he speaks of the journey as carrying him to "the edge of the Deep Canyon," [18] and he feels it as nothing less than death itself. While he is there he sees a universe where everything is not only animate, but a person, and not only a person but a kinsman. On his return from the journey he is reborn; he is no longer the same person he was before. Having seen for himself the reality of the other world, he now has what William Blake called "the *double* vision," as opposed to "the *single* vision" of Newton. Alfonso Ortiz describes this double vision in the teachings of his Tewa elders, who "saw the whole of life as consisting of the dual quest for wisdom and for divinity." [19] It is not that the Indian has an older, simpler view of the world, to which we as Newtonian thinkers have added another dimension, but that he has a comprehensive, double view of the world, while we have lost sight of one whole dimension.

The difference between the Indian view and our own is illustrated by an exchange which took place not long ago between an old man and a schoolboy in Montezuma Canyon on the Navajo Reservation. The boy asked where snow came from, and the old man told a long story about an ancestor who found a mysterious burning object and looked after it until some spirits came to claim it. They would not allow him to keep even a part of it, but instead put him to a series of tests. When he was successful at these tests, they promised they would throw all the ashes from their fireplace into Montezuma Canyon each year. "Sometimes they fail to keep their word, and sometimes they throw down too much; but in all, they turn their attention toward us regularly, here in Montezuma Canyon." With the story over, the boy had a retort: "It snows at Blanding, too. Why is that?" The old man quickly replied, "I don't know. You'll have to make up your own story for that." To the anthropologist who had witnessed this exchange the old man later commented that "it was too bad the boy did not understand stories," and he explained that this was not really a story about the historical origin of snow in Montezuma Canyon or in any other place, but a story about the properly reciprocal relationship between man and other beings. He attributed the boy's failure to grasp the story to the influences of white schooling.[20]

It would not have been the Indian way for the old man to have given the schoolboy a lecture about the true meaning of the story then and there, although he clearly could have. The proper exegesis of the story, if it comes, can only come from the boy's own experience in life. As Larry Bird, a young Keres, explains, "You don't ask questions when you grow up. You watch and listen and wait, and the answer will come to you. It's *yours* then, not like learning in school." What we learn in school is never ours; lectures by the experts can never produce in us the light which comes when suddenly and all alone, we know. In our growing reliance on formal education, Beeman Logan tells us, we have come to underestimate our own potential as human beings:

> You don't *respect* yourselves.
> You don't believe anything unless you can read it in a *book*.
> You have to learn to use your *eyes*.
> You have to learn to see with your eyes *shut*.

When we reflect about the way Indian religion has been studied, we can see the single vision in action. We have studied it solely with the eyes open and kept it outside. Our museums place

A Midewiwin diagram of the life road, from youth to old age. The tangents are the temptations a man encounters at sharp bends in the road. If he overcomes all seven of them, he will live to a proper old age. Engraving on birch bark, from Bulletin 45 of the Bureau of American Ethnology, p. 24.

once-sacred objects on display, so schoolchildren can examine their outward forms. Groups of hobbyists perform exact replicas of Indian ceremonies, with everything there but the meaning. Many anthropologists can only tell us that meaning lies in historical contexts, or is revealed by logical or mathematical transformations of the outward forms. All of this amounts to a hermetic seal between the Indian and ourselves. When an Indian voice penetrates this seal, whether indirectly through Joseph Epes Brown's *The Sacred Pipe,* or directly through Hyemeyohsts Storm's *Seven Arrows,* the experts do no better than quarrel about the "accuracy" of details. Vine Deloria, who has a clearer vision, comments on *Seven Arrows* as follows: "Storm in great measure succeeded in stepping outside of a time-dominated interpretation of Indian tribal religion and created a series of parabolic teachings concerning the nature of religion. Few people have understood him—or forgiven him." [21] The teachings of American Indian religion have always been parabolic; their meaning is discovered by reflection, not through historical exactness. As a Zuñi once said to an anthropologist who was carefully transcribing each word of a traditional story, "When I tell these stories, do you *see* it, or do you just write it down?"

Our road, if we now wish to hear the Indian and learn to think, to see like him, is not an easy one. Even if we succeed in abandoning a purely historical approach, there is a further pitfall. In attempting a straight intellectual experiment with Indian thought, we might assume, for the sake of argument, that "everything is alive." If we were to do that, we might get a response like the one an old Ojibwa gave the anthropologist who asked, "Are all the stones we see about us here alive?" The answer was, "No! But *some* are." [22]

This old man had the double vision. He did not live solely in the other world, where indeed *all* stones are alive, but he had the capacity to recognize that world in the appearances of this one. The way to his understanding is not found with the road maps of the measurable world. One begins by finding the four roads that run side by side and choosing the middle one. The Road, once found, is cut by an impassable ravine that extends to the ends of the world. One must go right through. Then there is an impenetrable thicket. Go right through. Then there are birds making a terrible noise. Just listen. Then there is a place where phlegm rains down. Don't brush it off. Then there is a place where the earth is burning. Pass right through. Then a great cliff face rises up, without a single foothold. Walk straight through.[23]

If you travel as far as this and someone threatens you with death, say, "I have already died."

Notes

1. Virgil J. Vogel, *American Indian Medicine* (New York: Ballantine, 1973), pp. 227–30.

2. See chapter 14, where Radin puts this realization into practice.

3. *Shamanism* (New York: Pantheon, 1964), pp. xviii–xix.

4. John Fire/Lame Deer and Richard Erdoes, *Lame Deer Seeker of Visions* (New York: Simon and Schuster, 1972), p. 246.

5. Martin Heidegger, *Discourse on Thinking,* trans. John M. Anderson and E. Hans Freund (New York: Harper & Row, 1966). For further Papago descriptions of vision seeking, see chapter 4.

6. For cosmological journeys, see Part One; for descriptions of various cosmologies, see Part Two.

7. Leo Simmons, ed., *Sun Chief* (New Haven: Yale University Press, 1942), pp. 47–50; for Talayesva's other visions, which were also unsought, see pp. 121–27 and 331–33 in this same autobiography.

8. John G. Neihardt, *Black Elk Speaks* (Lincoln: University of Nebraska Press, 1961), p. 43.

9. *Black Elk Speaks,* p. 30. For a discussion of Ojibwa transformations, see chapter 10 in the present book.

10. For a general discussion of ultimate beings, see chapter 14. For further details about *Tirawa* in particular, see Alice C. Fletcher, *The Hako: A Pawnee Ceremony,* Annual Report of the Bureau of American Ethnology 22 (1904).

11. For a full treatment of medicine bundles, see Clark Wissler, *Ceremonial Bundles of the Blackfoot Indians,* Anthropological Papers of the American Museum of Natural History 7, pt. 2 (1912).

12. For a general treatment of the guardian, see Ruth Benedict, *The Concept of the Guardian Spirit in North America,* Memoirs of the American Anthropological Association 29 (1923).

13. Father Berard Haile, "A Note on the Navaho Visionary," *American Anthropologist* 42 (1940), p. 359; Arthur C. Parker, "Secret Medicine Societies of the Seneca," *American Anthropologist* 11 (1909), pp. 161–85; Ruth Landes, *Ojibwa Religion and the Midewiwin* (Madison: University of Wisconsin Press, 1968); Leslie A. White, "A Comparative Study of Keresan Medicine Societies," *Proceedings of the International Congress of Americanists* 23 (1928), pp. 604–19.

14. Landes, *Ojibwa Religion,* p. 21.

15. Paul Radin, *The Autobiography of a Winnebago Indian* (New York: Dover, 1963), p. 70.

16. Benedict, *The Concept of the Guardian Spirit,* pp. 39–40; Charles H. Lange, *Cochiti* (Carbondale: Southern Illinois University Press, 1959), pp. 233–36.

17. See chapter 6.

18. Vera Laski, *Seeking Life,* Memoirs of the American Folklore Society 50 (1958), p. 128.

19. "Look to the Mountaintop," in *Essays in Reflection II,* ed. E. Graham Ward (Boston: Houghton Mifflin, 1973), p. 97.

20. J. Barre Toelken, "The 'Pretty Language' of Yellowman," *Genre* 2, no. 3 (1969), p. 213. Whole schools of "myth" interpretation have been based on a misunderstanding very much like that of this schoolboy.

21. *God Is Red* (New York: Grosset & Dunlap, 1973), p. 52.

22. See chapter 10, which includes an excellent discussion of "animism."

23. For more about roads, see Ruth L. Bunzel, *Zuñi Ritual Poetry,* Annual Report of the Bureau of American Ethnology 47 (1932), pp. 721–56; Paul Radin, *The Culture of the Winnebago as Described by Themselves,* Special Publications of the Bollingen Foundation 1 (1949); Paul Radin, *The Road of Life and Death* (New York: Pantheon, 1945).

Part One

SEEING AND CURING

1

The Career of a Medicine-Man

Isaac Tens, through Marius Barbeau

Thirty years after my birth was the time when I began to be a *swanassu* (medicine-man). I went up into the hills to get fire-wood. While I was cutting up the wood into lengths, it grew dark towards the evening. Before I had finished my last stack of wood, a loud noise broke out over me, ch^u—————, and a large owl appeared to me. The owl took hold of me, caught my face, and tried to lift me up. I lost consciousness. As soon as I came back to my senses I realized that I had fallen into the snow. My head was coated with ice, and some blood was running out of my mouth.

I stood up and went down the trail, walking very fast, with some wood packed on my back. On my way, the trees seemed to shake and to lean over me; tall trees were crawling after me, as if they had been snakes. I could see them. Before I arrived at my father's home, I told my folk what had happened to me, as soon as I walked in. I was very cold and warmed myself before going to bed. There I fell into a sort of trance. It seems that two *halaaits* (medi-

From Marius Barbeau, *Medicine Men of the North Pacific Coast,* Bulletin 152 (Ottawa: National Museum of Man of the National Museum of Canada, 1958). Reproduction authorized by Information Canada. Barbeau took down this story in 1920, at Hazelton, British Columbia. Isaac Tens was a member of the Gitenmaks division of the Gitksan.

cine-men) were working over me to bring me back to health. But it is now all vague in my memory. When I woke up and opened my eyes, I thought that flies covered my face completely. I looked down, and instead of being on firm ground, I felt that I was drifting in a huge whirlpool. My heart was thumping fast.

The medicine-men working over me were Kceraw'inerh (*Kceraw'inerhlorhs:* the sun shines out, in the morning) of the household of Lutkudzius, Gyedemraldo, and Meeky. While I was in a trance, one of them told me that the time had arrived for me to become a *halaait* (medicine-man) like them. But I did not agree; so I took no notice of the advice. The affair passed away as it had come, without results.

Another time, I went to my hunting grounds on the other side of the river here,[1] opposite Temlarham (the Good-land-of-yore),[2] at the foot of Rocherdéboulé. After I reached there, I caught two fishers in my traps, took their pelts, and threw the flesh and bones away. Farther along I looked for a bear's den amid the tall trees. As I glanced upwards, I saw an owl, at the top of a high cedar. I shot it, and it fell down in the bushes close to me. When I went to pick it up, it had disappeared. Not a feather was left; this seemed very strange. I walked down to the river, crossed over the ice, and returned to the village at Gitenmaks. Upon arriving at my fishing station on the point, I heard the noise of a crowd of people around the smoke-house, as if I were being chased away, pursued. I dared not look behind to find out what all this was about, but I hastened straight ahead. The voices followed in my tracks and came very close behind me. Then I wheeled round and looked back. There was no one in sight, only trees. A trance came over me once more, and I fell down, unconscious. When I came to, my head was buried in a snowbank. I got up and walked on the ice up the river to the village. There I met my father who had just come out to look for me, for he had missed me. We went back together to my house. Then my heart started to beat fast, and I began to tremble, just as had happened a while before, when the *halaaits* (medicine-men) were trying to fix me up. My flesh seemed to be boiling, and I could hear S^u—————. My body was quivering. While I remained in this state, I began to sing. A chant was coming out of me without my being able to do anything to stop it. Many things appeared to me presently: huge birds and other animals. They were calling me. I saw a *meskyawawderh* (a kind of bird), and a *mesqagweeuk* (bullhead fish). These were visible only to me, not to the others in my house. Such visions happen when a man is about to become a *halaait;* they occur of their own accord. The songs force themselves out complete without any attempt to compose them. But I learned and memorized these songs by repeating them.

During the following year I composed more songs and devoted all my time to my new experience, without doing any other work. I would lie down in my father's house, for I felt sick. Four people looked after me all the time in order to hear me sing my new songs, and they were not satisfied until they had learned them too.

My attendants were Kaldirhgyet (Split Person), Andawlerhsemhlorhs pistæi (The Grouse-warms-itself-in-the-sun), Waralsawal (Crazy or idiot, a *narhnorh* or spirit), and 'Arhkawdzem-Tsetsauts (the Tsetsaut-is-thoughtless, also a *narhnorh*). They were cousins of mine; all four were, like me, members of the Wolf (*Larhkibu*) clan. All the time they kept watching over me.

One day a year later, my father summoned the *halaaits* (medicine-men) in the village to come down and act over me. The first thing they did was to *sedarhgyætu* (to strengthen me), that is, they raised me from my couch and walked me round the room. Then I was really strengthened. To pay for their services my father distributed a great amount of property to all those who had assembled there to witness the event.

That was the time when I became a *swanassu* (medicine-man). This was the fasting period, when one aspires to become a *halaait*. I had to have dreams before being able to act. This period lasted a year, in seclusion at my father's house, out of touch with other folk excepting the four attendants.

The instructions which the medicine-men gave me were: "We look at the patient and diagnose his ailment. Sometimes, it is a bad song within him or her, sometimes a *narhnorh* (a spirit)."

When later I attended a patient for the first time, on my own, I had a new vision. The *halaait* doctors were still training me, teaching me. For this reason I was invited to all the *swanassu* activities.

As soon as I was able to go out by myself, I began to diagnose the cases by dreaming (*wawq:* sleeping, or *ksewawq:* dreaming), with the help of my instructors. I acquired charms, that is, things I would dream of: the *Hogwest* (snare for the bear), *Hlorhs* (the Moon), and *Angohawtu* (Sweat-house). And besides, I had also dreamed of charms: the Mink (*nes'in*), the Otter (*watserh*), and Canoe (*'mal*).

I acquired charms when I attended a patient. I used a charm (*aatirh*) and placed it over me first, then over the body of the person from whom I was to extract the disease or illness. It was never an actual object, but only one that had appeared in a dream. In a dream I once had over the hills, I saw a canoe (*'mal*). Many times it appeared to me in my dreams. The canoe sometimes was floating on the water, sometimes on the clouds. When any trouble occurred anywhere, I was able to see my canoe in visions.

My first patient was a woman, the wife of chief Gitemraldaw. Her full name was Niskyaw-romral'awstlegye'ns (Small-wooden-box-to-gather-berries; the grizzly has a bladder like it).[3] She was seriously ill, had been for a long time, and she had been treated before by various *halaaits* in turn, but without avail. I was called in to see whether I could undertake to do something for her. So I went into her house and instructed the people there to light a fire first. As I began to sing over her, many people around me were hitting sticks on boards and beating skin drums for me. My canoe came to me in a dream, and there many people sitting in it. The canoe itself was the Otter (*watserh*). The woman whom I was doctoring sat with the others inside this Otter canoe. By that time, about twenty other *halaaits* were present in the house. To them I explained what my vision was, and asked, "What shall I do? There the woman is sitting in the canoe, and the canoe is the Otter."

They answered, "Try to pull her out."

I told them, "Spread the fire out, into two parts, and make a pathway between them." I walked up and down this path four times, while the other *halaaits* kept singing until they were very tired. Then I went over to the couch on which the sick woman was lying. There was a great upheaval in the singing and the clapping of drums and the sticks on the boards. I placed my hand on her stomach and moved round her couch, all the while trying to draw the canoe out of her. I managed to pull it up very close to the surface of her chest. I grasped it, drew it out, and put it in my own bosom. This I did.

Two days later, the woman rose out of bed; she was cured. My prestige as a *halaait* gained greatly. This, because the others had failed to accomplish anything with her, and I had succeeded. More demands came to me from other parts, as far as the village of Gitsegyukla. Everything usually went well in my work. The fees for doctoring might be ten blankets, prepaid, for each patient, or it might be as little as one blanket. But if the doctored person died afterwards, the blankets were returned. The fees depended upon the wealth of the family calling for services, also upon the anxiety of the relatives of the sick person who wanted to urge the doctor to do his utmost. Should a *halaait* or *swanassu* refuse to doctor a patient, he might be suspected of being himself the cause of the sickness, or of the death should it occur. In this eventuality, the relatives would seek revenge and kill the one suspected. This was the hard law of the country. But the doctors were not known to decline any invitation to serve the people in need.

Swanassu Songs

These songs have words with a meaning that anybody can usually understand. Each *halaait* may own fifteen or twenty of them. Isaac Tens himself possessed three groups of songs—twenty-three in all.

First song which he used on patients is as follows:

(First verse): "He weakens, the spirit (*apwiltu narhnorh*), when I weaken (*tsuwin apwilturhwi*)." That is, "The spirit Salmon weakens when I do." This song was dreamt formerly and handed down to him, Tens, in a dream; it formed part of a myth (*adaaorh*) about a Salmon, the chief of all the Salmon at the canyon.

(Second verse): "Shall be cured (*temalemawturh*) the large

village (*weetsap*), when towards it floats (*'wenhagwegyawturh*) the Spirit (*narhnorh*).'' That is, ''The large village shall be cured when my Salmon spirit floats in.''

(Third verse): ''In floating (*lurawrawhl*), the chief Salmon (*mianhl hawn*) in the canyon (*'altsemtselaasu*) under me (*'ahlaa-wee*).'' That is: ''The chief of the Salmon is floating in the canyon underneath me.''

(Fourth verse): ''Woman Robin (*ksemgyilarhgyaw*) has flown away with me (*tantigyipæyigwee*).'' That is: ''The She Robin has flown away with me.'' This cannot be explained rationally, because it is a vision, and visions are not always intelligible. In my vision I dreamt that I was very sick, and my spirit became sick like me; it was like a human being but had no name. In the same dream I saw that there had been a heavy run of salmon headed by a large Salmon. This would bring relief to the people who were starving. The huge Salmon appeared to me in my vision, although he was way down deep in the canyon. The She Robin came to me, and she lifted me out of my sickness. That is how I was cured.

Second song. ''*Wahawhala . . . iyaw yaw' ehehe.*'' (Burthen):

(First verse): ''Will round walk (*temgutkwiyay*) the Grizzly (*legyai' ns*) a long way (*waræt*) behind the sky (*'andaairhlarhæ*).'' That is: ''The Grizzly shall go a long way from here behind the sky.'' Singing this, the actual words were not uttered, only the meaningless syllables of the burthen. But their meaning was kept in the thoughts, although they were not considered a secret.

(Second verse): ''Through fire (*galeksemihlmihl*) underneath the house (*hlakuhl wilp*) these fires (*hlaraluklaukhl*) the ordinary people (*'amgigyet*).'' That is: ''The *halaait* or medicine-man in his vision sees the fires of the common people through the ground.''

When getting ready for the songs, I fell into a trance and saw a vast fine territory. In the middle of it a house stood. I stepped into it, and I beheld my uncle Tsigwee who had been a medicine-man (*halaait*). He had died several years before. Then another uncle appeared—Gukswawtu. Both of them had been equally famous in their day. The songs above are those I heard them sing. While they were singing, the Grizzly ran through the door, and went right round. Then he rose into the air behind the clouds, describing a circle, and came back to the house. Each of my uncles took a rattle and placed it into one of my hands. That is why I always use two rattles in my performances. In my vision I beheld many fires burning under the house. As soon as I walked out of the house, my trance ended. From then on I sang those chants just as I had learned them in my vision.

Third song:

(First verse): "In held fast (*ludarhdawtuth*) feet (*sesæ'ee*) large spring (*weegwaaneks*)." That is: "My feet are held fast in the large spring."

(Second verse): "It is shellfish like a knife ('*nihlhagyeesta*) doing it to me (*hawelaakute*)." That is: "It is the mussel-shell that is holding my feet." In the vision for this chant, I dreamt of a lake or a large pool, and I put my feet into it. I sank down, way over my knees, and I was unable to get out.

Fourth song: heyuwaw haye . . . hayawa'nigwawhs . . . eyiwaw! (Exclamation):

(First verse): "The spirit (*dinarhnawraw*) of the bee-hives ('*ande'abewaw*) is shooting (*angurhkurhl*) my body (*tramaw'ee*)." That is: "The bee-hives' spirit stings my body."

(Second verse): "Growing up, grandmother ('*masensts'eets*) is doing it to me ('*anwulaakute*) in the head (*tsemtemris*)." That is: "Grandmother is making me grow, in my vision." It is as if she were looking after a small boy. In my vision, I went round in a strange land which cannot be described. There I saw huge bee-hives, out of which the bees darted and stung me all over my body. The reason why the words "in my head" were added on one occasion is that the patient then being treated had pains in the head.

Fifth song:

(First verse): "Where together talking (*wennededalres*) the mountain (*skanis*) where I walk about (*wilegyeyai*)." That is: "The mountains were talking to each other, as I was walking about."

(Second verse): "Where a loud noise (*weenasarhtowtst*) the canyon (*tsalaasu*) where into I went (*wunlawromda'uhle'*)." That is: "I went into the river where it makes the noise of the canyon."

(Third verse): "Where steep incline (*wunsa'ansuut*) my trail (*hlarainee'*)." That is: "I walk about on my trail down a steep incline." In my vision of this part, I was standing on the brink of the canyon, and I could not draw away from its edge, because behind me stood the steep mountain. A great noise was rising out of the canyon. I fell into the water, but I landed in the canoe that was there. I drifted in it further; then it rose with me into the mountain. Two mountain peaks stood there. I drifted between them. These peaks made a noise like bells, and I knew that they were speaking to each other. Now I found myself on a steep incline on the side of one of the mountains. I made a trail down for myself to the bottom.

Sixth song:

(First verse): "Whose canoe (*'nahl'maltu*) where in stands (*wenluheturh*) I don't know." That is: "Whose canoe is it where I stand with a stranger?"

(Second verse): "About floating (*legyi'nigyawt*) where floods (*wenbephtal*) in water (*'aks*)." That is: "It floats about among the whirlpools." In my vision, I was taken in my canoe to many places, among the trees where I was left; but they were receding from under my canoe. My canoe kept floating about, on land or in the water.

When I am called to treat a patient, I go into something like a trance, and I compose a song, or I revive one for the occasion.

As a last resort, I would use my charms (*hogwest*), only when in great difficulties. Then I put on a bear robe, I use a bear-claw head-dress, and I pass a snare (*hogwest*) round my neck. I suspend myself by the neck with it. That is, I would not actually hang by it, but I would be tied by this collar, and the cord would be held in hands by the people present. We would fall down side by side. And I would throw my weight on my neck. Four *halaaits* together are in action, one at each corner. The chief *halaait* would take water and throw it over my head. Then the four of us stand over the pool of water and hold a consultation among ourselves; this is called *silin*. While this happens, another *halaait* performs over the patient. After we have stepped over the pool of water, we cover ourselves up with a mat. If the patient is very weak, the chief doctor captures his spirit into his hands and blows quietly on it to give it more breath. If weaker still, the *halaait* takes a hot stone from the fireplace and holds the spirit over it. Perhaps a little fat is put on the hot stone to melt. The hands turn from one side to the other, thus feeding the sick spirit. After this is done, the *halaait* sits the spirit, then places it on the patient's head.

When a *halaait* is himself the patient, the treatment is called "Returning-the-catch" or "Returning-the-man" (*guksmugu'e*), or "Causing-the-man-to-recover." A cedar collar (*luirh*) is placed around the neck of the sick medicine-man. All the other doctors get together and intone their chants. In the middle of their songs, they raise the sick man, pulling him by the *luirh* (red cedar-bark collar). In time the patient may be able himself to sing; that is, after he has fully recovered. All the medicine-men eventually die a very hard death, because they are not truly human. They are bad spirits.

Now I use a different method in treating my patients. I employ nothing but prayers which I have learned at the church. I pray like the minister—the Lord's Prayer. It has been translated into Gitksan by the Rev. Mr. Price of Kitwanga. I have entirely given up the practice of the *halaait*. My two children became sick—Philip (*Piyawsu*) and Mary (*Tsigumnæq*). The folk around here agitated me and urged me to use the *halaait* over them. They blamed me for my refusal and declared that they would consider me responsible for their deaths. So I tried to revive one of my old charms—the Sun or the Moon (*hlorhs*). But my body was altogether different from what it used to be. I was sure that I had lost my powers as a *swanassu*. I was unable to act on my children. Being too weak, I had to quit. Then I spent $50 on medicine-men (*halaaits*) to assist me in my trial. But like me they could do nothing. My charms were of no use to them. So I have finally trusted my children to the treatment of the white man's doctor. One of the two is still sick at the hospital. But the other has recovered.

Notes

1. At the junction of the Skeena and Buckley rivers at Hazelton.
2. Paradise Lost, in Gitksan mythology.
3. She was a member of the family of Yael, in the Fireweed phratry, in Gitenmaks village.

2

A Shaman's Journey to the Sea Spirit Takánakapsâluk

Knud Rasmussen

The girl who was thrown into the sea by her own father and had her finger joints so cruelly cut off as she clung in terror to the side of the boat has in a strange fashion made herself the stern goddess of fate among the Eskimos. From her comes all the most indispensable of human food, the flesh of sea beasts; from her comes the blubber that warms the cold snow huts and gives light in the lamps when the long arctic night broods over the land. From her come also the skins of the great seal which are likewise indispensable for clothes and boot soles, if the hunters are to be able to move over the frozen sea all seasons of the year. But while Takánakapsâluk gives mankind all these good things, created out of her own finger joints, it is she also who sends nearly all the misfortunes

Knud Rasmussen, *Intellectual Culture of the Iglulik Eskimos* from vol. VII, no. 1 of *Report of the Fifth Thule Expedition, 1921–24* (Copenhagen: Gyldendalske Boghandel, Nordisk Forlag, 1929). Reprinted by permission of the estate of Knud Rasmussen. Dr. Rasmussen was born and raised among the Greenland Eskimos. The Iglulik, the Eskimos of the present account, are on the Melville Peninsula and Baffin Island, in the Northwest Territories.

which are regarded by the dwellers on earth as the worst and direst. In her anger at men's failing to live as they should, she calls up storms that prevent the men from hunting, or she keeps the animals they seek hidden away in a pool she has at the bottom of the sea, or she will steal away the souls of human beings and send sickness among the people. It is not strange, therefore, that it is regarded as one of a shaman's greatest feats to visit her where she lives at the bottom of the sea, and so tame and conciliate her that human beings can live once more untroubled on earth.

When a shaman wishes to visit Takánakapsâluk, he sits on the inner part of the sleeping place behind a curtain, and must wear nothing but his kamiks and mittens. A shaman about to make this journey is said to be ɴak·a·ɔ̃q: one who drops down to the bottom of the sea. This remarkable expression is due perhaps in some degree to the fact that no one can rightly explain how the journey is made. Some assert that it is only his soul or his spirit which makes the journey; others declare that it is the shaman himself who actually, in the flesh, drops down into the underworld.

The journey may be undertaken at the instance of a single individual, who pays the shaman for his trouble, either because there is sickness in his household which appears incurable, or because he has been particularly unsuccessful in his hunting. But it may also be made on behalf of a whole village threatened by famine and death owing to scarcity of game. As soon as such occasion arises, all the adult members of the community assemble in the house from which the shaman is to start, and when he has taken up his position—if it is winter, and in a snow hut, on the bare snow; if in summer, on the bare ground—the men and women present must loosen all tight fastenings in their clothes, the lacings of their footgear, the waistbands of their breeches, and then sit down and remain still with closed eyes, all lamps being put out, or allowed to burn only with so faint a flame that it is practically dark inside the house.

The shaman sits for a while in silence, breathing deeply, and then, after some time has elapsed, he begins to call upon his helping spirits, repeating over and over again: "The way is made ready for me; the way opens before me!"

Whereat all present must answer in chorus: "Let it be so!"

And when the helping spirits have arrived, the earth opens

under the shaman, but often only to close up again; he has to struggle for a long time with hidden forces, ere he can cry at last: "Now the way is open."

And then all present must answer: "Let the way be open before him; let there be way for him."

And now one hears, at first under the sleeping place: "Halala—he—he—he, halala—he—he—he!" and afterwards under the passage, below the ground, the same cry: "Halele—he!" And the sound can be distinctly heard to recede farther and farther until it is lost altogether. Then all know that he is on his way to the ruler of the sea beasts.

Meanwhile, the members of the household pass the time by singing songs in chorus, and here it may happen that the clothes which the shaman has discarded come alive and fly about round the house, above the heads of the singers, who are sitting with closed eyes. And one may hear deep sighs and the breathing of persons long since dead; these are the souls of the shaman's namesakes, who have come to help. But as soon as one calls them by name, the sighs cease, and all is silent in the house until another dead person begins to sigh.

In the darkened house one hears only sighing and groaning from the dead who lived many generations earlier. This sighing and puffing sounds as if the spirits were down under water, in the sea, as marine animals, and in between all the noises one hears the blowing and splashing of creatures coming up to breathe. There is one song especially which must be constantly repeated; it is only to be sung by the oldest members of the tribe, and is as follows:

> We reach out our hands
> to help you up;
> We are without food,
> we are without game.
> From the hollow by the entrance
> you shall open,
> you shall bore your way up.
> We are without food,
> and we lay ourselves down
> holding out hands
> to help you up!

An ordinary shaman will, even though skillful, encounter many dangers in his flight down to the bottom of the sea; the most dreaded are three large rolling stones which he meets as soon as he has reached the sea floor. There is no way round; he has to pass between them, and take great care not to be crushed by these stones, which churn about, hardly leaving room for a human being to pass. Once he has passed beyond them, he comes to a broad, trodden path, the shaman's path; he follows a coastline resembling that which he knows from on earth, and entering a bay finds himself on a great plain, and here lies the house of Takánakapsâluk, built of stone, with a short passageway, just like the houses of the tunit. Outside the house one can hear the animals puffing and blowing, but he does not see them; in the passage leading to the house lies Takánakapsâluk's dog stretched across the passage taking up all the room; it lies there gnawing at a bone and snarling. It is dangerous to all who fear it, and only the courageous shaman can pass by it, stepping straight over it as it lies; the dog then knows that the bold visitor is a great shaman, and does him no harm.

These difficulties and dangers attend the journey of an ordinary shaman. But for the very greatest, a way opens right from the house whence they invoke their helping spirits; a road down through the earth, if they are in a tent on shore, or down through the sea, if it is in a snow hut on the sea ice, and by this route the shaman is led down without encountering any obstacle. He almost glides as if falling through a tube so fitted to his body that he can check his progress by pressing against the sides, and need not actually fall down with a rush. This tube is kept open for him by all the souls of his namesakes, until he returns on his way back to earth.

Should a great shelter wall be built, outside the house of Takánakapsâluk, it means that she is very angry and implacable in her feelings towards mankind, but the shaman must fling himself upon the wall, kick it down and level it to the ground. There are some who declare that her house has no roof, and is open at the top, so that she can better watch, from her place by the lamp, the doings of mankind. All the different kinds of game: seal, bearded seal, walrus, and whale are collected in a great pool on the right of her lamp, and there they lie puffing and blowing. When the shaman enters the house, he at once sees Takánakapsâluk, who, as a sign of anger, is sitting with her back to the lamp and with her back to all the animals in the pool. Her hair hangs down loose all over one side of her face, a tangled, untidy mass hiding her eyes, so that she cannot see. It is the misdeeds and offenses committed by men which gather in dirt and impurity over her body. All the foul emanations from the sins of mankind nearly suffocate her. As the shaman moves towards her, Isarrataitsoq, her father, tries to grasp hold of him. He thinks it is a dead person come to expiate offenses before passing on to the Land of The Dead, but the shaman must then at once cry out: "I am flesh and blood" and then he will not be hurt. And he must grasp Takánakapsâluk by one shoulder and turn her face towards the lamp and towards the animals, and stroke her hair, the hair she has been unable to comb out herself, because she has no fingers; and he must smooth it and comb it, and as soon as she is calmer, he must say:

"Those up above can no longer help the seals up by grasping their foreflippers."

Then Takánakapsâluk answers in the spirit language: "The secret miscarriages of the women and breaches of taboo in eating boiled meat bar the way for the animals."

The shaman must now use all his efforts to appease her anger, and at last, when she is in a kindlier mood, she takes the animals one by one and drops them on the floor, and then it is as if a whirlpool arose in the passage, the water pours out from the pool and the animals disappear in the sea. This means rich hunting and abundance for mankind.

It is then time for the shaman to return to his fellows up above, who are waiting for him. They can hear him coming a long way off; the rush of his passage through the tube kept open for him by the spirits comes nearer and nearer, and with a mighty "Plu—a—he—he" he shoots up into his place behind the curtain: "Plu-plu," like some creature of the sea, shooting up from the deep to take breath under the pressure of mighty lungs.

Then there is silence for a moment. No one may break this silence until the shaman says: "I have something to say."

Then all present answer: "Let us hear, let us hear."

And the shaman goes on, in the solemn spirit language: "Words will arise."

And then all in the house must confess any breaches of taboo they have committed.

"It is my fault, perhaps," they cry, all at once, women and men together, in fear of famine and starvation, and all begin telling of the wrong things they have done. All the names of those in the house are mentioned, and all must confess, and thus much comes to light which no one had ever dreamed of; everyone learns his neighbors' secrets. But despite all the sin confessed, the shaman may go on talking as one who is unhappy at having made a mistake, and again and again break out into such expressions as this:

"I seek my grounds in things which have not happened; I speak as one who knows nothing."

There are still secrets barring the way for full solution of the trouble, and so the women in the house begin to go through all the names, one after another; nearly all women's names; for it was always their breaches of taboo which were most dangerous. Now and again when a name is mentioned, the shaman exclaims in relief:

"Taina, taina!"

It may happen that the woman in question is not present, and in such a case, she is sent for. Often it would be quite young girls or young wives, and when they came in crying and miserable, it was always a sign that they were good women, good penitent women. And as soon as they showed themselves, shamefaced and weeping, the shaman would break out again into his cries of self-reproach:

"I seek, and I strike where nothing is to be found! I seek, and I strike where nothing is to be found! If there is anything, you must say so!"

And the woman who has been led in, and whom the shaman has marked out as one who has broken her taboo, now confesses:

"I had a miscarriage, but I said nothing, because I was afraid, and because it took place in a house where there were many."

She thus admits that she has had a miscarriage, but did not venture to say so at the time because of the consequences involved, affecting her numerous housemates; for the rules provide that as soon as a woman has had a miscarriage in a house, all those living in the same house, men and women alike, must throw away all the house contains of qituptɔq: soft things, i.e., all the skins on the sleeping place, all the clothes, in a word all soft skins, thus including also ilupɛrɔq: the sealskin covering used to line the whole interior of a snow hut as used among the Iglulingmiut. This was so serious a matter for the household that women sometimes dared not report a miscarriage; moreover, in the case of quite young girls who had not yet given birth to any child, a miscarriage might accompany their menstruation without their knowing, and only when the shaman in such a case as this, pointed out the girl as the origin of the trouble and the cause of Takánakapsâluk's anger, would she call to mind that there had once been, in her menstruation skin (the piece of thick-haired caribou skin which women place in their underbreeches during menstruation) something that looked like "thick blood." She had not thought at the time that it was anything particular, and had therefore said nothing about it, but now that she is pointed out by the shaman, it recurs to her mind. Thus at last the cause of Takánakapsâluk's anger is explained, and all are filled with joy at having escaped disaster. They are now assured that there will be abundance of game on the following day. And in the end, there may be almost a feeling of thankfulness towards the delinquent. This then was what took place when shamans went down and propitiated the great Spirit of the Sea.

3

Hanblecheyapi:
Crying for a Vision

Black Elk, through Joseph Epes Brown

The "Crying for a Vision" ritual, like the purification rites of the *Inipi*, was used long before the coming of our most sacred pipe. This way of praying is very important, and indeed it is at the center of our religion, for from it we have received many good things, even the four great rites which I shall soon describe.

Every man can cry for a vision, or "lament"; and in the old days we all—men and women—"lamented" all the time. What is received through the "lamenting" is determined in part by the character of the person who does this, for it is only those people who are very qualified who receive the great visions, which are interpreted by our holy man, and which give strength and health to our nation. It is very important for a person who wishes to "lament" to receive aid and advice from a *wichasha wakan* (holy

From Joseph Epes Brown, ed., *The Sacred Pipe: Black Elk's Account of the Seven Rites of the Oglala Sioux* (Norman: University of Oklahoma Press, 1953). Copyright © 1953 by the University of Oklahoma Press. Black Elk (1862–1950), best known from John J. Neihardt's *Black Elk Speaks*, was a member of the Oglala division of the Teton Sioux. Brown spent the winter of 1947–1948 with Black Elk and his family near Manderson, South Dakota.

man),[1] so that everything is done correctly, for if things are not done in the right way, something very bad can happen, and even a serpent could come and wrap itself around the "lamenter."

You have all heard of our great chief and priest Crazy Horse, but perhaps you did not know that he received most of his great power through the "lamenting" which he did many times a year, and even in the winter when it is very cold and very difficult. He received visions of the Rock, the Shadow, the Badger, a prancing horse (from which he received his name), the Day, and also of *Wanbli Galeshka,* the Spotted Eagle, and from each of these he received much power and holiness.[2]

There are many reasons for going to a lonely mountaintop to "lament." Some young men receive a vision when they are very young and when they do not expect it,[3] and then they go to "lament" that they might understand it better. Then we "lament" if we wish to make ourselves brave for a great ordeal such as the Sun Dance or to prepare for going on the warpath. Some people "lament" in order to ask some favor of the Great Spirit, such as curing a sick relative; and then we also "lament" as an act of thanksgiving for some great gift which the Great Spirit may have given to us. But perhaps the most important reason for "lamenting" is that it helps us to realize our oneness with all things, to know that all things are our relatives; and then in behalf of all things we pray to *Wakan-Tanka* that He may give to us knowledge of Him who is the source of all things, yet greater than all things.

Our women also "lament," after first purifying themselves in the *Inipi;* they are helped by other women, but they do not go up on a very high and lonely mountain. They go up on a hill in a valley, for they are women and need protection.

When a person wishes to "lament," he goes with a filled pipe to a holy man; he enters the tipi with the stem of the pipe pointing in front of him, and sits before the old man who is to be his guide. The "lamenter" then places the pipe on the ground with its stem now pointing towards himself, for it is he who wishes to gain knowledge. The holy man raises his hands above to *Wakan-Tanka* and to the four directions, and, taking up the pipe, he asks the man what he wishes.

"I wish to 'lament' and offer my pipe to *Wakan-Tanka*. I need your help and guidance, and wish you to send a voice for me to the Powers above."

To this the old man says: *"How!"* (It is good); and then they leave the tipi, and, walking a short distance, they face the west, the young man standing to the left of the holy man, and they are joined by any others who may happen to be present. All raise their right hands, and the old man prays, holding the stem of the pipe to the heavens.

"Hee-ay-hay-ee-ee! [four times.] Grandfather, *Wakan-Tanka,* You are first and always have been! Everything belongs to You. It is You who have created all things! You are One and alone, and to You we are sending a voice. This young man here is in difficulty, and wishes to offer the pipe to You. We ask that You give help to him! Within a few days he will offer his body to You. Upon the sacred Earth, our Mother and Grandmother, he will place his feet in a sacred manner.

"All the Powers of the world, the heavens and the star peoples, and the red and blue sacred days; all things that move in the universe, in the rivers, the brooks, the springs, all waters, all trees that stand, all the grasses of our Grandmother, all the sacred peoples of the universe: Listen! A sacred relationship with you all will be asked by this young man, that his generations to come will increase and live in a holy manner.

"O You, winged One, there where the sun goes down, who guards our sacred pipe, help us! Help us to offer this pipe to *Wakan-Tanka,* that He may give a blessing to this young man!"

To this all the people cry *"How!"* and then they sit in a circle upon the ground. The old man offers the pipe to the six directions, lights it, and passes it first to the young man who is to "lament." The "lamenter" offers it up with a prayer, and then it is smoked by everybody in the circle. When the pipe is smoked out, it is handed back to the holy man, who cleans and purifies it and hands it back to the young man, asking him when he wishes to "lament," and a day is then decided upon.

When this chosen day arrives, the young man wears only his

buffalo robe, breech cloth, and moccasins, and he goes with his pipe to the tipi of the holy man. Crying as he walks, he enters the lodge and places his right hand on the head of the old man, saying: *"Unshe ma la ye!"* (Be merciful to me!) He then lays the pipe in front of the holy man and asks for his help.

The old man replies: "We all know that the pipe is sacred, and with it you have now come crying. I shall help you, but you must always remember what I am going to tell you; in the winters to come you must walk with the instructions and advice which I give to you. You may "lament" from one to four days, or even longer if you wish; how many days do you choose?"

"I choose two days."

"Good! This, then, is what you must do: First you should build an *Inipi* lodge in which we shall purify ourselves, and for this you must select twelve or sixteen small willows. But before you cut the willows remember to take to them a tobacco offering; and as you stand before them you should say: 'There are many kinds of trees, but it is you whom I have chosen to help me. I shall take you, but in your place there will be others!' Then you should bring these trees back to where we shall make the lodge.

"In a sacred manner you must also gather the rocks and sage, and then you must make a bundle of five long sticks and also five bundles of twelve small sticks, all of which will be used as offerings. These sticks you should lean against the west side of the sweat lodge until we are ready to purify them. We shall also need the Ree twist tobacco, *kinnikinnik,* a tobacco cutting board, buckskin for the tobacco-offering bags, sweet grass, a bag of sacred earth, a knife, and a stone hatchet. These things you must secure yourself, and when you are ready we shall purify ourselves. *Hetchetu welo!"*

When the purification lodge has been built, and all the equipment gathered, the holy man enters the lodge and sits at the west; the "lamenter" enters next and sits at the north, and then a helper enters and sits just to the south of the holy man. A cold rock is brought into the lodge and is placed on the north side of the central altar, where it is purified with a short prayer by the holy man; it is then taken outside by a helper. This is the first rock to be placed on the fire (*peta owihankeshni*) which has been built to the east of the lodge.

Just east of the central altar, within the purification lodge, the helper scrapes a sacred place upon the earth, and upon this he places a hot coal. The holy man now moves around to the east, and, bending over the coal, he holds up a bit of sweet grass and prays in this manner:

"O Grandfather, *Wakan-Tanka*, behold us! Upon the sacred earth I place this Your herb. The smoke that rises from the earth and fire will belong to all that moves in the universe: the four-leggeds, the wingeds, and everything that moves and everything that is. This offering of theirs will now be given to You, O *Wakan-Tanka!* We shall make sacred all that we touch!"

As the sweet grass is put upon the coal, the other two men in the lodge cry, *"Hi ye!"* (Thanks), and as the smoke rises, the holy man rubs his hands in it and then rubs them over his body. In the same manner the "lamenter" and the helper purify themselves with the sacred smoke. The little bag of earth is also purified, and then the three men take their places at the west, every movement being made, of course, in a sun-wise manner. The purified earth is now very carefully spread all around inside the sacred central hole, and this is done slowly and reverently for this earth represents the whole universe. The helper hands a stick to the holy man, who uses it to mark four places around the hole, the first at the west, and then at the north, east, and south. Next a cross is made by drawing a line on the ground from west to east, then one from the north to the south. All this is very sacred, for it establishes the four great Powers of the universe, and also the center which is the dwelling place of *Wakan-Tanka*. A helper now enters from the outside carrying a hot coal in a split stick; he walks slowly, stopping four times, and the last time the coal is placed upon the center of the cross.

Holding a pinch of sweet grass over the coal, the holy man prays: "My Grandfather, *Wakan-Tanka*, You are everything. And my Father, *Wakan-Tanka*, all things belong to You! I am about to place Your herb on this fire. Its fragrance belongs to You."

The old man then slowly lowers the sweet grass to the fire.

The helper now takes up the pipe, and moving with it in [a] direction, hands it to the holy man who prays with it [in] words: "O *Wakan-Tanka,* behold Your pipe! I hold it ove[r] smoke of this herb. O *Wakan-Tanka,* behold also this sacred pla[ce] which we have made. We know that its center is Your dwelling place. Upon this circle the generations will walk. The four-leggeds, the two-leggeds, the wingeds, and the four Powers of the universe, all will behold this, Your place."

The holy man holds the pipe over the smoke, pointing the stem first to the west, and then to the north, the east, the south, and to heaven, then he touches the earth with its foot. He purifies all the sacred equipment: the buffalo robe and all the offering sticks; and then he makes little bags of tobacco which he ties on the ends of the offering sticks.

The old holy man, now seated at the west, takes the tobacco cutting board and begins to chop and mix the *kinnikinnik*. He first judges carefully the size of the pipe, for he must make just enough to fill the pipe bowl and no more. Each time that he shaves off a little piece of the tobacco, he offers it to one of the quarters of the world, taking great care that no piece jumps off the board, for this would make the Thunder-beings very angry. When the mixing has been finished, the old man takes up the pipe with his left hand, and holding up a pinch of the *kinnikinnik* with his right hand, he prays.

"O *Wakan-Tanka,* my Father and Grandfather, You are first, and always have been! Behold this young man here who has a troubled mind. He wishes to travel upon the sacred path; he will offer this pipe to You. Be merciful to him and help him! The four Powers and the whole universe will be placed in the bowl of the pipe, and then this young man will offer it to You, with the help of the wingeds and all things.

"The first to be placed in the pipe is You, O winged Power of the place where the sun goes down. You with Your guards are ancient and sacred. Behold! There is a place for You in the pipe; help us with Your two sacred blue and red days!"

The holy man places this tobacco in the pipe, and then he holds up another pinch towards the place in the north where *Waziah* the Giant lives.

d Power, there where the Giant has His lodge,
he strong purifying winds: there is a place for
us with the two sacred days which you have!''
his direction is placed in the pipe, and a third
eld towards the east.

the sun comes up, who guard the light and
who give knowledge, this pipe will be offered to *Wakan-Tanka!*
There is a place here for You too; help us with Your sacred days!''

In the same manner the Power of the east is placed in the pipe;
and now a pinch of tobacco is held towards the south, the place
towards which we always face.

''O You who control the sacred winds, and who live there
where we always face, Your breath gives life; and it is from You
and to You that our generations come and go. This pipe is about to
be offered to *Wakan-Tanka;* there is a place in it for You. Help us
with the two sacred days which You have!''

In this manner all the Powers of the four directions have been
placed within the bowl of the pipe, and now a pinch of the sacred
tobacco is held up towards the heavens, and this is for *Wanbli
Galeshka,* the Spotted Eagle, who is higher than all other created
beings, and who represents *Wakan-Tanka:*

''O *Wanbli Galeshka,* who circles in the highest heavens, You
see all things in the heavens and upon the earth. This young man is
about to offer his pipe to *Wakan-Tanka,* in order that he may gain
knowledge. Help him, and all those who send their voices to
Wakan-Tanka through You. There is a place for You in the pipe;
give to us Your two sacred red and blue days.''

With this prayer the Spotted Eagle is placed in the bowl of the
pipe, and now a pinch of the tobacco is held towards Earth, and the
old man continues to pray:

''O *Unchi* and *Ina,* our Grandmother and Mother, You are
sacred! We know that it is from You that our bodies have come.
This young man wishes to become one with all things; he wishes to
gain knowledge. For the good of all Your peoples, help him! There
is a place for You in the pipe; give to us Your two sacred red and
blue days!''

Thus the Earth, which is now in the tobacco, is placed in the pipe, and in this manner all the six Powers of the universe have here become one. But in order to make sure that all the peoples of the world are included in the pipe, the holy man offers small grains of tobacco for each of the following winged peoples: "O sacred King Bird, who flies on the two sacred days; You who raise families so well, may we increase and live in the same manner. This pipe will soon be offered to *Wakan-Tanka!* There is a place here for You. Help us!" With the same prayer, small grains of tobacco are offered and placed in the pipe, for the meadow lark, the blackbird, the woodpecker, the snowbird, the crow, the magpie, the dove, the hawk, the eagle hawk, the bald eagle, and finally what is left of the tobacco is offered for the two-legged who is about to "lament," offering himself up to *Wakan-Tanka*.

The pipe is then sealed with tallow, for the "lamenter" will take it with him when he goes to the top of the mountain, and there he will offer it to *Wakan-Tanka;* but it will not be smoked until he finishes the "lamenting" and returns to the holy man.

All the offering poles and the equipment which have been purified, are now taken and are placed outside the lodge at the west. The three men leave the lodge and prepare for the *Inipi* by taking off all their clothes except the breech cloth. Any other men who may now be present are permitted to take part in this purification rite.

The "lamenter" enters the *Inipi* first and, moving around sunwise, sits at the west of the lodge. He takes up his pipe which had been left in the lodge (with its stem pointing to the east) and, turning it around sun-wise, holds it up in front of him; and he remains in this position for the first part of the rite. The holy man enters next and, passing behind the "lamenter," sits at the east, just beside the door. Any other men who wish to take part in the rite then fill in the remaining places; two men remain outside to act as helpers.

One of the helpers fills a pipe in a ritual manner, and this is handed in to the man who sits just at the left of the "lamenter." The rock which had previously been purified is also handed in—on a forked stick, for it is now very hot—and is placed at the center of the sacred hole. A second rock is then placed at the west in the sacred place, and the others are placed at the north, east, and south. As the rocks are put in place, the person who holds the pipe to be smoked in the rite touches its foot to each rock, and as he does this all the men cry: *"Hi ye! Hi ye!"* The pipe is then lit, offered to Heaven, Earth, and the four directions, and is smoked around the circle. As it passes around, each man mentions his relationship to the person next to him, and after everybody has smoked they all say together: *"Mitakuye oyasin!"* (We are all relatives!). The one who lit the pipe now empties it, placing the ashes upon the center altar, and after purifying it he hands it to the left, and it is passed out of the lodge. The helper again fills the pipe and leans it on the sacred mound with the stem pointing to the west. The door of the lodge is closed, and the holy man at the east begins to pray in the darkness: "Behold! All that moves in the universe is here!" This is repeated by everybody in the lodge, and at the end they all say: *"How!"*

"*Hee-ay-hay-ee-ee!* [four times] I am sending a voice! Hear me! [four times] *Wakan-Tanka,* Grandfather, behold us! O *Wakan-Tanka,* Father, behold us! On this great island there is a two-legged who says that he will offer a pipe to You. On this day his promise will be fulfilled. To whom could one send a voice except to You, *Wakan-Tanka,* our Grandfather and Father. O *Wakan-Tanka,* this young man asks You to be merciful to him. He says that his mind is troubled and that he needs Your help. In offering this pipe to You, he will offer his whole mind and body. The time has now come; he will soon go to a high place, and there he will cry for Your aid. Be merciful to him!

"O You four Powers of the universe, you wingeds of the air, and all the peoples who move in the universe—you have all been placed in the pipe. Help this young man with the knowledge which has been given to all of you by *Wakan-Tanka.* Be merciful to him! O *Wakan-Tanka,* grant that this young man may have relatives; that he may be one with the four winds, the four Powers of the world, and with the light of the dawn. May he understand his relationship with all the winged peoples of the air. He will place his feet upon the sacred earth of a mountaintop; may he receive understanding there; may his generations to come be holy! All things give thanks to You, O *Wakan-Tanka,* who are merciful, and who help us all. We ask all this of You because we know that You are the only One, and that You have power over all things!''

As a little water is poured on the red hot rocks, all the men sing:

> *Grandfather, I am sending a voice!*
> *To the Heavens of the universe, I am sending a voice;*
> *That my people may live!*

As the men sing this, and as the hot steam rises, the ''lamenter'' cries, for he is humbling himself, remembering his nothingness in the presence of the Great Spirit.[4]

After a short time the door of the lodge is opened by the helper, and the ''lamenter'' now embraces his pipe, holding it first to one shoulder and then to the other, and crying all the time to the Great Spirit: ''Be merciful to me! Help me!'' This pipe is then passed around the circle, and all the other men embrace it and cry in the same manner. It is then passed out of the lodge to the helpers, who also embrace it and then lean it on the little mound, with its stem to the east; for this direction is the source of light and understanding.

The second pipe which is being used for the purification rite, and which had been leaning on the sacred mound with its stem to the west, is now handed into the lodge, and is given to the person sitting just to the left of the ''lamenter.'' This pipe is lit, and after it has been smoked by everybody in the circle, it is passed out of the lodge. After this, water is passed around, and the ''lamenter'' is now allowed to drink all that he wishes, but he must be careful not to spill any or to put any on his body, for this would anger the Thunder-beings who guard the sacred waters, and then they might visit him every night that he ''laments.'' The holy man tells the ''lamenter'' to rub his body with the sage, and then the door is closed once more. A prayer is said by the next holiest man in the lodge, one who has had a vision.

''On this sacred earth, the Thunder-beings have been merciful to me, and have given to me a power from where the Giant *Waziah* lives. It was an eagle who came to me. He will see you too when you go to cry for a vision. Then from the place where the sun comes up, they sent to me a Baldheaded Eagle; he too will see you. From the place towards which we always face, they sent to me a winged one. They were very merciful to me. In the depths of the heavens there is a winged being who is next to *Wakan-Tanka;* He is the Spotted Eagle, and He too will behold you. You will be seen by all the Powers and by the sacred earth upon which you stand. They have given to me a good road to follow upon this earth; may you too know this way! Set your mind upon the meanings of these things, and you will see! All this is so; do not forget! *Hechetu welo!"*

This old man then sings:

> *They are sending a voice to me.*
> *From the place where the sun goes down,*
> *Our Grandfather is sending a voice to me.*
> *From where the sun goes down,*
> *They are talking to me as they come.*
> *Our Grandfather's voice is calling to me.*
> *That winged One there where the Giant lives,*
> *Is sending a voice to me. He is calling me.*
> *Our Grandfather is calling me!*

As the old man chants this song, water is put on the rocks, and after the men have been in the hot fragrant steam and darkness for a short time, the door is opened, and the fresh air and light fill the little lodge. Once again the pipe is taken from the sacred mound and is handed in to the man at the north of the lodge. After it has been smoked it is placed again on the mound with its stem pointing to the east. The door is closed, and this time it is the holy man at the east who prays.

"O *Wakan-Tanka,* behold all that we do and ask here! O You, Power, there where the sun goes down, who control the waters: with the breath of your waters this young man is purifying himself. And you too, O very aged rocks who are helping us here, listen! You are firmly fixed upon this earth; we know that the winds cannot shake you. This young man is about to send his voice, crying for a vision. You are helping us by giving to him some of your power; through your breath he is being made pure.

"O eternal fire there where the sun comes up, from you this young man is gaining strength and light. O you standing trees, *Wakan-Tanka* has given you the power to stand upright. May this young man always have you as an example; may he hold firmly to you! It is good. *Hechetu welo!*"

All the men now chant again, and after a little while the door is opened, and the pipe is sent to the holy man at the east, who lights it, and after smoking for a few puffs, hands it around the circle. When the tobacco has been smoked up, the helper again takes the pipe and places it on the earth mound, with the stem leaning to the south. The door of the *Inipi* is closed for the last time, and now the holy man addresses his prayer to the rocks.

"O you ancient rocks who are sacred, you have neither ears nor eyes, yet you hear and see all things. Through your powers this young man has become pure, that he may be worthy to go to receive some message from *Wakan-Tanka*. The men who guard the door of this sacred lodge will soon open it for the fourth time, and we shall see the light of the world. Be merciful to the men who guard the door! May their generations be blessed!"

Water is placed on the rocks, which are still very hot, and after the steam has penetrated throughout the lodge for a short time, the door is opened, and all the men cry: *"Hi ho! Hi ho!* Thanks!"

The "lamenter" leaves the lodge first, and goes and sits upon the sacred path, facing the little mound, and crying all the while. One of the helpers then takes up the buffalo robe, which had been purified, and places it over the shoulders of the "lamenter"; and another helper takes the pipe which has been leaning all this time on the mound, and hands it to the "lamenter," who is now ready to go up to the high mountain, there to cry for a vision.

Three horses are brought, and upon two of these the bundles of offering sticks and some sacred sage are loaded; the "lamenter" rides on the third horse, and all this time he is crying most pitifully and is holding his pipe in front of him. When they arrive at the foot of the chosen mountain, the two helpers go on ahead with all the equipment in order to prepare the sacred place on the mountaintop.

When they arrive they enter the chosen place by walking in a direction always away from their camping circle, and they go directly to the spot which they have chosen to be the center and place all the equipment here. At this center they first make a hole, in which they place some *kinnikinnik,* and then in this hole they set up a long pole with the offerings tied at the top. One of the helpers now goes about ten strides to the west, and in the same manner he sets up a pole here, tying offerings to it. He then goes to the center where he picks up another pole, and this he fixes at the north again returning to the center. In the same manner he sets up poles at the east and at the south. All this time the other helper has been making a bed of sage at the center, so that when the "lamenter" is tired he may lie with his head against the center pole, and his feet stretching towards the east. When everything has been finished the helpers leave the sacred place by the north path, and then return to the "lamenter" at the foot of the mountain.

The "lamenter" now takes off his moccasins and even his breech cloth—for if we really wish to "lament" we must be poor in the things of this world—and he walks alone up to the top of the mountain, holding his pipe in front of him, and carrying his buffalo robe which he will use at night. As he walks he cries continually: *"Wakan-Tanka onshimala ye oyate wani wachin cha!"* (O Great Spirit, be merciful to me that my people may live!)

Entering the sacred place, the "lamenter" goes directly to the center pole, where he faces the west, and holding up his pipe with both hands he continues to cry: "O *Wakan-Tanka,* have pity on me, that my people may live!" Then walking very slowly he goes to the pole at the west, where he offers up the same prayer, and then returns to the center. In the same manner he goes to the poles at the north, east, and south, always returning to the center each

The arrangement of the five poles at the sacred place of the lamenter, and the lines of his movements within that place.

time. After completing one of these rounds, he raises his pipe to the heavens asking the wingeds and all things to help him, and then pointing the pipe stem to the Earth, he asks aid from all that grows upon our Mother.

All this takes very little time to tell, yet the "lamenter" should do it all so slowly and in such a sacred manner that often he may take an hour or even two to make one of these rounds. The "lamenter" can move in no other manner than this, which is in the form of a cross, although he may linger at any one place as long as he wishes; but all day long this is what he does, praying constantly, either out loud or silently to himself, for the Great Spirit is everywhere; He hears whatever is in our minds and hearts, and it is not necessary to speak to Him in a loud voice. The "lamenter" need not always use this prayer that I have given, for he may remain silent with his whole attention directed to the Great Spirit or to one of His Powers. He must always be careful lest distracting thoughts come to him, yet he must be alert to recognize any messenger which the Great Spirit may send to him, for these people often come in the form of an animal, even one as small and as seemingly insignificant as a little ant. Perhaps a Spotted Eagle may come to him from the west, or a Black Eagle from the north, or the Bald Eagle from the east, or even the Redheaded Woodpecker may come to him from the south. And even though none of these may speak to him at first, they are important and should be observed. The "lamenter" should also notice if one of the little birds should come, or even perhaps a squirrel. At first the animals or winged peoples may be wild, but soon they become tame, and the birds will sit on the poles, or even little ants or worms may crawl on the pipe. All these people are important, for in their own way they are wise and they can teach us two-leggeds much if we make ourselves humble before them. The most important of all the creatures are the wingeds, for they are nearest to the heavens, and are not bound to the earth as are the four-leggeds, or the little crawling people.

It may be good to mention here that it is not without reason that we humans are two-legged along with the wingeds; for you see the birds leave the earth with their wings, and we humans may also leave this world, not with wings, but in the spirit. This will help you to understand in part how it is that we regard all created beings as sacred and important, for everything has a *wochangi* or influence which can be given to us, through which we may gain a little more understanding if we are attentive.

All day long the "lamenter" sends his voice to *Wakan-Tanka* for aid, and he walks as we have described upon the sacred paths which form a cross. This form has much power in it, for whenever we return to the center, we know that it is as if we are returning to *Wakan-Tanka,* who is the center of everything; and although we may think that we are going away from Him, sooner or later we and all things must return to Him.

In the evening the "lamenter" is very tired, for you should remember that he may neither eat nor drink during the days that he cries for a vision. He may sleep on the bed of sage which had been prepared for him, and must lean his head against the center pole, for even though he sleeps he is close to *Wakan-Tanka,* and it is very often during sleep that the most powerful visions come to us; they are not merely dreams, for they are much more real and powerful and do not come from ourselves, but from *Wakan-Tanka*. It may be that we shall receive no vision or message from the Great Spirit the first time that we "lament," yet we may try many times, for we should remember that *Wakan-Tanka* is always anxious to aid those who seek Him with a pure heart. But of course much depends on the nature of the person who cries for a vision, and upon the degree to which he has purified and prepared himself.

In the evenings the Thunder-beings may come, and although they are very terrifying, they bring much good, and they test our strength and endurance. Then too they help us to realize how really very small and insignificant we are compared to the great powers of *Wakan-Tanka*.

I remember one time when I "lamented," and a great storm came from the place where the sun goes down, and I talked with the Thunder-beings who came with hail and thunder and lightning and much rain, and the next morning I saw that there was hail all piled up on the ground around the sacred place, yet inside it was perfectly dry. I think that they were trying to test me. And then, on one of the nights the bad spirits came and started tearing the offerings off the poles; and I heard their voices under the ground, and one of them said: "Go and see if he is crying." And I heard rattles, but all the time they were outside the sacred place and could not get in, for I had resolved not to be afraid, and did not stop sending my voice to *Wakan-Tanka* for aid. Then later, one of the bad spirits said from somewhere under the ground: "Yes, he is surely crying," and the next morning I saw that the poles and offerings were still there. I was well prepared, you see, and did not weaken, and so nothing bad could happen.

The "lamenter" should get up in the middle of the night, and he should again go to the four quarters, returning to the center each time, and all the while he should be sending his voice. He should always be up with the morning star, and he should walk towards the east, and, pointing his pipe stem towards this sacred star, he should ask it for wisdom; this he should pray silently in his heart, and not out loud. All this the "lamenter" should do for the three or four days.

At the end of this period the helpers come with their horses and take the "lamenter" with his pipe back to the camp, and there he immediately enters the *Inipi* which has already been made ready for him. He should sit at the west, holding his pipe in front of him all the time. The holy man—the spiritual guide of the "lamenter"—enters next and, passing behind the "lamenter," sits at the east, and all the other men fill the remaining places.

The first sacred rock, which has already been heated, is brought into the lodge and is placed at the center of the altar, and then all the other rocks are brought in, as I have described before. All this is done very solemnly but more rapidly than before, for all the men are anxious to hear what the "lamenter" has to tell and to know what great things may have come to him up there on the mountain. When all has been made ready, the holy man says to the "lamenter":

"Ho! You have now sent a voice with your pipe to *Wakan-Tanka*. That pipe is now very sacred, for the whole universe has seen it. You have offered this pipe to all the four sacred Powers; they have seen it! And each word that you said up there was heard, even by our Grandmother and Mother Earth. The coming generations will hear you! These five ancient rocks here will hear you! The winged Power of the place where the sun goes down, who controls the waters, will hear you! The standing trees who are present here will hear you! And also the most sacred pipe which was given to the people will hear you; so tell us the truth, and be sure that you make up nothing! Even the tiny ants and the crawling worms may have come to see you up there when you were crying for a vision; tell us everything! You have brought back to us the pipe which you offered; it is finished! And since you are about to put this pipe to your mouth, you should tell us nothing but the truth. The pipe is *wakan* and knows all things; you cannot fool it. If you lie, *Wakinyan-Tanka,* who guards the pipe, will punish you! *Hechetu welo!*"

The holy man rises from his position at the east and, moving around the lodge sun-wise, sits just at the right of the "lamenter." Dried buffalo chips are placed in front of the "lamenter," and upon these the pipe is placed with its stem pointing towards the heavens. The holy man now takes the tallow seal off the bowl of the pipe and places it upon the buffalo chips. He lights the pipe with a coal from the fire and, after offering it up to the Powers of the six directions, points the stem towards the "lamenter," who just touches it with his mouth. The holy man then makes a circle in the air with the stem of the pipe, smokes it a little himself, and again touches it to the mouth of the "lamenter." Then he again waves the pipe stem in a circle and again smokes it a little himself. This is done four times, and then the pipe is passed around the circle for all the men to smoke. When it returns to the holy man, with four motions he empties it upon the top of the tallow seal and the buffalo chips and then purifies it. Holding the pipe up in front of himself, the holy man says to the "lamenter": "Young man, you left here three days ago with your two helpers, who have set up for you the five posts upon the sacred place. Tell us everything that happened to you up there after these helpers left! Do not omit anything! We have prayed much to *Wakan-Tanka* for you and have asked the pipe to be merciful. Tell us now what happened!"

The "lamenter" replies, and after each time he says something of importance all the men in the lodge cry *"Hi ye!"*

"I went up on the mountain, and, after entering the sacred place, I walked continually to each of the four directions, always returning to the center as you had instructed me. During the first day, as I was facing the place where the sun goes down, I saw an eagle flying towards me, and when it came nearer I saw that it was a sacred Spotted Eagle. He rested on a tree near me but said nothing; and then he flew away to the place where the Giant *Waziah* lives."

To this all the men cry: *"Hi ye!"*

"I returned to the center, and then I went to the north, and as I stood there I saw an eagle circling above, and as he lighted near me I noticed that he was a young eagle, but it, too, said nothing to me, and soon he circled and soared off towards the place towards which we always face.

"I went back to the center where I cried and sent my voice, and then I went towards the place where the sun comes up. There I saw something flying towards me, and soon I saw that it was a baldheaded eagle, but he too said nothing to me.

"Crying, I returned to the center, and then when I went towards the place which we always face, I saw a red-breasted woodpecker standing on the offering pole. I believe he may have given to me something of his *wochangi*, for I heard him say to me very faintly yet distinctly: 'Be attentive! [*wachin ksapa yo!*] and have no fear; but pay no attention to any bad thing that may come and talk to you!' "

All the men now say more loudly: *"Hi ye!"*; for this message which the bird gave is very important.

The "lamenter" continues: "Although I was crying and sending my voice continually, this was all that I heard and saw that first day. Then night fell, and I lay down with my head at the center and went to sleep; and in my sleep I heard and saw my people, and I noticed that they were all very happy.

"I arose in the middle of the night, and again walked to each of the four directions, returning to the center each time, continually sending my voice. Just before the morning star came up, I again visited the four quarters, and just as I reached the place where the sun rises, I saw the Morning Star, and I noticed that at first it was all red, and then it changed to blue, and then into yellow, and finally I saw that it was white, and in these four colors I saw the four ages. Although this star did not really speak to me, yet it taught me very much.

"I stood there waiting for the sun to rise, and just at dawn I saw the world full of little winged people, and they were all rejoicing. Finally the sun came up, bringing its light into the world, and then I began to cry and returned to the center where I lay down, leaning my pipe against the center offering-pole.

"As I lay there at the center I could hear all sorts of little wingeds who were sitting on the poles, but none of them spoke to me. I looked at my pipe and there I saw two ants walking on the stem. Perhaps they wished to speak to me, but soon they left.

"Often during the day as I was crying and sending my voice, birds and butterflies would come to me, and once a white bufferfly came and sat on the end of the pipe stem, working his beautiful wings up and down. During this day I saw no large four-leggeds, just the little peoples. Then just before the sun went down to rest, I saw that clouds were gathering, and the Thunder-beings were coming. The lightning was all over the sky, and the thunder was terrifying, and I think that perhaps I was a little afraid. But I held my pipe up and continued to send my voice to *Wakan-Tanka;* and soon I heard another voice saying: *'Hee-ay-hay-ee-ee! Hee-ay-hay-ee-ee!'* Four times they said this, and then all the fear left me, for I remembered what the little bird had told me, and I felt very brave. I heard other voices, also, which I could not understand. I stood there with my eyes closed—I do not know how long—and when I opened them everything was very bright, brighter even than the day; and I saw many people on horseback coming towards me, all riding horses of different colors. One of the riders even spoke to me saying: 'Young man, you are offering the pipe to *Wakan-Tanka;* we are all very happy that you are doing this!' This is all that they said, and then they disappeared.

"The next day, just before the sun came up, as I was visiting the four quarters, I saw the same little red-breasted bird; he was sitting on the pole there where we always face, and he said almost the same thing to me as before: 'Friend, be attentive as you walk!' That was all. Soon after this the two helpers came to bring me back. This is all that I know; I have told the truth and have made nothing up!''

Thus the "lamenter" finishes his account. Now the holy man gives to him his pipe, which he embraces, and it is then passed around the circle, and a helper takes it and leans it, with its stem to the west, against the sacred mound at the east of the lodge. More hot rocks are handed into the lodge; the door is closed; and the *Inipi* begins.

The holy man prays, giving thanks to *Wakan-Tanka:* "*Hee-ey-hay-ee-ee!* [four times] O Grandfather, *Wakan-Tanka,* today You have helped us. You have been merciful to this young man by giving him knowledge and a path which he may follow. You have made his people happy, and all the beings who move in the universe are rejoicing!

"Grandfather, this young man who has offered the pipe to You, has heard a voice which said to him, 'be attentive as you walk!' He wants to know what this message means; it must now be explained to him. It means that he should always remember You, O *Wakan-Tanka,* as he walks the sacred path of life; and he must be attentive to all the signs that You have given to us. If he does this always, he will become wise and a leader of his people. O *Wakan-Tanka,* help us all to be always attentive! [5]

"This young man also saw four ages in that star there where the sun comes up. These are the ages through which all creatures must pass in their journey from birth to death.

"O *Wakan-Tanka,* when this young man saw the dawn of the day, he saw Your light coming into the universe; this is the light of wisdom. All these things You have revealed to us, for it is Your will that the peoples of the world do not live in the darkness of ignorance.

"O *Wakan-Tanka,* You have established a relationship with this young man; and through this relationship he will bring strength to his people. We who are now sitting here represent all the people, and thus we all give thanks to You, O *Wakan-Tanka.* We all raise our hands to You and say: '*Wakan-Tanka*, we thank You for this understanding and relationship which You have given to us.' Be merciful to us always! May this relationship exist until the very end!''

All the men now sing this sacred chant.

Grandfather, behold me!
Grandfather, behold me!
I held my pipe and offered it to You,
That my people may live!

Grandfather, behold me!
Grandfather, behold me!
I give to You all these offerings,
That my people may live!

Grandfather, behold me!
Grandfather, behold me!
We who represent all the people,
Offer ourselves to You,
That we may live!

After this chant, water is put on the rocks, and the *Inipi* is continued in the same manner that I have described before. This young man who has cried for a vision for the first time, may perhaps become *wakan;* if he walks with his mind and heart attentive to *Wakan-Tanka* and His Powers, as he has been instructed, he will certainly travel upon the red path which leads to goodness and holiness. But he must cry for a vision a second time, and this time the bad spirits may tempt him; but if he is really a chosen one, he will stand firmly and will conquer all distracting thoughts and will become purified from all that is not good. Then he may receive some great vision that will bring strength to the nation. But should the young man still be in doubt after his second ''lamenting,'' he may try a third and even a fourth time; and if he is always sincere, and truly humiliates himself before all things, he shall certainly be aided, for *Wakan-Tanka* always helps those who cry to Him with a pure heart.

Notes

1. Throughout this work I have translated *wichasha wakan* as "holy man" or "priest," rather than "Medicine man," which has been used incorrectly in many books on the Indians. [See the discussion of this term in the first part of chapter 13—eds.]

2. The Indian actually identifies himself with, or becomes, the quality or principle of the being or thing which comes to him in a vision, whether it be a beast, a bird, one of the elements, or really any aspect of creation. In order that this "power" may never leave him, he always carries with him some material form representing the animal or object from which he has received his "power." These objects have often been incorrectly called fetishes, whereas they actually correspond more precisely to what the Christian calls guardian angels, since for the Indian, the animals and birds, and all things, are the "reflections"—in a material form—of the Divine principles. The Indian is only attached to the form for the sake of the principle which is contained within the form.

3. Black Elk himself received his great vision when he was only nine years old. For a description of this vision, see Neihardt's *Black Elk Speaks,* chap. III.

4. This humiliation in which the Indian makes himself "lower than even the smallest ant," as Black Elk once expressed it, is the same attitude as that which, in Christianity, is called the "spiritual poverty"; this poverty is the *faqr* of the Islamic tradition or the *balya* of Hinduism and is the condition of those who realize that in relation to the Divine principle their own individuality is as nothing.

5. This message—"Be attentive!"—well expresses a spirit which is central to the Indian peoples; it implies that in every act, in every thing, and in every instant, the Great Spirit is present, and that one should be continually and intensely "attentive" to this Divine presence.

This presence of *Wakan-Tanka,* and one's consciousness of it, is that which the Christian saints have termed "living in the moment," the "eternal now," or what in the Islamic tradition is termed the *Waqt.* In Lakota this presence is called *Taku Skanskan,* or simply *Skan* in the sacred language of the holy men. [See the discussion of these terms in chapter 13—eds.]

4

The Salt Pilgrimage

Ruth Underhill

Along the northern beaches of the Gulf of California there are salt deposits, left in the low sandy stretches by the high tides. The country is waterless and uninhabited, and few whites have penetrated it even to the present day. Records have been left of this forbidding waste of sand dunes by Kino, by Anza,[1] and later by Lumholtz,[2] and all thought they were lucky to get themselves and their animals through alive. But the Papago, since prehistoric times, have been visiting this wilderness to fetch salt, both for use and for trade. Velarde reports: "There is salt in the inlets on the coast. The Pimas take some to distribute to friends and relatives, especially the Pimas of the west (Papago). Those of the north care little about it." [3]

To this day the Papago continue their pilgrimages to the salt beds.[4] They have, through the centuries, worked out routes which take them past the few hidden "tanks," or rocky reservoirs, of rain water to be found in the wastes of sand. Even so, the last lap of the journey which brings them to the gulf must be made with no other

From Ruth Underhill, *Papago Indian Religion* (New York: Columbia University Contributions to Anthropology 33 [1946]), pp. 211–42. Reprinted by permission of the author and Columbia University Press. The Papago are in south-central Arizona and in the adjoining portion of Sonora; the Pimas are their neighbors to the north. The account is based on field work done in the 1930s.

drinking water than that in their canteens. Though they take canny means to compass the journey safely, they make no attempt to minimize its hardships. Rather, these are emphasized to the last degree and used as an occasion for heroism. Even in the days of gourd canteens, they carried only the minimal quantity of water. Now that they have horses, they use them neither for carrying extra water nor extra quantities of salt. They fast voluntarily, almost to starvation. They run until men have been known to die from the effects. The south, which is the direction of the gulf, is often designated in their poetry, not by a color, but as "the painful direction."

The hardships, which have been thus raised from an accident into an institution, constitute one of the principal opportunities for gaining power. The journey is hedged about with ceremonial restrictions, from the time it is first proposed till long after the return. The salt pilgrimage is, in fact, very like a war party, and some of its rules are even more stringent. It is as though the Papago, who had so little to do with war, had transferred some of the magical elements connected with it to this safer and more regular form of ordeal.

The returned pilgrims were purified, like the enemy slayer and the eagle killer, and they achieved the same title: "ripe man." Their endeavor, like that of the other power seekers, resulted ultimately in rain. Pilgrims are thought to bring back with them the moist wind from the ocean, and the songs used for their purification are the same as those for the growth of crops. During the ritual the salt is ceremonially spoken of as corn. Yet it is not, in itself, sacred, any more than are the crops. After a little of it has been purified, just as specimen crops are purified at the cleansing ceremony, salt may be eaten, given away, or even traded, without further ritual. The Pima, who do not make the salt pilgrimage, used to get all their salt from the Papago by trade.

Preparation

All the Papago villages, in the old days, made the salt pilgrimage. Now, some have dropped it, and others may have dropped most of the ritual. Only Santa Rosa and Anegam have a full set of songs and speeches, and the others admit that "they know how to get salt. The rest of us just do what we can."

Each main village had for the salt expedition a recognized leader who was known as *síiwanyi,* the old name for rain magician. His functions were both practical and priestly, for not only must he know the route and the water holes but also must make ritual recitations and guide his party through a long series of ceremonial acts. He was usually chosen by the former leader from among the older men who had many trips to their credit, and he was expected to learn his duties by observation *en route.* As a leader grew old, he would begin to enlist the assistance of one of the more mature men, and finally the latter would step into his place without further formality. According to Papago pattern, the chosen assistant was a relative if possible.

The season for fetching salt was summer, after the high tides of spring had left a deposit on the beach. At this time the leader, after consultation with the keeper of the smoke, announced a meeting and told the conditions of the trip. "Now we are going down there. You will follow and obey everything. If you are lucky, you will be a good singer, a hunter, a fighter, a shaman."

Young men with their careers before them volunteered for the expedition, especially if they had not had a chance to go to war, for salt gathering ranked almost with war as an opportunity for dreaming and acquiring power. Having volunteered for his first trip, a man must continue to go for four successive years or he would be ill. During these first four trips he ranked as a neophyte and must be purified on his return. Afterward purification was shorter, but he observed the ceremonial restrictions on the trail. After ten trips, there were no restrictions or purification, and he was eligible as a leader.

Any village which had decided on a trip would send messengers to its neighbors, inviting recruits. The neighbors held meetings in their turn and reported the number of volunteers; then a date was set when all the parties should meet at the first stop along the way. If there were many men, the date might be eight days later; if only a few, four days. From the night of the meeting all the future pilgrims remained sexually continent. The neophytes practiced running, since when they reached the ocean it was by running that they would obtain a vision. They collected their equipment, which must all be new, since used property might have come under the influence of a menstruating woman.

Since the coming of horses, a horse has been the first requisite for the salt pilgrimage. But the Papago use this convenience sparingly. Each man took only one horse, rode it to the salt beds, loaded it, and walked home. Each pilgrim must keep his horse fresh for the trip. If he had none, he might borrow, and no one would dare refuse. The compensation to the horse's owner was half a load of salt, or one saddlebagfull. The saddlebags taken were the ancient netted receptacles of maguey fiber. Inside these the salt was wrapped in handwoven cotton sheets or, in old days, fiber mats. Each pilgrim must make ropes of hair or of maguey fiber, for a bridle and for hobbling his horse. He wore, in the old days, only breech cloth and sandals. At his waist he carried two canteens, made of gourds, covered with rabbit skin, and slung in a grass net. He also carried a pouch of parched corn meal and the small watertight basket which was his only utensil for eating and drinking. Beside the corn meal, "ripe men" might carry as much dried squash, tortillas, or any other food as they could manage.

For all equipment there was a special vocabulary, analogous to that used on the warpath. The horse was called the partner; the gourd, the jar; the basket, the dish; pinole, gruel; hay, weeds; salt, corn. For other common terms there were words showing a similar slight variation. These words the neophyte must learn and not misuse, under pain of accident on the journey.

Each village took prayer sticks in some form, to be offered to the ocean. The following list will show the variety introduced under the general heading prayer-stick offering:

> *Komarik:* prayer sticks with two turkey or eagle feathers. Left at each camping place, and one thrown by each man into the sea.
> *Pisinimo:* eagle down; no sticks. Each man brings his own down and throws it into the sea.
> *Anegam and Santa Rosa:* peeled white sticks of western

willow; no feathers. Carried by leader. One placed at every camp, and one given each man to throw in the sea.

Akchin: sticks with turkey or eagle feathers carried by leader, placed at each camp along the way and given men to carry into the sea and to bring back again. One large stick, with streamer of red cloth, planted on the beach.

San Miguel: strips of red cloth thrown into ocean.

All the villages took sacred corn meal as an offering. It must be made from flat-headed corn (two ears growing together, so that each had one flat side). Each man brought his own in a small pouch of rabbit skin carried at the waist.

During the period of preparation a meeting was held every night, at which the leader received reports of progress. When the last day arrived the leader asked: "Are you ready? Is everything new?" Next morning, when the dawn star rose, they started.

The Journey

There were two accessible salt deposits, reached by different routes. One route led straight south, through Quijotoa and Sharp Mountain, requiring only two days and a half. However, this meant forced marches, when the men had sometimes to travel half the night in order to reach the one camp which had water. The village of Akchin, which followed this route, took the minimum time for ceremonials and recited no long speeches. The other route led west to Ajo Mountain and then south, past the present Pinacate. This took four days; Santa Rosa and Anegam, which followed it, had long rituals for each of the watering places.

They rode single file, with the leader ahead "like a quail with her young." All the contingencies of the journey were dealt with by forms of sympathetic magic. They must never step off the trail, for that might "ruin somebody's [some animal's] house," and the animal would become their enemy. They must never think of home and their women, for this would delay their progress. For the same reason, they must always sleep with their heads to the ocean that it might "draw them on." They must never spill a drop of the precious water from their canteens, or they would be punished by a flood. This happened to one informant. As a result, the party had to ride in a cloudburst, and they found the salt beds so flooded that they could scarcely excavate any salt.

They observed the usual ceremonial restriction of speaking slowly and in a low voice, and Santa Rosa men were not allowed to speak at all. For the neophytes there were other rules. They must obey every direction instantly and must never walk, but always run. They had two meals a day, noon and evening, and these were special occasions for the exhibition of fortitude. They sat in a circle, each holding his basket, but not touching the corn meal he carried, while the leader stood in the center and spoke:

1. Was not this our purpose—that we should indeed make this journey on behalf of all? Thus we may attain much: great industry; great endurance of hunger; great energy. Something each man desires: to be a great runner, a shaman, a great singer, a great hunter. After having seen many things, look you, it is thus [as I have described] that each man will feel, look you, as he returns home [that is, he will have attained his heart's desire].

This he said that "the men might realize the seriousness of the occasion." If they took it lightly, there would be an accident: a horse might escape or die, or a man might be injured.

After the leader had spoken, he went to the first neophyte. Taking from the man's pouch a little corn meal, he placed it in the basket held ready and added water from the man's gourd, the man himself not touching anything. The leader stirred the mixture and handed it to its owner to drink, but the latter, if he was brave, would let the corn meal settle and drink the thin solution on top, throwing the rest away. It was not etiquette for a man to turn his back to the circle; "he might eat too much." "Ripe men" were not subject to these restrictions, but ate as they pleased. They might also smoke, a privilege forbidden the neophytes. They puffed toward the sun, with a long "A-a-ah!" and the usual invocation: "You stand there [pointing]. Give me blessing. Give me life."

Each stage of the journey had its appointed ceremonial procedure, varying from the planting of prayer sticks with a very brief invocation, to the presentation of long ritual speeches. Komarik and Anegam left a prayer stick at each water hole, the Anegam invocation being:

> 2. Lo, it is my own offering, which already I have carefully made and finished. I have come bringing it, and thus I do: I will offer it. See it and do for me increasingly [what I ask]. Grant powers to me: great speed in running; great industry; great skill in hunting. Grant powers to me: great lightness in running; great industry. I will take them; I will journey back, and I will attain my desire. Not hard will it be to turn homeward, not hard to reach my land.

This speech was impromptu. The one quoted was made by an informant who had special ambitions to be a runner.

Anegam and Santa Rosa made ritual speeches, those now preserved at Anegam being the most elaborate. On the second night of the journey (the first having ended a forced march), the Anegam crier called his men together.

> 3. Already has again leaped down [the sun] the gift of God, and shadow covers us. Already has arrived [Coyote] our shining-eyed comrade, our burning-eyed comrade. Around us four times he went, swiftly circling, then he stood still. His shining and his circling seemed of good omen. Then hurry! Gather quickly! Come together! That we may speed our ceremonies.[5]

The men seated themselves in a circle with arms folded and heads bowed. Each removed his sandals and tied a buckskin thong around his hair, that it might not blow and cause him to raise his hands, disturbing the meeting. The leader made an introductory speech known as The Heartening.

> 4. Already has again leaped down [the sun] the shining traveler, and shadow begins to cover us. Already has arrived [Coyote] our shining white comrade and four times around us he went circling. Already has he strengthened our hearts and perfected them; he

has strengthened our hands and perfected them; he has strengthened our legs and perfected them. He has done the same for our beasts. He has strengthened their hearts and perfected them; he has strengthened their hands (forelegs) and perfected them; he has strengthened their legs (hind legs) and perfected them.

Then followed the speech known as The Preparation. This is actually a psychological preparation for receiving visions at the ocean. More than that, it is in the nature of a pattern for such visions. A neophyte, even though he completely lacked imagination, could hardly fail, when in a state of exhaustion and with this speech in memory, to imagine the experience expected of him.

The speech is one of those known as *s'hámpataki nyió'k* (wise talks), which refer only to salt. The introduction is spoken in the usual oratorical style, with emphasis on the last word of sentence or phrase. This introduction describes at length the approach to the supernatural through tobacco smoke. But when the smoke has done its work and the suppliant finds himself before the supernatural, there begins the "throwing words" in monotonous panting form, which is the characteristic of salt orations.

5. Food she cooked for me;
   I did not eat.
   Water she poured for me;
   I did not drink.
   Then, thus to me she said:
   "What, then, is it?
   You did not eat the food which I have cooked,
   The water which I fetched you did not drink."
   Then, thus I said:
   "It is a thing I feel."

   I rose, and across the bare spaces did go walking;
   Did peep through the openings in the scrub,
   Looking about me, seeking something.
   Thus I went on and on.
   Where there was a tree that suited me,
   Beneath it prone and solitary I lay;
   My forehead upon my folded arms, I lay.

There was an ancient woman.
Some lore she had somehow learned,
And quietly she went about telling it.
To me she spoke, telling it.
Then did I raise myself upon my hands:
I put them to my face and wiped away the dust;
I put them to my hair and shook out twigs and rubbish.
I rose. I reached the shade before my house,
And there did try to sit; not like itself it seemed.
Then did I make myself small and squeeze through my narrow
        door.
On my bed I tried to lie; not like itself it seemed.
About me with my hand I felt;
About the withes that bound the walls I felt,
Seeking my jointed reed [cigarette].

Then, thus I did.
Within my hut I tried to feel about with my fingers,
At the base of my hut, in the dirt,
I tried to feel about with my fingers,
Seeking my jointed reed.
I could not find it.
To the center of the house did I go crawling [ceiling being low],
And the center post
Seemed a white prayer stick,
So like it was.
At its base did I go feeling in the dirt,
Seeking my jointed reed;
I could not find it.

There did I seize my flat stick [for hoeing].
I leaned upon it.
I made myself small and squeezed out the door.
Lo, I saw my ashes in many piles;
Already were they all hardened and all cracked.
I sat down, and with the hoe I went to breaking them.
Among them, somehow, did I find my reed joint.

Then did I scratch it.
Lo, there still tobacco lay.
There beside me, then, I saw
Near me lying a shaman ember charred.

Long ago had it grown moldy and full of holes.
I took it up, and four times hard did shake it.
Within a spark burst out and brightly burned.
Then the reed joint did I light, and to my lips I put it,
And somehow tried to move toward my desire.

Begin "throwing words."
In what direction shall I first breathe out?
To eastward did I breathe.
It was my reed smoke in white filaments stretching.
I followed it, and I went on and on.
Four times I stopped, and then I reacched
The rainhouse standing in the east.
Delightful things were done there.
All kinds of white clouds thatch it.
All kinds of rainbows form the binding withes.
The winds upon its roof fourfold are tied.
Powerless was I there.
It was my reed smoke;
Therewith did I go untying them.
Quietly I peeped in.
Lo, there I saw
Him (the rainmaker), my guardian
Yonder; far back in the house, facing away from me, he sat.
My reed smoke toward him did circling go
Toward the door; it did cause him to turn his eyes
And set him there.

Then did I say:
"What will you do, my guardian?
Yonder see,
The earth which you have spread thus wretched seems.
The mountains which you placed erect now crumbling stand.
The trees you planted have no leaves.
The birds you threw into the air
Wretchedly flit therein and do not sing.
The beasts that run upon the earth
At the tree roots go digging holes
And make no sound.
The wretched people
See nothing fit to eat." Thus did I say.

There did the entrails within him crack with pity.
"Verily nephew, for so I name you,
   Do you enter my house, and do you tell me Something?
   The people are afraid; none dares to enter.
   But you have entered and have told me,
   And Something, indeed, I will cause you to see."

"But let me reach my house [I said], then let it happen."
   Then in his breast he put his hand and brought forth seed:
   White seed, blue seed, red seed, smooth seed.
   Then did I fold it tight and grasp it and rush forth.

I saw the land did sloping lie.
Before I had gone far the wind did follow and breathe upon me.
Then, down at the foot of the east there moved the clouds,
And from their breasts the lightning did go roaring.
Though the earth seemed very wide,
Straight across it fell the rain
And stabbed the north with its drops.
Straight across it fell the rain
And stabbed the south with its drops.
The flood channels, lying side by side,
Seemed many;
But the water from all directions went filling them to the brim.
The ditches lying side by side
Seemed many;
But the water along them went bubbling.
The magicians on the nearby mountains
Went rushing out, gathering themselves together.
The storm went on and on.
It reached the foot of the west, it turned and faced about.
It saw the earth spongy with moisture.

Thus beautifully did my desire end;
Thus perchance will you also feel, my kinsman.

This speech, unlike most of the other orations and narratives, does not refer to anything in the origin myth. The "guardian" is not Elder Brother, and informants, when asked about him, could supply no further information: "the words of the speech were *given.''* But an Aztec prayer quoted by Sahagún [6] and addressed to the Tlalocs, or rain gods, has phraseology that is strikingly similar.

> No one has been able to escape the suffering and tribulation of the present famine. The animals and the birds themselves are in need on account of the great drought. It is pitiable to see the birds, of whom some have their wings falling and dragging on the earth as a result of their privations. Others fall and cannot stand on their feet. Others have their mouths open, panting to eat and drink.
>
> As for the other animals, O Lord, it is grievous to see them walking and falling down with weakness, licking the earth, their tongues hanging out, their gullets open, panting with hunger and thirst. . . .
>
> It is grievous, O Lord, to see everywhere the surface of the earth dry and unable to produce either grass or tree or anything which may serve for nourishment.

The Aztec has no parallel to the vivid Papago description of the desert and the hut. The phrases quoted, if they are indeed a heritage from some Nahua prayer, have undergone many permutations before inclusion in the salt ritual.

Santa Rosa gives an abbreviated version of the same material.

SALT SPEECH IN CAMP

6. Thus was my desire.
   Then hastily I ate the food which my wife had cooked;
   Hastily I took my child in my arms.
   "What is it?
   What has he learned that he is acting thus?
   The day has dawned when I must go."

Begin "throwing words."

Ready!
Then forth I stepped upon the west-lying road.
Utterly weary I was when evening fell.
Then I pushed together the remaining embers of my fire.
Beside them, with head bowed, I sat.
Within my pouch I thrust my hand

And brought forth my reed joint [cigarette].
I stood it up [in the fire, to light it].
I wet it.
Strongly I breathed out upon the west-lying road.
I asked of him, my guardian, many kinds of power.
I asked to be hunger enduring, thirst enduring, cold enduring.
I asked for swift-leaping legs,
Strong-grasping hands,
Keen eyes.
Four times the dawn poured over me
As I trod the west-lying road.
Then I reached him, my guardian,
And more than I asked he did for me.
A mixture he made that was like white clay.
With it on my breast he marked me;
On my back he marked me;
On my shoulder tops, both sides, he marked me.
Then most perfectly did he purify me,
So that nowhere do I take any hurt,
Wherever I go.
Thus should you, too, do and think,
All you my kinsmen.

On both routes a mountain was passed, just at the edge of the sandy waste which led to the gulf. The climbing of this peak and the first view of the "outspread water" was surrounded with ritual.

On the southern route, it was Sharp Mountain, reached on the second night. When the party was a mile or so from its base, the leader stopped them; bade the men tie everything tight on their horses and line up for a race. They galloped to the base of the mountain, where there was a tank, but when they reached it, no one must drink or water his horse. They waited till the leader arrived, having picked up any of the precious equipment dropped on the way. Then the neophytes must dismount and race on foot to the top of the mountain. "Part of the way you couldn't run. You had to crawl in the sand."

When each man reached the top, he turned to get his first view of the gulf and stretched out his right arm toward it; then moved the arm down his face and body, receiving power. The man with the prayer stick waved it. Then each planted a prayer stick, with the invocation:

> 7. I have brought the thing which I promised you. Now we are drawing close, and I desire something. I shall indeed remember that which I promised you, and I shall give it. Give me a good life and power.

When they returned to the tank, they might drink. Here they filled their canteens, for it was the last fresh water they would find. At a little distance grew the last tree they would see, and from it they cut scratching sticks, to be used as soon as they had touched salt.

Then they went as far as possible that night, so that they might get to the ocean and back the next day. It would be a waterless twenty-four hours, and they had drunk all they could at the tank in preparation. At this last camping place they left all extra equipment, and each man deposited one of his canteens. When they returned from their day of salt gathering, they would be sure of a drink.

The peak where Anegam and Santa Rosa performed their ritual was Black Mountain,[7] the Ararat where Elder Brother is said to have landed in his olla after the flood. Here, also, there was water, which the neophytes might not drink until they had raced up the hill. The fleetest of them carried one prayer stick for all. He waved it four times toward the ocean, then four times across his breast from right to left and four times down, while the others "cleansed" themselves with a similar motion. The man with the prayer stick then sat down and pounded it into the earth, with the usual invocation. Santa Rosa and Anegam also left prayer sticks at the tree where they cut scratching sticks.

On this last night, both Santa Rosa and Anegam made speeches which prefigured the purification of the neophyte and his acquisition of power. The Anegam speech describes most vividly the neophyte's entrance into the water and the ceremonial throwing of corn meal, which was the actual procedure. In the visions of Anegam, Coyote was the traditional protector, while with Santa

Rosa it is the unnamed "guardian" himself. The "marking" described is the same as that which is used in naming a child and in purifying a girl at puberty. It seems to stand for purification, though it is not now used for the salt pilgrim.

After the crier's call and "The Heartening," the Anegam speaker said:

8. Thus was fulfilled my desire.
   Toward the west a black road did lie.
   Then upon it did I tread and follow it.
   Four times did I camp and then did reach the wide-spreading
       water.

   Already had arrived the woolly comrade [Coyote].
   Around us four times did he go circling,
   And lo, already the white clay was mixed for me,
   The owl feather for painting laid upon it.

   To him did Coyote pull the young man and set him there.
   With the clay across the heart he marked him.
   Back he turned, and on the right shoulder marked him.
   In front he crossed, and on the left shoulder marked him.
   Back he turned, and on the back he marked him.
   Then well he purified him.

   There was corn meal, made from flat-headed corn.
   I sprinkled a handful, and again a handful,
   As I ran into the wide-spreading water.
   Though dangerously it crashed toward me,
   I did not reck,
   But I walked near and cast the sacred meal.

   There followed another wave.
   I did not reck.
   I walked nearer and cast the sacred meal.
   Though dangerously it roared, crashing and falling,
   I did not reck.
   I cast the sacred meal.

   There followed a fourth wave.
   Dangerously it roared;
   It crashed, it rolled over me, it broke behind me,
   But firm I stood and sought what I might see.

Then did I come forth
And along the beach begin to run,
And somewhere there did come upon
[Coyote], our woolly comrade,
Our comrade with burning eyes.

Dangerously he turned upon me,
But I ran toward him and did not reck.
Nearer I came and cast the sacred meal.
Then did he run, did run and run,
Till at last he only walked
And I did follow, and did come upon him.
In a circle did I run and come behind him.
I did not reck, but cast the sacred meal.

Again he dashed away.
I followed and did overtake him.
Then wild he barked and, crouching, turned to bite.
I did not reck, but cast the sacred meal.
Then he stood still and said:
"Verily, nephew, you will take away
All of my powers together,
And more and more a seer you will be
Of mysteries."

He took me, then, he took me;
He made me stand
Beside the wide-spreading water.
Under the spray that rose like smoke he took me.
Across on the other side he brought me out
To a pool of water thick as cactus juice.
He set me before it.

"Ready, nephew!
Now, if you are brave
You will drink all and you will take away
All of my powers together."
Then down I threw myself.
I drank and drank.
I drank it empty; then I scraped the dregs,
Folded them up, and carried them away.

Then, next, he took me
To a pool of water, thick with greenish scum;

He set me before it.
"Ready, nephew!
Now if you are brave
You will drink all and you will take away
All of my powers together."
Then down I threw myself.
I drank and drank.
I drank it empty, then I scraped the dregs,
Folded them tight, and carried them away.

Then, next, he took me
To a pool of yellow water
And set me before it.
"Ready, nephew!
Now if you are brave
You will drink all and you will take away
All of my powers together."
Then down I threw myself.
I drank and drank.
I drank it empty, then I scraped the dregs,
Folded them tight, and carried them away.

Then next he took me
To a pool of bloody water
And set me before it.
"Ready, nephew!
Now, if you are brave
You will drink all and you will take away
All of my powers together."
Then down I threw myself.
I drank and drank.
I drank it empty, then I scraped the dregs,
Folded them tight, and carried them away.

Then he stood still and said:
"If you shall take away
All of my powers together,
Then more and more a seer shall you be
Of mysteries."

Then he went, taking me,
And reached a land
Which lies before the sunset.

There abides the bitter wind.
Not slowly did we go.
About the wind's house dust lay scattered wildly.
Not slowly did he go and bring me there.
Then, leaping up, did I stretch out my hand.
I grasped the wind and slowly bent him down,
Till blood drops trickled from him.
Then from that house I seized
A leather shield and a short club,
A well-strung bow and smooth, straight-flying arrow,
A sharp-cutting sword.
These did I bind together
And did return whence I had come.

That water did I reach
Which was thick like cactus juice,
And there a magician sat.
Coyote made me stand before him, saying:
"What will you do for this my nephew?
I have brought him here."
Then forth he brought his white magic power
And placed it in my heart.

Then did I reach
The pool of water thick with greenish scum.
There a magician sat.
Coyote made me stand before him saying:
"What will you do for this my nephew?
I have brought him here."
Then forth he brought his green magic power
And placed it in my heart.

Then did I reach
The pool of yellow water.
Therein a magician sat.
Coyote made me stand before him, saying:
"What will you do for this my nephew?
I have brought him here."
Then forth he took his yellow magic power
And placed it in my heart.

Then did I reach
The pool of bloody water.

Therein a magician sat.
Coyote made me stand before him, saying:
"What will you do for this my nephew?
I have brought him here."
Then forth he brought his red magic power
And placed it in my heart.

Then back Coyote took me whence we came,
And reached the wide-spreading ocean.
Under the smoke-like spray he carried me,
Even to that place where I had run along the beach,
And there he left me.
Then down I fell, but rose and toward the east came running.
He had not slept [the leader of the expedition].
Straight to him walking, into his hands I put
The power I had won, tight pressing it.

Then I saw emerge
[The sun], the gift of God.
Then up I looked, I followed the road,
I camped four times, and reached my land.

The powers I had won beneath my bed I placed.
I lay upon them and lay down to sleep.
Then, in a little time mysteriously there came to me
Beautiful drunken songs;
Beautiful songs for the circling dance;
Beautiful songs for the maidens' dance,
Wherewith the maiden I might cozen,
My songs the stay-at-home youths did learn and sing,
Scarce permitting me to be heard.

With my songs the evening spread echoing,
And the early dawn emerged with a good sound,
The firm mountains stood echoing therewith,
And the trees stood deep rooted.

Again, the Santa Rosa version was abridged.

SALT SPEECH AT OCEAN (*Santa Rosa*)

9. It was mysteriously hidden.
   Wanting it, I could not find it.

In behind my house post I thrust my hand;
I could not find it.
There was a short leftover stick.
With this, feeling my way, I went out the door.
At the door my ashes were piled high.
Then, hard I struck them and out I took it,
My jointed reed [cigarette].
Burnt out, it seemed.
Then I scratched it.
There at the side charred blackness lay.
Four times I struck it,
And out a great spark shone.
I lit it in the fire;
I put it to my lips;
I smoked.
Right swiftly white filaments stretched out
Until they reached the sunrise.

Begin "throwing words."

I followed, and I reached the sacred house
That stands within the east.
All kinds of cloudiness were there bound up,
And I could not unloose it.
It was my cigarette smoke,
Floating beneath the clouds, it did unbind.
I tried to see him, my guardian,
But squarely turned away from me he sat.
It was my cigarette smoke
Circling about; it turned him
And set him facing me.
What will he do, my guardian?
"Most wretched lies the earth which you have made.
The trees which you have planted leafless stand.
The birds you threw into the air
Alight in vain and do not sing.
The springs of water are gone dry.
The beasts that run upon the earth,
They make no sound."

"Indeed, indeed, my nephew;
Is this so hard to change?

Not hard it is if all think and act with one accord.
Know this and go back whence you came."

Then home I turned me.
Westward the land was sloping laid;
Across it slowly did I go.
I reached my sleeping place.
Four dawns I passed.
Then, at the east a wind arose,
Well knowing whither it should blow.
The standing trees it went shaking;
The rubbish at the foot of the trees it piled.
All the way to the west it went, and there, back looking,
Turned itself and saw
The land well smoothed and finished.

Leaves on it there came forth.
A shining cloud toward the sky upreared
And touched it with its head.
All kinds of clouds together their crests upreared,
And with it they did go.
Although the north seemed very far,
Clear to the edge of it did they go.
Although the south seemed more than far,
Clear to the very edge of it did they go.
Then, within the great Rainy Mountains
A black cloud rose.
With them it mixed, and with them it did go.
Pulling out their white breast feathers
Did they go.

Then they stood still and looked.
Although the ditches seemed deep enough,
And needing no more digging,
Full to the brim they were,
With rubbish high piled on the edges.
Although the flood channels seemed deep enough
And needing no more digging,
Full to the brim, they were,
With rubbish high piled at the edges.
All the way to the west went [the clouds],

And there they turned and looked back.
They saw the land lying beautifully moist and finished.

Then on it old men in a circle sat
And held their meeting.
Then they scattered seed, and it came forth.
A thick root came forth;
A thick stalk came forth;
Great broad leaves came forth;
A fair tassel came forth,
And well it ripened.
Therewith were delightful the evenings;
Delightful the dawns.

Thus, indeed, should you think and desire, all you my kinsmen.

Salt Gathering and Sea Power

Akchin reached the salt beds on the day after viewing them
from the peak. The procedure was brief, for the men had left their
extra canteens several hours' march away and must reach them
before night. As they neared the salt beds, the leader urged them to
hurry. They dismounted without ceremony; grubbed into the earth
for the long stones embedded there, and with them smashed salt
lumps and proceeded to load them. As they did so, they adjured the
salt: "Be light! We are going back to see the old women." [8]

When each man finished loading his horse, he approached the
leader. The latter had, laid out before him, the sacred corn meal,
the peeled prayer sticks, and the newly cut scratching sticks, also a
piece of red cloth (in old days one of the hand woven headbands).
This cloth he tied to a large unfeathered stick, which he planted in
sight of the sea, with the usual invocation. Then he gave to each
man a pinch of corn meal in his left hand and a prayer stick in his
right. He also gave him a scratching stick to tie on his belt, with the
instructions:

10. I give you, as your property, this stick for scratching. You
will run, and you will reach the water. You will see how it con-

tinually comes toward you. You will approach it, and you will throw corn meal; corn meal you will pour upon it. There will come another wave: you will throw corn meal. There will come another (wave): you will throw corn meal. There will come another (wave): you will throw corn meal.

The men walked into the sea, throwing corn meal on the approaching waves, as they were bidden. To these desert people the waves had a peculiar horror, and the mere facing them was considered an act of bravery. Men who seem to make no great matter of battle or starvation have recounted to the writer with deep pride how they walked in up to their necks. They have heard but vaguely of swimming, from the Seri and the Yuma. To them the ocean is the edge of the world, fraught with power and death.

The Akchin men retained the prayer sticks in their hands as a protection. After they had faced the fourth wave, they went back to the leader. They gave him the prayer sticks to be used on another occasion and dusted off any corn meal that had remained on their hands into his pouch. Then they left, walking behind their horses. Any visions which the ocean might vouchsafe would appear on the journey home or during the subsequent purification.

Santa Rosa and the other villages of the western route traveled two days after viewing the ocean, since they must go along the coast some distance before reaching salt. The place they used, called Salty Badger, was a bed a quarter of a mile long and half a mile from the gulf. On reaching it, the neophytes dismounted and Akchin planted a prayer stick. Then the neophytes ran four times around the salt bed, counterclockwise while the older men galloped around on their horses.

Then they began to break up the lumps of salt and spread them to dry on sheets or mats. As each man picked up his first lump, he made the motion of passing it over his body, saying: "Give me power. Let me safely reach my home." Some addressed the salt bed: "We mean no harm. We have only come to gather salt."

While the salt was drying, the neophytes went into the sea. In some villages each man had his prayer stick and corn meal; in some the leader provided it. One, San Miguel, threw into the sea only scraps of red cloth.

Pisinimo ran to the top of the first sand dunes, whence the waves could be seen, and there strewed corn meal, saying: "Be favorable to me. Be smooth. Let me run and see what I shall see." When they reached the water, Pisinimo again gave an invocation: "Be favorable to me. Give me life. Let me be a runner; a shaman; a singer; a hunter."

All those who had their prayer sticks threw them into the sea. If, for some reason, a man was not acceptable to the supernatural, the waves would return the prayer stick. The most usual reasons for rejection were failure in sexual continence during the preparations for the journey or the fact that a man's wife might be menstruating. However, "the sea cleans the sticks." If a man persevered and threw in his offering four times, it would be accepted.

Sometimes a man himself was taken by the sea and engulfed like the prayer sticks. Speech No. 8 speaks of such an experience. No one attempted to rescue the drowning man, for he was being summoned by the supernatural. He might reappear after many years as a powerful shaman, or he might be turned into a bird or a fish.

Any object which a man saw while in the sea was a special gift to him from the supernatural. If he noticed a strand of seaweed, a shell, or a pebble, he sprinkled corn meal on the object, then took it home as a token, very powerful in cleansing salt pilgrims. A kind of seaweed known as "ocean foam" was particularly desired. Sometimes a man took hold of something which, when he found it in his hand, lost its beauty, and in that case he must put it back exactly where he found it, again sprinkling corn meal.

After their entry into the sea, the neophytes ran on the beach: a strenuous test of their powers. There was a headland some twenty miles from the salt bed, according to informants, and the men ran to this and back, not stopping except on the headland itself. Some men are reported to have perished from cold and exhaustion during this run, but all trained for it during their whole boyhood, for it was here that a magic experience was expected.

Everything that a man saw while running was an omen for his future career. One informant saw a flock of white cranes, which seemed to him to be men running. He followed them and was able to keep pace, and from this he knew that he would be a great runner. One saw the white cranes playing with a kickball, and knew that he would excel in this sport. One, exhausted from running, saw the mountain ahead of him revolving, and composed a series of songs about it which made him one of the popular leaders for the skipping dance. A legendary case recounts the story of a hero who heard a voice call to him: "The sea shaman wants to see you." He went into a cave, where he was taught songs, and when he emerged found that four years had passed. His house and property had been destroyed, as at death, and his wife considered herself a widow. But he was now a powerful shaman, so highly paid that he soon made good the losses.

There are no tales of men who failed to receive a vision. The aids to the experience, both material and spiritual, were so many that few could fail to have some sight or some emotion that might be regarded as a message from the supernatural. In the subsequent weeks of fasting this could easily magnify itself into a vision.

The runners returned late at night, and the leader waited for them. Speech No. 8 describes him sitting, half dead with cold and weariness. They gave him the objects they had picked up, which must be purified before their power could be used.

Purification

Early next morning they loaded the horses and left, adjuring the salt to be light, when they placed it in the saddlebags. As they turned to go home, the leader addressed the ocean: "I shall now return. Do you make it easy! Blow me along that I may arrive safely." They started with the elders ahead, then the neophytes, and last the leader, "to push them with his power." They must not look back or think of the salt, because this would impede their journey. They might hear singing behind them, which was the ocean trying to tempt them, but if they heeded it, they would be unable to move. The prohibition against noise was particularly rigid. "It would make the ocean angry." The neophytes must use their scratching sticks and, at the first opportunity, cut new ones to replace those which had been touched by ocean air.

On nearing the home village, they camped just outside, so that they could make an entry in the morning, and sent a messenger to announce their arrival, as after a war party. The small boys came out to meet them with bull roarers, which imitate the rain coming from the ocean. The old women came out in a group, begging: "Give me salt," and each man threw them gifts.

Each owned the salt which he had brought, except for two handfuls, which he must contribute to the common pile to be used for that evening's ceremonies. The rest he took to his house, where his family had spread a mat in the sun to receive it. Each member of the family took a handful, from which he breathed in to receive its power, and then the salt was dried; finally it was used or traded.

The family of each neophyte had prepared a shelter where he could pass the days of his purification, and his wife or mother made the new clay dishes which he was to use. An old man had been selected to act as his guardian. This man met him and conducted him immediately to the shelter, where he spent the day in sleep.

That night a public purification was held, for in this instance the sixteen days of retreat followed the purification ceremony instead of preceding it. Since the salt pilgrimage usually took place in summer, the ceremony was held out-of-doors. A fire was built to the east of the council house and in the intervening space was placed a pile of salt, to which each pilgrim contributed two handfuls. If the men brought tokens, such as seaweed and shells, these were ranged beside the fire and, in some villages, prayer sticks were placed with them.

At the north of the fire sat the older men who had made the pilgrimage more than four times and who needed no purification but were competent to purify others. They were the singers of the evening and were furnished with scraping sticks and basket drums. Opposite them, at the south, sat the returned neophytes while the spectators sat at the east and the shaman at the west, outside the door of the ceremonial house.

The keeper of the smoke had charge of the ceremonies. He first passed a ceremonial cigarette around the circle to the right, each man taking four puffs, then passing it to his neighbor, who received it and called the giver by the proper kinship term. When

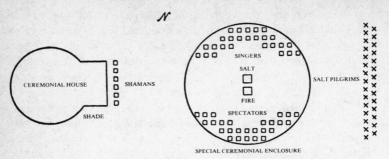

Arrangement for the public purification of the returned salt pilgrims.

the cigarette had passed around the whole circle, all bowed their heads, and a purification speech was made. No one was found who knew the Santa Rosa speech. The one recited is a variation of the material used in the previous speech, The Marking.

FOR SALT PURIFICATION (*Santa Rosa*)

11. The remains of a cigarette did I place upright [in the fire, to light it].
    I put it to my lips,
    I smoked.

    To the rain house standing in the west I came.
    All kinds of mist were bound up there,
    And I could not (unbind them).
    It was my cigarette smoke.
    Circling around it, it entered and unbound them.
    I tried to see him, my guardian,
    But squarely turned away from me he sat.
    It was my cigarette smoke.
    Circling around, it turned him toward me.

    Thus I spoke, to him, my guardian.
    "What will happen?
    Most wretched lies the earth which you have made.
    The trees which you have planted, leafless stand.
    The birds you threw into the air,
    They perch and do not sing.
    The springs of water are gone dry.

The beasts which run upon the earth,
They make no sound."
Thus I said.
"What will befall the earth which you have made?"
Then, thus spake he, my guardian.
"Is this so difficult?
You need but gather and recite the ritual.
Then, knowing all is well,
Go to your homes."

Then back I turned.
Eastward, I saw, the land was sloping laid.
Slowly along I went.
I reached my former sleeping place and laid me down.
Thus, four days did I travel toward the east.
Then in the west a wind arose,
Well knowing whither it should blow.
Up rose a mist and towered toward the sky,
And others stood with it, their tendrils touching.
Then they moved.
Although the earth seemed very wide,
Clear to the edge of it did they go.
Although the north seemed very far,
Clear to the edge of it did they go.
Although the south seemed very far,
Clear to the edge of it did they go.
Then to the east they went, and, looking back,
They saw the earth lie beautifully moist and finished.

Then out flew Blue Jay shaman;
Soft feathers he pulled out and let them fall.
The earth was blue (with flowers).
Then out flew Yellow Finch shaman;
Soft feathers he pulled out and let them fall,
Till earth was yellow (with flowers).
Thus was it fair, our year.

Thus should you also think,
All you my kinsmen.

After the speech, scraping-stick songs were sung. These have
the same introduction and ending as the songs to promote growth,

and in them the salt is spoken of as corn. . . . The introductory songs are the same on both occasions. Here these are omitted, and only those songs which refer to salt are quoted from the writer's collection.

SCRAPING-STICK SONGS FOR
THE PURIFICATION OF SALT PILGRIMS

12. *Hí híanai hu!*
    Here we pour it out and sing for it [the salt].
    Here we pour it out and sing for it.
    We shall pour it all out and eat it.
    The blue fetishes we have brought;
    We pour it out and sing for it.
    We shall eat it all,
    Hítcia háhina!

    Hí híanai hu!
    Here we pour it out and sing for it.
    Here we pour it out and sing for it.
    We shall pour it all out and eat it.
    The yellow fetishes we have brought;
    We pour it out and sing for it
    We shall eat it all,
    Hítcia háhina!

13. *Hí híanai hu!*
    The blue prayer stick,
    Met me there.
    Beside the corn
    Black [birds] in a row are singing.
    The kernels are blue.
    Hítcia háhina!

14. *Hí híanai hu!*
    Blue evening
    Knows all.
    Then I take the blue corn kernel [a prayer stick]
    And sing for it.
    Hítcia háhina!

    Hí híanai hu!
    Yellow evening

Knows all.
I take the yellow corn kernel
And sing for it.
Hítcia háhina!

15. Now I am ready to go.
The ocean wind from far off
Overtakes me.
It bends down the tassels of the corn.

The ocean wind,
From far it reaches me,
Far it blows and reaches me.
The squash leaves it has broken down.
Hítcia háhina!

16. *Hí híanai hu!*
The ocean water hurts my heart.
Beautiful clouds bring rain upon our fields.
Hítcia háhina!

17. *Hí híanai hu!*
The outspread water!
Running along it,
I seized the corn.
Hítcia háhina!

Hí híanai hu!
The outspread water [ocean]!
Running along it,
I seized the squash.
Hítcia háhina!

A song is included here which was made on a recent pilgrimage, as a joke, by men wearing modern clothes. It was not sung at the purification, but is passed around privately, with much amusement. The rhythm and the refrain are correct.

18. *Hí híanai hu!*
Pink shirt!
Braid on his hat!
Bowlegged!
Hítcia háhina!

After each two songs two of the singers walked over to perform an act of purification on the neophytes. They approached each
one and laid a scraping stick on his breast and back, pressing down
four times. As they did this, they breathed out, while the neophyte
breathed in the power being given him. Each singer then spoke to
him:

19. Hail! Thus do I to you. You will be like me. You will do
much. You will go about much. You will be like me in action.

Any other virtue of the singer might be augured for the neophyte.

As the singers returned to their seats, one man who was a he-
reditary sprinkler of corn meal, rose and strewed the sacred meal
made from flat-headed corn over their baskets and their scraping
sticks, also over the piles of salt and of tokens. During all this performance, the shaman sat by the fire, looking into the salt and then
around the village in order to perceive any sickness or evil which
might be present. He had his magic crystal in his hand and used it
to "give light." The songs continued until morning, when the
basket of salt was carried around by one of the pilgrims and distributed to the bystanders. As each took a lump, he breathed in from it
to obtain power.

BEFORE SALT IS DISTRIBUTED

20. *Hí híanai hu!*
    Morning is lulled to sleep.
    Hítcia háhina!
    Morning is lulled to sleep.
    Hítcia háhina!
    Finely ground corn [salt]
    By daylight we will give.
    Morning is lulled to sleep.
    Hítcia háhina!

After the distribution the meeting broke up.

The neophytes now passed the usual period of seclusion to
make safe the power they had acquired for failure to do so would
bring on them and their families a disease called yellow vomit. The

writer has not identified this disease, but has found it frequently mentioned by old Spanish writers as a pest of the country. The Papago say: "It comes from the smell of the ocean or the smell of the Apache. The Whites don't know that: that's why they have it so much."

The length of the period of seclusion varied. At Komarik it was one month the first time, then four days. At Akchin, eight days the first time, then four. At Pisinimo it was sixteen days, with a move nearer the house after every four. At Anegam it was four days away from the house, with diet restrictions for four days after the return.

In any case, after each four-day period the neophyte was bathed by his guardian in cool water. His face was not blacked as for purification after war, but otherwise he was under the same restrictions. He was not allowed to eat meat, salt, or grease. He must not look at the sun or go near the fire. For the first day and night, until after the public purification, he was allowed no fire at all. Afterward he could have a small one, but he must fan, not blow it. Every four days the dishes he had used were thrown away, each being "killed" by making a hole in the bottom, and new ones were provided by the women of the family. The women cooked for him, but on a separate fire, or a separate part of the fire, where none of the family food had been cooked. He must use the scratching stick—according to some, the same which he had brought from the ocean, according to others, a new one every four days. His wife was under no restrictions.[9]

Neophytes generally made their first pilgrimage at sixteen or seventeen, and this experience placed them within the ranks of adults. The seclusion during purification was the time when the fathers of eligible girls often approached the parents of neophytes to offer their daughters.

Notes

1. Herbert Bolton, *Anza's California Expedition* (Berkeley, 1930), vol. I, p. 90.

2. Carl Lumholtz, *New Trails in Mexico* (New York, 1912), pp. 196–254.

3. Luis Velarde, "Relación of Pimería Alta, 1716," ed. Rufus Kay Wyllys; trans. from Juan Matheo Manje, *Luz de tierra Incognita,* Libro II, *New Mexico Historical Review* 6 (1931), sec. 2, p. 127.

4. The Pima do not make the salt pilgrimage, but say they always traded for salt with the Papago.

5. In this speech circumlocutions are used instead of the important words "sun" and "coyote." In old days the sun was called the shining traveler, but Christian expressions have crept in.

6. Bernardino de Sahagún, *Histoire générale des choses de la Nouvelle-Espagne,* trans. and annotated by D. Jourdanet and Remi Siméon (Paris, 1880), pp. 344–48.

7. Mexican, Pinacate.

8. This refers to the old women who came out to meet the pilgrims on their return, begging for donations of salt.

9. This pilgrimage has obvious likenesses to the simpler ones made by Zuñi (Matilda Coxe Stevenson, *The Zuñi Indians,* Annual Report of the Bureau of American Ethnology 23 [1904], pp. 354–60); Acoma (Leslie A. White, *The Acoma Indians,* Annual Report of the Bureau of American Ethnology 47 [1932], p. 139); Laguna (Elsie Clews Parsons, *Laguna Genealogies,* Anthropological Papers of the American Museum of Natural History 19, part 5 [1923], p. 226); Cochiti (Esther Goldfrank, *The Social and Ceremonial Organization of Cochiti,* Memoirs of the American Anthropological Association 33 [1927], p. 9); and Hopi (Ernest Beaglehole, *Notes on Hopi Economic Life,* Yale University Publications in Anthropology 15 [1937], pp. 52–55). It also has many points in common with the Huichol expedition to gather *hikuli* or peyote (Carl Lumholtz, *Symbolism of the Huichol Indians,* Memoirs of the American Museum of Natural History 1, No. 2 [New York, 1900], pp. 126–236 and 268–80).

5

The Doctrine of the Ghost Dance

James Mooney

You must not fight. Do no harm to anyone. Do right always.
WOVOKA

The great underlying principle of the Ghost dance doctrine is that the time will come when the whole Indian race, living and dead, will be reunited upon a regenerated earth, to live a life of aboriginal happiness, forever free from death, disease, and misery. On this foundation each tribe has built a structure from its own mythology, and each apostle and believer has filled in the details

---

From James Mooney, *The Ghost-Dance Religion and the Sioux Outbreak of 1890*. Fourteenth Annual Report of the Bureau of American Ethnology (1896). In the late 1880s, Wovoka (Jack Wilson), a Paiute of western Nevada, received a revelation of the coming of a new world and of the dance that would prepare the way for it. The dance spread across the Great Basin and into the Plains, from Oklahoma to Canada, and the Bureau of American Ethnology sent James Mooney (1861–1921) to investigate it after the Sioux outbreak of 1890. Mooney himself was devoted to Irish nationalism and to the preservation of Irish culture among immigrants to the United States, and he was therefore in sympathy with the motives of the adherents of the Ghost Dance.

according to his own mental capacity or ideas of happiness, with such additions as come to him from the trance. Some changes, also, have undoubtedly resulted from the transmission of the doctrine through the imperfect medium of the sign language. The differences of interpretation are precisely such as we find in Christianity, with its hundreds of sects and innumerable shades of individual opinion. The white race, being alien and secondary and hardly real, has no part in this scheme of aboriginal regeneration, and will be left behind with the other things of earth that have served their temporary purpose, or else will cease entirely to exist.

All this is to be brought about by an overruling spiritual power that needs no assistance from human creatures; and though certain medicine-men were disposed to anticipate the Indian millennium by preaching resistance to the further encroachments of the whites, such teachings form no part of the true doctrine, and it was only where chronic dissatisfaction was aggravated by recent grievances, as among the Sioux, that the movement assumed a hostile expression. On the contrary, all believers were exhorted to make themselves worthy of the predicted happiness by discarding all things warlike and practicing honesty, peace, and good will, not only among themselves, but also toward the whites, so long as they were together. Some apostles have even thought that all race distinctions are to be obliterated, and that the whites are to participate with the Indians in the coming felicity; but it seems unquestionable that this is equally contrary to the doctrine as originally preached.

Different dates have been assigned at various times for the fulfillment of the prophecy. Whatever the year, it has generally been held, for very natural reasons, that the regeneration of the earth and the renewal of all life would occur in the early spring. In some cases July, and particularly the 4th of July, was the expected time. This, it may be noted, was about the season when the great annual ceremony of the sun dance formerly took place among the prairie tribes. The messiah himself has set several dates from time to time, as one prediction after another failed to materialize, and in his message to the Cheyenne and Arapaho, in August, 1891, he leaves the whole matter an open question. The date universally recognized among all the tribes immediately prior to the Sioux outbreak was the spring of 1891. As springtime came and passed, and summer grew and waned, and autumn faded again into winter without the realization of their hopes and longings, the doctrine gradually assumed its present form—that some time in the unknown future the Indian will be united with his friends who have gone before, to be forever supremely happy, and that this happiness may be anticipated in dreams, if not actually hastened in reality, by earnest and frequent attendance on the sacred dance.

On returning to the Cheyenne and Arapaho in Oklahoma, after my visit to Wovoka in January, 1892, I was at once sought by my friends of both tribes, anxious to hear the report of my journey and see the sacred things that I had brought back from the messiah. The Arapaho especially, who are of more spiritual nature than any of the other tribes, showed a deep interest and followed intently every detail of the narrative. As soon as the news of my return was spread abroad, men and women, in groups and singly, would come to me, and after grasping my hand would repeat a long and earnest prayer, sometimes aloud, sometimes with the lips silently moving, and frequently with tears rolling down the cheeks, and the whole body trembling violently from stress of emotion. Often before the prayer was ended the condition of the devotee bordered on the hysterical, very little less than in the Ghost dance itself. The substance of the prayer was usually an appeal to the messiah to hasten the coming of the promised happiness, with a petition that, as the speaker himself was unable to make the long journey, he might, by grasping the hand of one who had seen and talked with the messiah face to face, be enabled in his trance visions to catch a glimpse of the coming glory. During all this performance the bystanders awaiting their turn kept reverent silence. In a short time it became very embarrassing, but until the story had been told over and over again there was no way of escape without wounding their feelings. The same thing afterward happened among the northern Arapaho in Wyoming, one chief even holding out his hands toward me with short exclamations of *hŭ! hŭ! hŭ!* as is sometimes done by the devotees about a priest in the Ghost dance, in the hope, as he himself explained, that he might thus be enabled to go into a trance then and there. The hope, however, was not realized.

After this preliminary ordeal my visitors would ask to see the things which I had brought back from the messiah—the rabbit-skin robes, the piñon nuts, the gaming sticks, the sacred magpie feathers, and, above all, the sacred red paint. This is a bright-red ocher, about the color of brick dust, which the Paiute procure from the neighborhood of their sacred eminence, Mount Grant. It is ground, and by the help of water is made into elliptical cakes about six inches in length. It is the principal paint used by the Paiute in the Ghost dance, and small portions of it are given by the messiah to all the delegates and are carried back by them to their respective tribes, where it is mixed with larger quantities of their own red paint and used in decorating the faces of the participants in the dance, the painting being solemnly performed for each dancer by the medicine-man himself. It is believed to ward off sickness, to contribute to long life, and to assist the mental vision in the trance. On the battlefield of Wounded Knee I have seen this paint smeared on the posts of the inclosure about the trench in which are buried the Indians killed in the fight. I found it very hard to refuse the numerous requests for some of the paint, but as I had only one cake myself I could not afford to be too liberal. My friends were very anxious to touch it, however, but when I found that every man tried to rub off as much of it as possible on the palms of his hands, afterward smearing this dust on the faces of himself and his family, I was obliged in self-defense to put it entirely away.

The piñon nuts, although not esteemed so sacred, were also the subject of reverent curiosity. One evening, by invitation from Left Hand, the principal chief of the Arapaho, I went over to his tipi to talk with him about the messiah and his country, and brought with me a quantity of the nuts for distribution. On entering I found the chief and a number of the principal men ranged on one side of the fire, while his wife and several other women, with his young grandchildren, completed the circle on the other. Each of the adults in turn took my hand with a prayer, as before described, varying in length and earnestness according to the devotion of the speaker. This ceremony consumed a considerable time. I then produced the piñon nuts and gave them to Left Hand, telling him how they were used as food by the Paiute. He handed a portion to his wife, and before I knew what was coming the two arose in their places and stretching out their hands toward the northwest, the country of the messiah, made a long and earnest prayer aloud that *Hesûnanin,* "Our Father," would bless themselves and their children through the sacred food, and hasten the time of his coming. The others, men and women, listened with bowed heads, breaking in from time to time with similar appeals to "the Father." The scene was deeply affecting. It was another of those impressive exhibitions of natural religion which it has been my fortune to witness among the Indians, and which throw light on a side of their character of which the ordinary white observer never dreams. After the prayer the nuts were carefully divided among those present, down to the youngest infant, that all might taste of what to them was the veritable bread of life.

As I had always shown a sympathy for their ideas and feelings, and had now accomplished a long journey to the messiah himself at the cost of considerable difficulty and hardship, the Indians were at last fully satisfied that I was really desirous of learning the truth concerning their new religion. A few days after my visit to Left Hand, several of the delegates who had been sent out in the preceding August came down to see me, headed by Black Short Nose, a Cheyenne. After preliminary greetings, he stated that the Cheyenne and Arapaho were now convinced that I would tell the truth about their religion, and as they loved their religion and were anxious to have the whites know that it was all good and contained nothing bad or hostile they would now give me the message which the messiah himself had given to them, that I might take it back to show in Washington. He then took from a beaded pouch and gave to me a letter, which proved to be the message or statement of the doctrine delivered by Wovoka to the Cheyenne and Arapaho delegates, of whom Black Short Nose was one, on the occasion of their last visit to Nevada, in August, 1891, and written down on the spot, in broken English, by one of the Arapaho delegates, Casper Edson, a young man who had acquired some English education by several years' attendance at the government Indian school at Carlisle, Pennsylvania. On the reverse page of the paper was a duplicate in somewhat better English, written out by a daughter of Black

Short Nose, a school girl, as dictated by her father on his return. These letters contained the message to be delivered to the two tribes, and as is expressly stated in the text were not intended to be seen by a white man. The daughter of Black Short Nose had attempted to erase this clause before her father brought the letter down to me, but the lines were still plainly visible. It is the genuine official statement of the Ghost-dance doctrine as given by the messiah himself to his disciples. It is reproduced here in duplicate and verbatim, just as received, with a translation for the benefit of those not accustomed to Carlisle English. In accordance with the request of the Indians, I brought the original to Washington, where it was read by the Indian Commissioner, Honorable T. J. Morgan, after which I had two copies made, giving one to the commissioner and retaining the other myself, returning the original to its owner, Black Short Nose.

The Messiah Letter (Arapaho version)

What you get home you make dance, and will give you the same. when you dance four days and in night one day, dance day time, five days and then fift, will wash five for every body. He likes you flok you give him good many things, he heart been satting feel good. After you get home, will give good cloud, and give you chance to make you feel good. and he give you good spirit. and he give you al a good paint.

You folks want you to come in three [months] here, any tribs from there. There will be good bit snow this year. Sometimes rain's, in fall, this year some rain, never give you any thing like that. grandfather said when he die never no cry. no hurt anybody. no fight, good behave always, it will give you satisfaction, this young man, he is a good Father and mother, dont tell no white man. Jueses was on ground, he just like cloud. Every body is alive again, I dont know when they will [be] here, may be this fall or in spring.

Every body never get sick, be young again,—(if young fellow no sick any more,) work for white men never trouble with him until you leave, when it shake the earth dont be afraid no harm any body.

You make dance for six weeks night, and put you foot [food?]

in dance to eat for every body and wash in the water. that is all to tell, I am in to you. and you will received a good words from him some time. Dont tell lie.

The Messiah Letter (*Cheyenne version*)

When you get home you have to make dance. You must dance four nights and one day time. You will take bath in the morning before you go to yours homes, for every body, and give you all the same as this. Jackson Wilson likes you all, he is glad to get good many things. His heart satting fully of gladness, after you get home, I will give you a good cloud and give you chance to make you feel good. I give you a good spirit, and give you all good paint, I want you people to come here again, want them in three months any tribs of you from there. There will be a good deal snow this year. Some time rains, in fall this year some rain, never give you any thing like that, grandfather, said, when they were die never cry, no hurt any body, do any harm for it, not to fight. Be a good behave always. It will give a satisfaction in your life. This young man is a good father and mother. Do not tell the white people about this, Juses is on the ground, he just like cloud. Every body is a live again. I don't know when he will be here, may be will be this fall or in spring. When it happen it may be this. There will be no sickness and return to young again. Do not refuse to work for white man or do not make any trouble with them until you leave them. When the earth shakes do not be afraid it will not hurt you. I want you to make dance for six weeks. Eat and wash good clean yourselves [The rest of the letter had been erased].

The Messiah Letter (*free Rendering*)

When you get home you must make a dance to continue five days. Dance four successive nights, and the last night keep up the dance until the morning of the fifth day, when all must bathe in the river and then disperse to their homes. You must all do in the same way.

I, Jack Wilson, love you all, and my heart is full of gladness for the gifts you have brought me. When you get home I shall give you a good cloud [rain?] which will make you feel good. I give you a good spirit and give you all good paint. I want you to come again in three months, some from each tribe there [the Indian Territory].

There will be a good deal of snow this year and some rain. In the fall there will be such a rain as I have never given you before.

Grandfather [a universal title of reverence among Indians and here meaning the messiah] says, when your friends die you must not cry. You must not hurt anybody or do harm to anyone. You must not fight. Do right always. It will give you satisfaction in life. This young man has a good father and mother. [Possibly this refers to Casper Edson, the young Arapaho who wrote down this message of Wovoka for the delegation].

Do not tell the white people about this. Jesus is now upon the earth. He appears like a cloud. The dead are all alive again. I do not know when they will be here; maybe this fall or in the spring. When the time comes there will be no more sickness and everyone will be young again.

Do not refuse to work for the whites and do not make any trouble with them until you leave them. When the earth shakes [at the coming of the new world] do not be afraid. It will not hurt you.

I want you to dance every six weeks. Make a feast at the dance and have food that everybody may eat. Then bathe in the water. That is all. You will receive good words again from me some time. Do not tell lies.

Every organized religion has a system of ethics, a system of mythology, and a system of ritual observance. In this message from the high priest of the Ghost dance we have a synopsis of all three. With regard to the ritual part, ceremonial purification and bathing have formed a part in some form or other of every great religion from the beginning of history, while the religious dance dates back far beyond the day when the daughter of Saul "looked through a window and saw King David leaping and dancing before the Lord." The feasting enjoined is a part of every Indian ceremonial gathering, religious, political, or social. The dance is to continue four successive nights, in accord with the regular Indian system, in which *four* is the sacred number, as *three* is in Christianity. In obedience to this message the southern prairie tribes, after the return of the delegation in August, 1891, ceased to hold frequent one-night dances at irregular intervals as formerly without the ceremonial bathing, and adopted instead a system of four-night dances at regular periods of six weeks, followed by ceremonial bathing on the morning of the fifth day.

The mythology of the doctrine is only briefly indicated, but the principal articles are given. The dead are all arisen and the spirit hosts are advancing and have already arrived at the boundaries of this earth, led forward by the regenerator in shape of cloud-like indistinctness. The spirit captain of the dead is always represented under this shadowy semblance. The great change will be ushered in by a trembling of the earth, at which the faithful are exhorted to feel no alarm. The hope held out is the same that has inspired the Christian for nineteen centuries—a happy immortality in perpetual youth. As to fixing a date, the messiah is as cautious as his predecessor in prophecy, who declares that "no man knoweth the time, not even the angels of God." His weather predictions also are about as definite as the inspired utterances of the Delphian oracle.

The moral code inculcated is as pure and comprehensive in its simplicity as anything found in religious systems from the days of Gautama Buddha to the time of Jesus Christ. *"Do no harm to any one. Do right always."* Could anything be more simple, and yet more exact and exacting? It inculcates honesty—*"Do not tell lies."* It preaches good will—*"Do no harm to any one."* It forbids the extravagant mourning customs formerly common among the tribes—*"When your friends die, you must not cry,"* which is interpreted by the prairie tribes as forbidding the killing of horses, the burning of tipis and destruction of property, the cutting off of the hair and the gashing of the body with knives, all of which were formerly the sickening rule at every death until forbidden by the new doctrine. As an Arapaho said to me when his little boy died, "I shall not shoot any ponies, and my wife will not gash her arms. We used to do this when our friends died, because we thought we would never see them again, and it made us feel bad. But now we know we shall all be united again." If the Kiowa had held to the Ghost-dance doctrine instead of abandoning it as they had done, they would have been spared the loss of thousands of dollars in horses, tipis, wagons, and other property destroyed, with much of the mental suffering and all of the physical laceration that resulted in consequence of the recent fatal epidemic in the tribe, when for weeks and months the sound of wailing went up night and morning, and in every camp men and women could be seen daily, with dress disordered and hair cut close to the scalp, with blood hardened in clots upon the skin, or streaming from mutilated fingers and fresh gashes on face, and arms, and legs. It preaches peace with the whites and obedience to authority until the day of deliverance shall come. Above all, it forbids war—*"You must not fight."* It is hardly possible for us to realize the tremendous and radical change which this doctrine works in the whole spirit of savage life. The career of every Indian has been the warpath. His proudest title has been that of warrior. His conversation by day and his dreams by night have been of bloody deeds upon the enemies of his tribe. His highest boast was in the number of his scalp trophies, and his chief delight at home was in the war dance and the scalp dance. The thirst for blood and massacre seemed inborn in every man, woman, and child of every tribe. Now comes a prophet as a messenger from God to forbid not only war, but all that savors of war—the war dance, the scalp dance, and even the bloody torture of the sun dance—and his teaching is accepted and his words obeyed by four-fifths of all the warlike predatory tribes of the mountains and the great plains. . . .

The beliefs held among the various tribes in regard to the final catastrophe are as fairly probable as some held on the same subject by more orthodox authorities. As to the dance itself, with its scenes of intense excitement, spasmodic action, and physical exhaustion even to unconsciousness, such manifestations have always accompanied religious upheavals among primitive peoples, and are not entirely unknown among ourselves. In a country which produces magnetic healers, shakers, trance mediums, and the like, all these things may very easily be paralleled without going far from home. . . .

We may now consider details of the doctrine as held by different tribes, beginning with the Paiute, among whom it originated. The best account of the Paiute belief is contained in a report to the

War Department by Captain J. M. Lee, who was sent out in the autumn of 1890 to investigate the temper and fighting strength of the Paiute and other Indians in the vicinity of Fort Bidwell in northeastern California. We give the statement obtained by him from Captain Dick, a Paiute, as delivered one day in a conversational way and apparently without reserve, after nearly all the Indians had left the room:

> Long time, twenty years ago, Indian medicine-man in Mason's valley at Walker lake talk same way, same as you hear now. In one year, maybe, after he begin talk he die. Three years ago another medicine-man begin same talk. Heap talk all time. Indians hear all about it everywhere. Indians come from long way off to hear him. They come from the east; they make signs. Two years ago me go to Winnemucca and Pyramid lake, me see Indian Sam, a head man, and Johnson Sides. Sam he tell me he just been to see Indian medicine-man to hear him talk. Sam say medicine-man talk this way:
>
> "All Indians must dance, everywhere, keep on dancing. Pretty soon in next spring Big Man [Great Spirit] come. He bring back all game of every kind. The game be thick everywhere. All dead Indians come back and live again. They all be strong just like young men, be young again. Old blind Indian see again and get young and have fine time. When Old Man [God] comes this way, then all the Indians go to mountains, high up away from whites. Whites can't hurt Indians then. Then while Indians way up high, big flood comes like water and all white people die, get drowned. After that water go way and then nobody but Indians everywhere and game all kinds thick. Then medicine-man tell Indians to send word to all Indians to keep up dancing and the good time will come. Indians who don't dance, who don't believe in this word, will grow little, just about a foot high, and stay that way. Some of them will be turned into wood and be burned in fire." That's the way Sam tell me the medicine-man talk.

Lieutenant N. P. Phister, who gathered a part of the material embodied in Captain Lee's report, confirms this general statement and gives a few additional particulars. The flood is to consist of mingled mud and water, and when the faithful go up into the mountains, the skeptics will be left behind and will be turned to stone. The prophet claims to receive these revelations directly from God and the spirits of the dead Indians during his trances. He asserts also that he is invulnerable, and that if soldiers should attempt to kill him they would fall down as if they had no bones and die, while he would still live, even though cut into little pieces.

One of the first and most prominent of those who brought the doctrine to the prairie tribes was Porcupine, a Cheyenne, who crossed the mountains with several companions in the fall of 1889, visited Wovoka, and attended the dance near Walker lake, Nevada. In his report of his experiences, made some months later to a military officer, he states that Wovoka claimed to be Christ himself, who had come back again, many centuries after his first rejection, in pity to teach his children. He quotes the prophet as saying:

I found my children were bad, so I went back to heaven and left them. I told them that in so many hundred years I would come back to see my children. At the end of this time I was sent back to try to teach them. My father told me the earth was getting old and worn out and the people getting bad, and that I was to renew everything as it used to be and make it better.

He also told us that all our dead were to be resurrected; that they were all to come back to earth, and that, as the earth was too small for them and us, he would do away with heaven and make the earth itself large enough to contain us all; that we must tell all the people we met about these things. He spoke to us about fighting, and said that was bad and we must keep from it; that the earth was to be all good hereafter, and we must all be friends with one another. He said that in the fall of the year the youth of all good people would be renewed, so that nobody would be more than forty years old, and that if they behaved themselves well after this the youth of everyone would be renewed in the spring. He said if we were all good he would send people among us who could heal all our wounds and sickness by mere touch and that we would live forever. He told us not to quarrel or fight or strike each other, or shoot one another; that the whites and Indians were to be all one people. He said if any man disobeyed what he ordered his tribe would be wiped from the face of the earth; that we must believe everything he said, and we must not doubt him or say he lied; that if we did, he would know it; that he would know our thoughts and actions in no matter what part of the world we might be.

Here we have the statement that both races are to live together as one. We have also the doctrine of healing by touch. Whether or not this is an essential part of the system is questionable, but it is certain that the faithful believe that great physical good comes to them, to their children, and to the sick from the imposition of hands by the priests of the dance, apart from the ability thus conferred to see the things of the spiritual world.

Another idea here presented, namely, that the earth becomes old and decrepit, and requires that its youth be renewed at the end of certain great cycles, is common to a number of tribes, and has an important place in the oldest religions of the world. As an Arapaho who spoke English expressed it, "This earth too old, grass too old, trees too old, our lives too old. Then all be new again." Captain H. L. Scott also found among the southern plains tribes the same belief that the rivers, the mountains, and the earth itself are worn out and must be renewed, together with an indefinite idea that both races alike must die at the same time, to be resurrected in new but separate worlds.

The Washo, Pit River, Bannock, and other tribes adjoining the Paiute on the north and west hold the doctrine substantially as taught by the messiah himself. We have but little light in regard to the belief as held by the Walapai, Cohonino, Mohave, and Navajo to the southward, beyond the general fact that the resurrection and return of the dead formed the principal tenet. As these tribes received their knowledge of the new religion directly from Paiute apostles, it is quite probable that they made but few changes in or additions to the original gospel.

A witness of the dance among the Walapai in 1891 obtained from the leaders of the ceremony about the same statement of doctrine already mentioned as held by the Paiute, from whom also the Walapai had adopted many of the songs and ceremonial words used in connection with the dance. They were then expecting the Indian redeemer to appear on earth some time within three or four years.

They were particularly anxious to have it understood that their intentions were not hostile toward the whites and that they desired to live in peace with them until the redeemer came, but that then they would be unable to prevent their destruction even if they wished.

The manner of the final change and the destruction of the whites has been variously interpreted as the doctrine was carried from its original center. East of the mountains it is commonly held that a deep sleep will come on the believers, during which the great catastrophe will be accomplished, and the faithful will awake to immortality on a new earth. The Shoshoni of Wyoming say this sleep will continue four days and nights, and that on the morning of the fifth day all will open their eyes in a new world where both races will dwell together forever. The Cheyenne, Arapaho, Kiowa, and others, of Oklahoma, say that the new earth, with all the resurrected dead from the beginning, and with the buffalo, the elk, and other game upon it, will come from the west and slide over the surface of the present earth, as the right hand might slide over the left. As it approaches, the Indians will be carried upward and alight on it by the aid of the sacred dance feathers which they wear in their hair and which will act as wings to bear them up. They will then become unconscious for four days, and on waking out of their trance will find themselves with their former friends in the midst of all the oldtime surroundings. By Sitting Bull, the Arapaho apostle, it is thought that this new earth as it advances will be preceded by a wall of fire which will drive the whites across the water to their original and proper country, while the Indians will be enabled by means of the sacred feathers to surmount the flames and reach the promised land. When the expulsion of the whites has been accomplished, the fire will be extinguished by a rain continuing twelve days. By a few it is believed that a hurricane with thunder and lightning will come to destroy the whites alone. This last idea is said to be held also by the Walapai of Arizona, who extend its provisions to include the unbelieving Indians as well. The doctrine held by the Caddo, Wichita, and Delaware, of Oklahoma, is practically the same as is held by the Arapaho and Cheyenne from whom they obtained it. All these tribes believe that the destruction or removal of the whites is to be accomplished entirely by supernatural means, and they severely blame the Sioux for having provoked a physical conflict by their impatience instead of waiting for their God to deliver them in his own good time.

Among all the tribes which have accepted the new faith it is held that frequent devout attendance on the dance conduces to ward off disease and restore the sick to health, this applying not only to the actual participants, but also to their children and friends. The idea of obtaining temporal blessings as the reward of a faithful performance of religious duties is too natural and universal to require comment. The purification by the sweat-bath, which forms an important preliminary to the dance among the Sioux, while devotional in its purpose, is probably also sanitary in its effect.

Among the powerful and warlike Sioux of the Dakotas, already restless under both old and recent grievances, and more lately brought to the edge of starvation by a reduction of rations, the doctrine speedily assumed a hostile meaning and developed some peculiar features, for which reason it deserves particular notice as concerns this tribe. The earliest rumors of the new messiah came to the Sioux from the more western tribes in the winter of 1888–89, but the first definite account was brought by a delegation which crossed the mountains to visit the messiah in the fall of 1889, returning in the spring of 1890. On the report of these delegates the dance was at once inaugurated and spread so rapidly that in a few months the new religion had been accepted by the majority of the tribe.

Perhaps the best statement of the Sioux version is given by the veteran agent, James McLaughlin, of Standing Rock agency. In an official letter of October 17, 1890, he writes that the Sioux, under the influence of Sitting Bull, were greatly excited over the near approach of a predicted Indian millennium or "return of the ghosts," when the white man would be annihilated and the Indian again supreme, and which the medicine-men had promised was to occur as soon as the grass was green in the spring. They were told that the Great Spirit had sent upon them the dominant race to punish them for their sins, and that their sins were now expiated and the time of deliverance was at hand. Their decimated ranks were to be reinforced by all the Indians who had ever died, and these spirits were already on their way to reinhabit the earth, which had originally belonged to the Indians, and were driving before them, as they advanced, immense herds of buffalo and fine ponies. The Great Spirit, who had so long deserted his red children, was now once more with them and against the whites, and the white man's gunpowder would no longer have power to drive a bullet through the skin of an Indian. The whites themselves would soon be overwhelmed and smothered under a deep landslide, held down by sod and timber, and the few who might escape would become small fishes in the rivers. In order to bring about this happy result, the Indians must believe and organize the Ghost dance. . . .

The following extract is from a translation of a letter dated March 30, 1891, written in Sioux by an Indian at Pine Ridge to a friend at Rosebud agency:

> And now I will tell another thing. Lately there is a man died and come to life again, and he say he has been to Indian nation of ghosts, and tells us dead Indian nation all coming home. The Indian ghost tell him come after his war bonnet. The Indian (not ghost Indian) gave him his war bonnet and he died again.

The Sioux, like other tribes, believed that at the moment of the catastrophe the earth would tremble. According to one version the landslide was to be accompanied by a flood of water, which would flow into the mouths of the whites and cause them to choke with mud. Storms and whirlwinds were also to assist in their destruction. The Indians were to surmount the avalanche, probably in the manner described in speaking of the southern tribes, and on reaching the surface of the new earth would behold boundless prairies covered with long grass and filled with great herds of buffalo and other game. When the time was near at hand, they must assemble at certain places of rendezvous and prepare for the final abandonment of all earthly things by stripping off their clothing. In accordance with the general idea of a return to aboriginal habits, the believers, as far as possible, discarded white man's dress and utensils. Those who could procure buckskin—which is now very scarce in the Sioux country—resumed buckskin dress, while the dancers put on "ghost shirts" made of cloth, but cut and ornamented in Indian fashion. No metal of any kind was allowed in the dance, no knives, and not even the earrings or belts of imitation silver which form such an important part of prairie Indian costume. This was at variance with the custom among the Cheyenne and other southern tribes, where the women always wear in the dance their finest belts studded with large disks of German silver. The beads used so freely on moccasins and leggings seem to have been regarded as a substitute for the oldtime wampum and porcupine quill work, and were therefore not included in the prohibition. No weapon of any kind was allowed to be carried in the Ghost dance by any tribe, north or south, a fact which effectually disposes of the assertion that this was another variety of war dance. At certain of the Sioux dances, however, sacred arrows and a sacred bow, with other things, were tied on the tree in the center of the circle.

Valuable light in regard to the Sioux version of the doctrine is obtained from the sermon delivered at Red Leaf camp, on Pine Ridge reservation, October 31, 1890, by Short Bull, one of those who had been selected to visit the messiah, and who afterward became one of the prime leaders in the dance:

> My friends and relations: I will soon start this thing in running order. I have told you that this would come to pass in two seasons, but since the whites are interfering so much, I will advance the time from what my father above told me to do, so the time will be shorter. Therefore you must not be afraid of anything. Some of my relations have no ears, so I will have them blown away.
>
> Now, there will be a tree sprout up, and there all the members of our religion and the tribe must gather together. That will be the place where we will see our dead relations. But before this time we must dance the balance of this moon, at the end of which time the earth will shiver very hard. Whenever this thing occurs, I will start the wind to blow. We are the ones who will then see our fathers, mothers, and everybody. We, the tribe of Indians, are the ones who are living a sacred life. God, our father himself, has told and commanded and shown me to do these things.
>
> Our father in heaven has placed a mark at each point of the four winds. First, a clay pipe, which lies at the setting of the sun and represents the Sioux tribe. Second, there is a holy arrow

lying at the north, which represents the Cheyenne tribe. Third, at the rising of the sun there lies hail, representing the Arapaho tribe. Fourth, there lies a pipe and nice feather at the south, which represents the Crow tribe. My father has shown me these things, therefore we must continue this dance. If the soldiers surround you four deep, three of you, on whom I have put holy shirts, will sing a song, which I have taught you, around them, when some of them will drop dead. Then the rest will start to run, but their horses will sink into the earth. The riders will jump from their horses, but they will sink into the earth also. Then you can do as you desire with them. Now, you must know this, that all the soldiers and that race will be dead. There will be only five thousand of them left living on the earth. My friends and relations, this is straight and true.

Now, we must gather at Pass creek where the tree is sprouting. There we will go among our dead relations. You must not take any earthly things with you. Then the men must take off all their clothing and the women must do the same. No one shall be ashamed of exposing their persons. My father above has told us to do this, and we must do as he says. You must not be afraid of anything. The guns are the only things we are afraid of, but they belong to our father in heaven. He will see that they do no harm. Whatever white men may tell you, do not listen to them, my relations. This is all. I will now raise my hand up to my father and close what he has said to you through me.

The pipe here referred to is the most sacred thing in Sioux mythology. The sacred object of the Cheyenne is the "medicine arrow," now in the keeping of the band living near Cantonment, Oklahoma. The Crow and Arapaho references are not so clear. The Arapaho are called by the Sioux the "Blue Cloud" people, a name which may possibly have some connection with hail. The sprouting tree at which all the believers must gather refers to the tree or pole which the Sioux planted in the center of the dance circle. The cardinal directions here assigned to the other tribes may refer to their former locations with regard to the Sioux. The Cheyenne and Arapaho, who now live far west and south of the Sioux, originally lived north and east of them, about Red river and the Saskatchewan.

The most noted thing connected with the Ghost dance among

the Sioux is the "ghost shirt" which was worn by all adherents of the doctrine—men, women, and children alike. During the dance it was worn as an outside garment, but was said to be worn at other times under the ordinary dress. Although the shape, fringing, and feather adornment were practically the same in every case, considerable variation existed in regard to the painting, the designs on some being very simple, while the others were fairly covered with representations of sun, moon, stars, the sacred things of their mythology, and the visions of the trance. The feathers attached to the garment were always those of the eagle, and the thread used in the sewing was always the old-time sinew. In some cases the fringe or other portions were painted with the sacred red paint of the messiah. The shirt was firmly believed to be impenetrable to bullets or weapons of any sort. When one of the women shot in the Wounded Knee massacre was approached as she lay in the church and told that she must let them remove her ghost shirt in order the better to get at her wound, she replied: "Yes; take it off. They told me a bullet would not go through. Now I don't want it any more."

The protective idea in connection with the ghost shirt does not seem to be aboriginal. The Indian warrior habitually went into battle naked above the waist. His protecting "medicine" was a feather, a tiny bag of some sacred powder, the claw of an animal, the head of a bird, or some other small object which could be readily twisted into his hair or hidden between the covers of his shield without attracting attention. Its virtue depended entirely on the ceremony of the consecration and not on size or texture. The war paint had the same magic power of protection. To cover the body in battle was not in accordance with Indian usage, which demanded that the warrior should be as free and unincumbered in movement as possible. The so-called "war shirt" was worn chiefly in ceremonial dress parades and only rarely on the warpath.

Dreams are but incoherent combinations of waking ideas, and there is a hint of recollection even in the wildest visions of sleep. The ghost shirt may easily have been an inspiration from a trance, while the trance vision itself was the result of ideas derived from previous observation or report. The author is strongly inclined to the opinion that the idea of an invulnerable sacred garment is not original with the Indians, but, like several other important points pertaining to the Ghost-dance doctrine, is a practical adaptation by them of ideas derived from contact with some sectarian body among the whites. It may have been suggested by the "endowment robe" of the Mormons, a seamless garment of white muslin adorned with symbolic figures, which is worn by their initiates as the most sacred badge of their faith, and by many of the believers is supposed to render the wearer invulnerable. The Mormons have always manifested a particular interest in the Indians, whom they regard as the Lamanites of their sacred writings, and hence have made special efforts for their evangelization, with the result that a considerable number of the neighboring tribes of Ute, Paiute, Bannock, and Shoshoni have been received into the Mormon church and invested with the endowment robe. The Shoshoni and northern Arapaho occupy the same reservation in Wyoming, and anything which concerns one tribe is more or less talked of by the other. As the Sioux, Cheyenne, and other eastern tribes make frequent visits to the Arapaho, and as these Arapaho have been the great apostles of the Ghost dance, it is easy to see how an idea borrowed by the Shoshoni from the Mormons could find its way through the Arapaho first to the Sioux and Cheyenne and afterward to more remote tribes. Wovoka himself expressly disclaimed any responsibility for the ghost shirt, and whites and Indians alike agreed that it formed no part of the dance costume in Mason valley. When I first went among the Cheyenne and neighboring tribes of Oklahoma in January, 1891, the ghost shirt had not yet reached them. Soon afterward the first one was brought down from the Sioux country by a Cheyenne named White Buffalo, who had been a Carlisle student, but the Arapaho and Cheyenne, after debating the matter, refused to allow it to be worn in the dance, on the ground that the doctrine of the Ghost dance was one of peace, whereas the Sioux had made the ghost shirt an auxiliary of war. In consequence of this decision such shirts have never been worn by the dancers among the southern tribes. Instead they wear in the dance their finest shirts and dresses of buckskin, covered with painted and beaded figures from the Ghost-dance mythology and the visions of the trance.

The Ghost dance is variously named among the different tribes.

In its original home among the Paiute it is called *Nänigükwa,* "dance in a circle" (*nüka,* dance), to distinguish it from the other dances of the tribe, which have only the ordinary up-and-down step without the circular movement. The Shoshoni call it *Tänä'räyün* or *Tämanä'rayära,* which may be rendered "everybody dragging," in allusion to the manner in which the dancers move around the circle holding hands, as children do in their ring games. They insist that it is a revival of a similar dance which existed among them fifty years ago. The Comanche call it *A'p-anĕka'ra,* "the Father's dance," or sometimes the dance "with joined hands." The Kiowa call it *Mânposo'ti guan,* "dance with clasped hands," and the frenzy, *guan â'dalka-i,* "dance craziness." The Caddo know it as *A'ă kakï'mbawi'ut,* "the prayer of all to the Father," or as the *Nänisana ka au'-shan,* "nänisana dance," from *nänisana,* "my children," which forms the burden of so many of the ghost songs in the language of the Arapaho, from whom they obtained the dance. By the Sioux, Arapaho, and most other prairie tribes it is called the "spirit" or "ghost" dance (Sioux, *Wana'ghi wa'chipi;* Arapaho, *Thigû'nawat*), from the fact that everything connected with it relates to the coming of the spirits of the dead from the spirit world, and by this name it has become known among the whites.

6

The Peyote Way

J. S. Slotkin

Peyote (*Lophophora williamsi*) is a spineless cactus which grows in the northern half of Mexico and for a short distance north of the Texas border. It has attracted attention because it is used as a sacrament in religious rites conducted by Indians in the United States and Canada belonging to the Native American Church. The Peyote Religion or Peyote Way, as it is called by members, is the most widespread contemporary religion among the Indians, and is continually spreading to additional tribes.

From the viewpoint of almost all Peyotists, the religion is an Indian version of Christianity. White Christian theology, ethics, and eschatology have been adopted with modifications which make them more compatible with traditional Indian culture. The religion probably originated among the Kiowa and Comanche in Oklahoma about 1885.

The Peyote rite is an all-night ceremony, lasting approximately

From J. S. Slotkin, "The Peyote Way," *Tomorrow* IV, no. 3 (1956). Reprinted by permission of Perennial Books, Ltd. Slotkin (1913–1958) was an anthropologist who worked primarily among the Menomini of Wisconsin; he became a member and officer of the Native American Church, the chief body of Peyotists. The adherents of Peyotism are centered in the Great Plains and extend west into Arizona and Nevada, east to the Great Lakes, and north into the Mackenzie Basin.

from sunset to sunrise, characteristically held in a Plains type tipi. Essentially the rite has four major elements: prayer, singing, eating the sacramental Peyote, and contemplation. The ritual is well defined, being divided into four periods: from sunset to midnight, from midnight to three o'clock, from three o'clock to dawn, and from dawn to morning. Four fixed songs sung by the rite leader, analogous to the fixed songs in the Catholic mass, mark most of these divisions.

The rite within the tipi begins with the Starting Song; the midnight period is marked by the Midnight Water Song; there is no special song at three o'clock; at dawn there is the Morning Water Song, and the rite ends with the Quitting Song. At midnight sacred water is drunk again and a communion meal eaten.

Usually five people officiate at the rite. Four are men: the leader, often referred to as the Roadman because he leads the group along the Peyote Road (that is, the Peyotist way of life) to salvation; the drum chief who accompanies the leader when he sings; the cedar chief who is in charge of cedar incense; and the fire chief who maintains a ritual fire and acts as sergeant-at-arms. A close female relative of the leader, usually his wife, brings in, and prays over, the morning water.

In clockwise rotation, starting with the leader, each male parti-

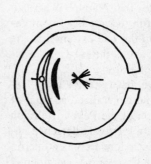

The arrangement of a tipi for the Peyote rite, with the door at the east. The large crescent is an earthen altar, with a place for the "Father" or "Chief" Peyote at its center; the line traversing it is the Peyote Road, from birth (at the south) to death (north). On the west side of the altar is the eagle bone whistle of the Roadman. At the center is the arrangement of sticks for the fire, and the small crescent west of the fire is made from its ashes. The participants sit in a circle around the walls of the tipi, and they light their cigarettes from the single stick shown just east of the fire. Together, the objects within the circle are the Waterbird.

cipant sings a set of four solo songs; he is accompanied on a water drum by the man to his right. The singing continues from the time of the Starting Song to that of the Morning Water Song; the number of rounds of singing therefore depends upon the amount of men present. On most occasions there are four rounds, so that each man sings a total of sixteen songs.

"God Pitied the Indian"

During the rite Peyote is taken in one of the following forms: the fresh whole plant except for roots (green Peyote), the dried top of the plant (Peyote button), or an infusion of the Peyote button in water (Peyote tea). Some people have no difficulty taking Peyote. But many find it bitter, inducing indigestion or nausea. A common complaint is, "It's hard to take Peyote."

The amount taken depends upon the individual, and the solemnity of the ritual occasion. There is great tribal variability in amount used, and accurate figures are virtually impossible to obtain. But in general one might say that under ordinary circumstances the bulk of the people take less than a dozen Peyotes. On the most serious occasions, such as rites held for someone mortally sick, those present take as much Peyote as they can; the capacity of most people seems to range from about four to forty Peyote buttons.

Peyotists have been organized into the Native American Church since 1918. These church groups run the gamut of comprehensiveness from the single local group on the one extreme, to the intertribal and international federation known as the Native American Church of North America, on the other extreme.

In a series of other publications I have discussed the early history of Peyotism, presented an historical and generalized account of the religion and given a detailed description of the Peyote Religion in a single tribe—all from the viewpoint of a relatively detached anthropologist.[1] The present essay is different. Here I concentrate on the contemporary uses of, and attitudes toward, sacramental Peyote, and write as a member and officer of the Native American

Church of North America. Of course the presentation is mine, but I think substantially it represents the consensus of our membership.

Long ago God took pity on the Indian. (Opinions vary as to when this happened: when plants were created at the origin of the world, when Jesus lived, or after the white man had successfully invaded this continent.) So God created Peyote and put some of his power into it for the use of Indians. Therefore the Peyotist takes the sacramental Peyote to absorb God's power contained in it, in the same way that the white Christian takes the sacramental bread and wine.

Lesson of Peyote

Power is the English term used by Indians for the supernatural force called *mana* by anthropologists; it is equivalent to the New Testament *pneuma,* translated as Holy Spirit or Holy Ghost. Power is needed to live. As a Crow Indian once remarked to me as we were strolling near a highway, man is like an auto; if the car loses its power it cannot go. Physically, power makes a person healthy, and safe when confronted by danger. Spiritually, power gives a person knowledge of how to behave successfully in everyday life, and what to make of one's life as a whole. The Peyotist obtains power from the sacramental Peyote.

Physically, Peyote is used as a divine healer and amulet.

For sick people Peyote is used in various ways. In a mild illness Peyote is taken as a home remedy. Thus when a man has a cold, he drinks hot Peyote tea and goes to bed. In more serious illnesses Peyote is taken during the Peyote rite. Such an illness is due not only to lack of sufficient power, but also to a foreign object within the body. Therefore a seriously sick person who takes Peyote usually vomits, thus expelling the foreign object which is the precipitating cause of the illness; then more Peyote is taken in order to obtain the amount of power needed for health. In cases of severe illness, the rite itself is held for the purpose of healing the patient; it is often referred to as a doctoring meeting. In addition to having the sick person take Peyote, as in less desperate cases, everyone else present prays to God to give the patient extra power so he or she will recover.

Members may keep a Peyote button at home, or on their person, to protect them from danger. The latter is particularly true of men in the armed forces. The power within the Peyote wards off harm from anything in the area of its influence. In cases of great danger, as when a young man is about to leave for military service, a prayer meeting is held at which everyone present beseeches God to give the man extra power to avoid harm.

Spiritually, Peyote is used to obtain knowledge. This is known as learning from Peyote. Used properly Peyote is an inexhaustible teacher. A stock statement is, "You can use Peyote all your life, but you'll never get to the end of what there is to be known from Peyote. Peyote is always teaching you something new." Many Peyotists say that the educated white man obtains his knowledge from books—particularly the Bible; while the uneducated Indian has to obtain his knowledge from Peyote. But the Indian's means of achieving knowledge is superior to that of the white man. The latter learns from books merely what other people have to say; the former learns from Peyote by direct experience.

A Comanche once said, "The white man talks *about* Jesus; we talk *to* Jesus." Thus the individual has a vividly direct experience of what he learns, qualitatively different from inference or hearsay. Therefore the Peyotist, epistemologically speaking, is an individualist and empiricist; he believes only what he himself has experienced.

A Peyotist maxim is, "The only way to find out about Peyote is to take it and learn from Peyote yourself." It may be interesting to know what others have to say; but all that really matters is what one has directly experienced—what he has learned himself from Peyote. This conception of salvation by knowledge, to be achieved by revelation (in this case, through Peyote) rather than through verbal or written learning, is a doctrine similar to that of early Middle Eastern Gnosticism.

The mere act of eating Peyote does not itself bring knowledge. The proper ritual behavior has to be observed before one is granted knowledge through Peyote. Physically, one must be clean, having bathed and put on clean clothes. Spiritually, one must put away all evil thought. Psychologically, one must be conscious of his personal inadequacy, humble, sincere in wanting to obtain the benefits of Peyote, and concentrate on it.

A Gift of Tongues

Peyote teaches in a variety of ways.

One common way in which Peyote teaches is by heightening the sensibility of the Peyotist, either in reference to himself or to others.

Heightened sensibility to oneself manifests itself as increased powers of introspection. One aspect of introspection is very important in Peyotism. During the rite a good deal of time is spent in self-evaluation. Finally the individual engages in silent or vocal prayer to God, confessing his sins, repenting, and promising to follow the Peyote Road (that is, the Peyotist ethic) more carefully in the future. If he has spiritual evil within him, Peyote makes him vomit, thus purging him of sin.

Heightened sensibility to others manifests itself as what might be called mental telepathy. One either feels that he knows what others are thinking, or feels that he either influences, or is influenced by, the thoughts of others. In this connection a frequent phenomenon is speaking in tongues, which results from the fact that people from different tribes participate in a rite together, each using his own language; Peyote teaches one the meaning of otherwise unknown languages.

For example, during the rite each male participant in succession sings solo four songs at a time. Recently a Winnebago sitting next to me sang a song with what I heard as a Fox text (Fox is an Algonquian language closely related to Menomini, the language I use in the rite), sung so clearly and distinctly I understood every word.

When he was through, I leaned over and asked, "How come you sang that song in Fox rather than Winnebago (a Siouan language unintelligible to me)?"

"I did sing it in Winnebago," he replied. The afternoon following the rite he sat down next to me and asked me to listen while he repeated the song; this time it was completely unintelligible to me because the effects of Peyote had worn off.

A second common way in which Peyote teaches is by means of revelation, called a vision. The vision is obtained because one has eaten enough Peyote under the proper ritual conditions to obtain the power needed to commune with the spirit world. The vision provides a direct experience (visual, auditory, or a combination of both) of God or some intermediary spirit, such as Jesus, Peyote Spirit (the personification of Peyote), or Waterbird.

The nature of the vision depends upon the personality and problems of the individual. The following are typical: He may be comforted by seeing or hearing some previously unexperienced item of Peyotist belief, or departed loved ones now in a happy existence. He may be guided on the one hand by being shown the way to solve some problem in daily life; on the other hand, he may be reproved for evil thoughts or deeds, and warned to repent.

Harmony and Healing

A third way in which Peyote teaches is by means of a mystical experience. This is relatively uncommon. It is limited to Peyotists of a certain personality type among the more knowledgeable members of the church; roughly speaking, they have what white people would call a mystical temperament. These Peyotists, in turn, rarely have visions, and tend to look upon them as distractions. The mystical experience may be said to consist in the harmony of all immediate experience with whatever the individual conceives to be the highest good.

Peyote has the remarkable property of helping one to have a mystical experience for an indefinite period of time, as opposed to most forms of mystical discipline under which the mystical experience commonly lasts for a matter of minutes. Actually, I have no idea of how long I could maintain such an experience with Peyote, for after about an hour or so it is invariably interrupted by some ritual detail I am required to perform.

What happens to the Peyotist phenomenologically that makes possible the extraordinary results I have described? It seems to depend on both the physiological and psychological effects of Peyote.

Physiologically, Peyote seems to have curative properties. Many times, after a variety of illnesses brought about by fieldwork conditions, I have left a Peyote meeting permanently well again.

Another physiological effect of Peyote is that it reduces fatigue to an astonishing extent. For instance, I am not robust, but after taking Peyote I can participate in the rite with virtually no fatigue—a rite which requires me to sit on the ground, cross-legged, with no back rest, and without moving, for ten to fourteen hours at a stretch; all this in the absence of food and water.

Final Warnings

Psychologically, Peyote increases one's sensitivity to relevant stimuli. This applies to both external and internal stimuli. Externally, for example, the ritual fire has more intense colors when I am under the influence of Peyote. Internally, I find it easier to introspect upon otherwise vague immediate experiences.

At the same time, Peyote decreases one's sensitivity to irrelevant external and internal stimuli. Very little concentration is needed for me to ignore distracting noises inside or outside the tipi. Similarly, extraneous internal sensations or ideas are easily ignored.

Thus, on one occasion I wrote in my field diary, "I could notice no internal sensations. If I paid very close attention I could observe a vague and faint feeling that suggested that without Peyote my back would be sore from sitting up in one position all night; the same was true of my crossed legs. Also, my mouth might be dry, but I couldn't be sure."

The combination of such effects as absence of fatigue, heightened sensitivity to relevant stimuli, and lowered sensitivity to irrelevant stimuli, should make it easier to understand how the individual is disposed to learn from Peyote under especially created ritual conditions.

To any reader who becomes intrigued by Peyote, two warnings should be given. First, I have discussed the effects of Peyote on those who used it as a sacrament under ritual conditions. The described responses of white people to Peyote under experimental conditions are quite different; in fact, they tend to be psychologically traumatic. Second, Peyote is a sacrament in the Native American Church, which refuses to permit the presence of curiosity seekers at its rites, and vigorously opposes the sale or use of Peyote for non-sacramental purposes.

Note

1. "Peyotism, 1521–1891," *American Anthropologist* 57 (1955), pp. 202–30; *The Peyote Religion* (Glencoe, Ill.: Free Press, 1956); "Menomini Peyotism," *Transactions of the American Philosophical Society* 42, pt. 4 (1952). See also Weston LaBarre, *The Peyote Cult* (New York: Schocken, 1969); and David F. Aberle, *The Peyote Religion Among the Navaho* (Chicago: Aldine, 1966)—eds.

7

The Clown's Way

Barbara Tedlock

Sacred clowns, although they are often portrayed as merely providing comic relief in otherwise deadly serious ceremonies, are in reality close to the heart of American Indian religion. As an Apache medicine man explained:

> People think that the clown is just nothing, that he is just for fun. That is not so. When I make other masked dancers and they do not set things right or can't find out something, I make that clown and he never fails. Many people who know about these things say that the clown is the most powerful.[1]

The Sioux clown, or *heyoka,* is a man or woman who has received the greatest possible vision, that of the Thunder Being, who is many but only one, moves counter-sunwise instead of sunwise, is shapeless but has wings, lacks feet but has huge talons, and is headless but has a huge beak; his voice is the thunderclap and the glance of his eye is lightning. During this great vision the person promised to work for the Thunder Being on earth in a human way, and until he fulfilled his promise by announcing that he would give the *Heyoka* Ceremony, the Thunder Being was "wearing" him, even as a medicine man wears an object or a symbol of an object which is subject to his commands. If he did not serve the Thunder

Being by clowning before his people, he would be struck and killed by a glance of the Thunder Being's eye.[2]

During a *heyoka* impersonation, the new *heyoka* does many seemingly foolish things, such as riding backwards on his horse with his boots on backwards so that he's coming when he's really going; if the weather is hot he covers himself with blankets and shivers as with the cold, and he always says "yes" when he means "no." These actions, while they expose him to the ridicule of the unthinking, have important meaning. As Lame Deer expressed it: "Fooling around, a clown is really performing a spiritual ceremony." [3] Indeed, these actions are a translation, as it were, of the knowledge of another reality: a non-objective, shapeless, unnatural world of pure power or energy symbolized by lightning. The contrary actions of the *heyoka* not only demonstrate some of the unnatural, anti-sunwise nature of the Thunder Being, but they also *open* people. As Black Elk said, the people are made "to feel jolly and happy at first, so that it may be easier for the power to come to them." [4] In the process of getting a good laugh at these backwards-forwards, cold-hot contraries, the people are opened to immediate experience.

In some tribes religious ceremonies cannot even begin until all the people, particularly any strangers, have laughed. Among the Eskimos, for example, it often takes an entire night of clowning for

During the winter of 1787–88, this man was going around a Sioux village as a *heyoka*, bedecked with feathers and singing to himself, when he decided to join a war party. Later the party sighted the enemy and he was warned to retreat, but he went forward instead and was killed. Part of a hide painting, from the 10th Annual Report of the Bureau of American Ethnology, p. 466.

the visitors from other villages or tribes to break down and laugh. During a festival in 1912, the Unalit of St. Michael performed several unsuccessful humourous episodes before the Malemuit and some Unalit from Unalakleet, until finally they presented an old man wearing a mask adorned with feathers and an enormous nose. This man was a caricature of a Yukon Indian; this tribe, called *ingkilik,* "louse-eater," was the chief enemy of both the hosts and visitors. Coming out and sitting down in the center of the floor, he placed his head on his breast and his hands in his lap. Then, raising his hand to his head, he cracked a louse audibly. This was too much for the guests and they howled with laughter. They had resisted so long because after laughing they would be at the mercy of their hosts, who could then theoretically demand anything from them. With the visitors completely *open* before their hosts, the religious drama could begin.[5] On the Northwest Coast the Haida symbolized this *opening* of their feast guests while greeting them on the shore: they burst open their baggage.

Although the guests of the Haida were prepared for a forceful greeting, they were more often than not annoyed with it.[6] Frequently, roaring laughter is neither the desired nor the actual response to ritual humor. For example, the Arapaho "Crazy Dancers" are said to "act as ridiculously as possible and annoy everyone in camp"; the Cahuilla "Funny Man" of Southern California "annoys people by throwing water on them or dropping live coals down their backs"; and the Iroquois "False Faces," on entering a house, scoop up handfuls of smoldering cinders from the fireplace and spray everyone in sight, sending them screaming in all directions.[7] The Assiniboine clowns are said to provoke laughter in their audience, but they also frighten them; when Navajo clowns approach too closely, "the smiles of the women and children quickly change to expressions of surprise, tempered with fear"; and Apache children are terrified by clowns, having been told that the clowns will put them in their baskets and carry them off to eat them.[8] The "Fool Dancers" of the Kwakiutl, when they are possessed by supernatural power, move from practical joking, as when they throw stones at the people or hit them with sticks, to outright terror, stabbing and even occasionally killing people.[9]

There is a clue to the potential terror of clowning in the visionary experience of the Plains clown. Black Elk, a Sioux Holy Man, explained it this way:

> When a vision comes from the thunder beings of the west, it comes with terror like a thunder storm; but when the storm of vision has passed, the world is greener and happier; for wherever the truth of vision comes upon the world, it is like a rain. The world, you see, is happier after the terror of the storm.[10]

A person who had this experience and became a *heyoka,* a visionary clown, could from then on strut before the lightning of his fear. Among the Cheyenne, as among the Sioux, men and women who had such a vision had to act it out by clowning before the entire tribe. These people, called "Contraries," put up a contrary lodge with its covering inside out, the lodge poles on the outside, and the smoke hole turned in the wrong direction. Dressed in rags, they backed in and out of the lodge, and sat against it upside down—that is to say, with head and body on the ground and legs against the wall—while all the people laughed at them. They did many other foolish things, such as run around wildly and pull weeds backwards: they backed up to weeds and pulled them from between their legs. They were said to act like lightning in a storm, thus becoming one with the sacred power they most feared.[11]

The clown's mystical liberation from ultimate cosmic fears brings with it a liberation from conventional notions of what is dangerous or sacred in the religious ceremonies of men. Among the northwestern Maidu of California, clowns interrupt the shaman whenever he tries to make a speech and parody everything he says.[12] In the Wintu *Hesi* Ceremony, the most important of all Wintu ceremonies, the clown, walking backwards, precedes the leader all around the inside of the dance house in perfect step with him, while delivering joking remarks about his bad singing.[13] Among the Zuñi of New Mexico, a *neweekwe* clown may lampoon a Beast Priest (shaman), wearing a bear paw on his left hand, a wolf snout on his nose, and acting wild. The clown of the Navajo Mountain Chant burlesques the sacred sleight-of-hand performances, clumsily revealing their secrets.[14]

Although the clown, by causing people to laugh at shamans and other religious authorities, might appear to weaken the very fabric of his society's religion, he may actually revitalize it by revealing higher truths. For example, the Navajo clown who reveals sleight-of-hand tricks is in effect reminding the people that these tricks are not in themselves the power which cures them, but are instead a symbolic demonstration of power which is itself invisible. A white man cured by a Navajo medicine man during a Red Ant ceremony asked him whether he *really* had red ants in his system. The curer told him, "No, not ants, but *ants*. We have to have a way of thinking strongly about disease." [15]

Because of the difficulty in seeing other than disruptive meanings for specific clown actions, I shall give a second example from my own knowledge of religious symbolism. The most common religious gesture among Pueblo Indians is the feeding of their kachina dancers (ancestors impersonated by initiated males) by sprinkling them with corn meal. On occasion, clowns have been known to substitute ashes or sweepings from the plaza for corn meal as their own "sacred" offering, which causes people to laugh. The clowns intend this immediate response, but their action also contains a hidden meaning. For ten days before each winter solstice every Zuñi woman saves her cooking and heating ashes and her sweepings and then on the solstice she and her daughters take them to the family corn field and deposit them, saying first to the sweepings: "I now deposit you as sweepings but in one year you will return to me as corn," and then to the ashes: "I now deposit you as ashes but in one year you will return to me as meal." [16] We can understand her assertion on the model of plant germination, which involves the bursting forth of life from the decay of the seed pod just as flames may suddenly spring forth from smoldering ashes. The clown's offering of ashes, then, can be understood as an esoteric substitute for corn meal. Here we see the clown's creative edge: no one else ever deviates from feeding the kachina dancers the corn meal, but the clown thinks of a possible variation, and one that is only apparently disrespectful.

The ability of American Indian religions to allow room for the disruptive, crazy, but creative power of the clown is perhaps their greatest strength. Within some Indian societies the clown is given his charter for "revolution" within the text of the sacred story of the creation itself. At Acoma Pueblo, the first *koshari* clown "was kind of crazy; he was active, picking around, talking nonsense, talking backwards," saying "I know everything," and speaking "loudly around the altar, even though it was supposed to be very quiet there." It was decided that he should live with his Sun Father because he was "not acting normally enough to be here with the people. He was different from the other people because he knew something about himself." From this time on he was to help the sun cross the sky, but he would be called upon from time to time to help on earth, and since he was not "afraid of anything," nor did he "regard anything as sacred," he was "to be allowed everywhere." So, although the people could not live with such a powerful bundle of energy all of the time, they did need him from time to time. When he was called upon to help on earth it was always for new ideas. For instance, when the people decided that they needed a harvest dance in order to "get away from the continuous solemnity of the secret ceremonies," Country Chief called upon *Koshari*, "because he knew of no new way to dance and he wanted to leave it to *Koshari* to arrange the dance and instruct the people in it. For *Koshari* had power to do this." [17] The Acoma avert the possibility of the stagnation of their religion in excessive esotericism by including the clown.

In other creation stories from the Southwest the clown leads the people out of the darkness of the underworld into the knowledge of daylight, thereby assuming an even more central position within the religion. At Isleta Pueblo *k'apyo shure* clowns used their horns in order to tunnel upwards to the earth's surface so that the people could come out. [18] At Zia both *koshairi* and *kwiraina* clowns helped the people emerge by leading them up through the four underworlds by means of four trees which they strengthened by their clowning:

They told him to make the tree firm and strong. So he climbed the tree doing funny things, shaking the branches as he went up.

> . . . Then he told them the tree was now ready and strong and they started to ascend. *Koshairi* went first and then the three mothers and all of the societies and the people in the order in which they had been created.[19]

By preparing the trees for climbing and making the tunnel through the earth these Pueblo clowns opened the way for their people to follow them out of the earth (ignorance) into the sunlight (knowledge).

The Jicarilla Apache, however, did not see this sunlight world as purely good, but as containing disease; the clown that led them up out of the dark earth (thought of as perfectly spiritiual and holy) was equipped with a ''horrible non-human laugh'' which scared away the sickness on the earth's surface.[20] In this origin story we learn a basic curing technique which is still practiced today by clowns in many tribes. Just as these Apache clowns kept smallpox and other epidemics away from the people with their sudden terrifying laugh, the Assiniboine, Plains Cree, and Plains Ojibwa clowns scare disease out of the people.[21] Navajo clowns during their Mud Dance all of a sudden stop dancing and rush up to a sick person and lift him high above their heads, sometimes tossing him into the air.[22] The Cheyenne ''Contraries'' also cure by quickly lifting people into the air, sometimes holding the head downward. Another curing method is to run up to a person very fast, in a threatening manner, and then either jump over him or else throw a piece of boiling-hot dog meat at him.[23]

By startling people in these ways clowns reverse their polarity, as it were, curing them by releasing them from any idle thoughts or worries. This clearing of worry from the mind is both an ethical value and an important preventative health concept. The Tewa beautifully express this ethic within one of their most important prayers:

> Now go to your homes
> Without worry
> Without weeping
> Without sadness.[24]

At Zuñi, before a man puts on his mask to impersonate the dead (an action which might well worry him), he is reminded to "make his mind a blank, just forget about worries"; otherwise he could be taken over by the terrible power of the mask and die. At Hopi the clown himself "must go out there with a happy heart, a heart without worry, to help his people." Releasing oneself from worry is central to much American Indian thought; as the Hopis have it, "disease and death are primarily caused by worry, which settles particularly in the stomach, causing it to harden." [25] The clown, as the enemy of worry, is also the curer of the stomach. The Zuñi *neweekwe* clowns are "the medicine men *par excellence* of the tribe, whose special province is the cure of all diseases of the stomach—the elimination of poisons from the systems of the victims of sorcery or imprudence." [26] At Acoma, where it is the *chayani* (magician or shaman) who actually makes the medicine for stomach troubles, the clown takes this medicine without permission and goes among the people, administering it to them through his own mouth. They prefer him to the *chayani* because "he knows no sadness, pain, or sickness." [27]

The clown himself is immune from stomach problems, that is, from poisoning. Among the California Maidu, the *pehei'pe* clown was the chief of the ceremony of *yomepa* or "poisons," powerful substances owned by shamans which killed on contact.[28] The Southwestern clown demonstrates his immunity by eating filth of all sorts without any visible harm. These scatalogical rites have quite naturally attracted much descriptive attention. As early as 1882 Adolph Bandelier, reporting on a clown performance at Cochiti Pueblo, noted that "the whole is a filthy, obscene affair. [They were] drinking urine out of bowls and jars used as privies on the house tops, eating excrements and dirt." [29]

At Zuñi Cushing described a *neweekwe* clown, or "glutton," as eating "bits of stick and refuse, unmentionable water, live puppies—or dead, no matter—peaches, stone and all, in fact everything soft enough or small enough to be forced down his gullet, including wood ashes and pebbles." [30] During the *koshari* initiation at Acoma, "one of the old members took a dish, urinated in it and mixed this with the medicine (herbs), another put phlegm from his nose in it, and the woman who was a *koshari* pulled out some pubic hair and threw it in." [31]

At Hopi during the Horned Water Serpent dance the seven *chükü* clowns eagerly drank three gallons of well aged, particularly foul-smelling urine, "rubbing their bellies after each draught and shouting, 'Very sweet!' " [32] The Jicarilla Apache clowns, whose name means "Striped Excrement," eat both dog and child feces; this makes their bodies very powerful, enabling them to dance ecstatically for hours, amusing and curing the people. Just before they eat this "medicine" they say, "Wa!" four times, imitating the sound people make when they are going to vomit. These clowns, known for their ability to cure vomiting, never give their "medicine" to anyone except themselves; for others, they chew small sun- and moon-shaped breads which they wear around their necks and then administer these, partially masticated, to the sick person. [33]

Thus the clown, even though he is a curer, has no medicine of his own; he either uses medicine that belongs to others, or else his "medicine" is nothing but common filth. All he has, otherwise, is himself and his own actions. In a word, clowns are poor, or at least they appear to be. All over North America they wear shabby clothing or even rags; they beg for and even steal food. Poor though they may be, they are also powerful and potentially terrifying, so that the people willingly give them anything when they go on begging tours. Zuñis, for example, give away whole dressed sheep or deer—or bushels of apples, cantaloups, and watermelons—to their *koyemshi* clowns, because "they are very dangerous, and whoever withholds food from them will injure himself—he will burn himself." [34] During the Iroquois Midwinter Ceremony, beggars wearing "False Face" masks and rags or a "parody of women's dress—very short skirts, out-size bras, girdles, and the like" go from house to house collecting tobacco or food. If anyone refuses them they throw dirt on them or else simply steal whatever they want. [35] The theft of food is common clown behavior in California, where the Miwok clowns are allowed to enter any home for this express purpose. [36]

The aggressive shamelessness the clowns display in their quest

for food is also extended to sex. They talk about, sing about, and
even perform shocking sexual displays in societies which are normally quite modest. For example, Jemez clowns "make advances
toward women"; Ponca clowns "crawl up and touch a woman's
genitalia in full daylight"; and Kwakiutl clowns jest with chiefs'
daughters, often making pointed references to sex.[37] In the South-
east, Creek clowns, while singing obscene songs during the Crazy
Dance, make sexual motions and even come into bodily contact
with women, touching and rubbing against their genitals.[38] The
Pueblo clowns formerly wore enormous dildos, and sometimes they
displayed their own genitals. Among the Arizona Tewa, Alexander
Stephen saw a clown snatch off another clown's breech clout and
"literally drag him by the penis nearly the whole length of the
dance court," and in California, Yuki clowns "hold each other's
penises during their frolics." [39] In the Plains, Crow clowns simu-
late intercourse with a horse made of willow bark; east of the
Plains, the Fox clowns, imitating stallions during the Mule Dance,
performed "indecent antics"; and in the Southwest the *koyemshi*
clowns tell the people at *Sha'lako,* the most important religious ceremony at Zuñi, to go out and "copulate with rams." [40]

From an 1880 entry in Bandelier's diary we learn of a particularly intense example of sexual display at Cochiti Pueblo:

> They chased after her, carried her back and threw her down in
> the center of the plaza, then while one was performing the coitus
> from behind, another was doing it against her head. Of course,
> all was simulated, and not the real act, as the woman was
> dressed. The naked fellow performed masturbation in the center
> of the plaza or very near it, alternately with a black rug and his
> hand. Everybody laughed.[41]

Such performances as this would have to get some response from
everyone present, including foreigners, and indeed they did. As the
American anthropologist Julian Steward noted, "funny as these are
to the natives, however, they have elicited only emotions of repug-
nance and disgust from even the ethnologist." [42] Whatever the attitudes of ethnologists, it is fortunate that at least some of them made

a record of such displays (often using Latin instead of English) while they still flourished. The objections and interferences of Protestant missionaries have been unrelenting, and during the 1920s the Bureau of Indian Affairs indulged in one last fling at religious persecution. "Obscene" practices were one of the principal targets of the Bureau's "religious crimes code," and clown performances have never been quite the same since.

My last example, reported from Hopi at the turn of the century by Alexander Stephen, contains an important detail suggesting an esoteric interpretation. A clown dressed as a woman comes into the plaza with a basin of water and proceeds to wash "her" legs while displaying a great false vulva and turning around so that all the spectators can see and laugh at it. Then another clown wearing a large false penis made of a gourd neck comes in, climbs on top of "her," and proceeds to "imitate copulation with her with the utmost grossness right on the sacred shrine." [43] This clowning episode, centering itself as it did on top of the shrine, might be interpreted as revealing the higher truth of a non-attachment to shrines, altars, or other religious objects; it certainly demonstrates the clown's own non-attachment.

Here, as at other clown performances, the onlookers are opened to immediate experience by laughter or shock; their minds are cleared of whatever worries they brought with them. It may be possible to attend a church service without so much as a smile, but American Indian religion, like Zen Buddhism, has a place for laughter, the laughter that goes with a sudden opening or dislocation in the universe. R. H. Blyth, one of the foremost Western students of Zen, has said that for him laughter is "a breakthrough of the intellectual barrier; at the moment of laughing something is understood; it needs no proof of itself. . . . When we laugh we are free of all the oppression of our personality, or that of others, and even of God, who is indeed laughed away." [44] Or, as a Zen monk explained, a well-placed, unexpected kick from his master helped him to attain enlightenment, and "since I received that kick from Ma Tsu, I haven't been able to stop laughing." [45] Or, as Black Elk put it, the people are made "to feel jolly and happy at first, so that it may be easier for the power to come to them." And, as the Acomas say of the first clown, "He knew something about himself."

Notes

1. Morris Opler, *An Apache Life Way* (Chicago: University of Chicago Press, 1941), p. 276.

2. For a description of the Thunder Being see Joseph Epes Brown, *The Sacred Pipe* (Baltimore: Penguin Books, 1971), p. 39; and Frances Densmore, *Teton Sioux Music,* Bulletin of the Bureau of American Ethnology 61 (1918), pp. 157–58.

3. John Fire/Lame Deer and Richard Erdoes, *Lame Deer Seeker of Visions* (New York: Simon and Schuster, 1972), p. 236.

4. John G. Neihardt, *Black Elk Speaks* (Lincoln: University of Nebraska Press, 1961), p. 192.

5. E. W. Hawkes, *The "Inviting-In" Feast of the Alaskan Eskimo,* Memoir of the Canada Department of Mines, Geological Survey, Anthropological series 45, no. 3 (1913), pp. 13–14.

6. John Swanton, *Contribution to the Ethnology of the Haida,* Memoirs of the American Museum of Natural History 8, pt. 1 (1909), p. 168.

7. Alfred Kroeber, *The Arapaho,* Bulletin of the American Museum of Natural History 18 (1902–1907), p. 192; William Strong, *Aboriginal Society in Southern California,* University of California Publications in American Archaeology and Ethnology 26 (1929), p. 166; De Cost Smith, "Witchcraft and Demonism of the Modern Iroquois," *Journal of American Folk-Lore* 1 (1888), p. 192.

8. Robert Lowie, *The Assiniboine,* Anthropological Papers of the American Museum of Natural History 4 (1909), pp. 62–65. Gladys Reichard, *Navaho Religion* (New York: Bollingen Foundation, 1963), p. 184. Opler, *An Apache Life Way,* p. 30.

9. Franz Boas, *The Social Organization of the Secret Societies of the Kwakiutl Indians,* Reports of the United States National Museum for 1895 (1897), pp. 468–71.

10. Neihardt, loc. cit.

11. George Grinnell, *The Cheyenne Indians* (New Haven, Conn.: Yale University Press, 1923), vol. II, pp. 204, 329.

12. Roland Dixon, *The Northern Maidu,* Bulletin of the American Museum of Natural History 17 (1905), p. 316.

13. S. A. Barrett, *The Wintun Hesi Ceremony,* University of California Publications in American Archaeology and Ethnology 14 (1919), p. 457.

14. Washington Matthews, *The Mountain Chant, a Navajo Ceremony,* Annual Report of the Bureau of American Ethnology 5 (1887), p. 447.

15. J. Barre Toelken, "The 'Pretty Language' of Yellowman," *Genre* 2, no. 3 (1969), p. 231.

16. Matilda Coxe Stevenson, *The Zuñi Indians,* Annual Report of the Bureau of American Ethnology 23 (1904), p. 132.

17. Matthew Stirling, *Origin Myth of Acoma and Other Records,* Bulletin of the Bureau of American Ethnology 135 (1942), pp. 33, 37, and 42–43.

18. Elsie Clews Parsons, *Isleta, New Mexico,* Annual Report of the Bureau of American Ethnology 47 (1932), p. 360.

19. Leslie White, *The Pueblo of Sia, New Mexico,* Bulletin of the Bureau of American Ethnology 184 (1962), p. 116.

20. Opler, *An Apache Life Way,* p. 276.

21. Alanson Skinner, *Political and Ceremonial Organization of the Plains-Ojibway,* Anthropological Papers of the American Museum of Natural History 11 (1914), p. 529.

22. Gladys Reichard, *Social Life of the Navaho Indians* (New York: Columbia University, 1928), p. 132.

23. Grinnell, op. cit., pp. 205, 210.

24. Vera Laski, *Seeking Life,* Memoirs of the American Folklore Society 50 (1958), p. 81.

25. Leo Simmons, *Sun Chief* (New Haven, Conn.: Yale University Press, 1942), p. 411.

26. Frank Hamilton Cushing, *Zuñi Breadstuff,* Indian Notes and Monographs, Heye Foundation 8 (1920), p. 620.

27. Stirling, op. cit., pp. 33–37, 65.

28. Dixon, op. cit., pp. 271–74.

29. Charles Lange, *Cochiti* (Carbondale: Southern Illinois University Press, 1968), p. 304.

30. Cushing, op. cit., p. 621.

31. Stirling, op. cit., p. 113.

32. Alexander Stephen, *Hopi Journal,* ed. Elsie Clews Parsons, Columbia University Contributions to Anthropology 25, vol. I, p. 328.

33. Morris Opler, *Myths and Tales of the Jicarilla Apache Indians,* Memoirs of the American Folklore Society 31 (1938), pp. 18, 189.

34. Ruth Bunzel, *Zuñi Texts,* Publications of the American Ethnological Society 15 (1933), p. 66.

35. Elizabeth Tooker, *The Iroquois Ceremonial of Midwinter* (Syracuse, N.Y.: Syracuse University Press, 1970), pp. 53, 129, 138.

36. E. W. Gifford, *Central Miwok Ceremonies,* Anthropological Records, no. 14 (1955), p. 270.

37. Albert Reagan, "Masked Dances of the Jemez Indians," *The Southern Workman* (1915), pp. 423–27; Alanson Skinner, *Ponca Societies and Dances,* Anthropological Papers of the American Museum of Natural History 11 (1915), p. 789; Boas, p. 546.

38. Frank Speck, *The Creek Indians of Taskagi Town,* Memoirs of the American Anthropological Association 2 (1907), p. 136.

39. Stephen, p. 491; Alfred Kroeber, *Handbook of the Indians of California,* Bulletin of the Bureau of American Ethnology 78 (1925), p. 186.

40. Robert Lowie, *Military Societies of the Crow Indians,* Anthropological Papers of the American Museum of Natural History 11 (1913), p. 217; Julian Steward, "Indian Ceremonial Buffoon," *Papers of the Michigan Academy of Science Arts and Letters* (1931), p. 194; Ruth Bunzel, *Zuñi Katcinas,* Annual Report of the Bureau of American Ethnology 47 (1932), p. 952.

41. Lange, op. cit., p. 303.

42. Steward, op. cit., p. 199.

43. Stephen, op. cit., p. 386.

44. Nancy Wilson Ross, *The World of Zen* (New York: Vintage Books, 1960), pp. 184–85.

45. Chang Chen-chi, *The Practice of Zen* (New York: Harper and Brothers, 1959), p. 52.

Part Two

THINKING ABOUT THE WORLD

8

An American Indian Model of the Universe

Benjamin Lee Whorf

I find it gratuitous to assume that a Hopi who knows only the Hopi language and the cultural ideas of his own society has the same notions, often supposed to be intuitions, of time and space that we have, and that are generally assumed to be universal. In particular, he has no general notion or intuition of TIME as a smooth flowing continuum in which everything in the universe proceeds at an equal rate, out of a future, through a present, into a past; or, in which, to reverse the picture, the observer is being carried in the stream of duration continuously away from a past and into a future.

After long and careful study and analysis, the Hopi language is seen to contain no words, grammatical forms, constructions or

From John M. Carrol, ed., *Language, Thought, and Reality, Selected Writings of Benjamin Lee Whorf* (Cambridge, Mass.: M.I.T. Press, 1956), pp. 57–64. Reprinted by permission of the M.I.T. Press, Cambridge, Massachusetts. Copyright © 1956 by The Massachusetts Institute of Technology. The Hopi are in northeastern Arizona. Whorf (1897–1941) is best known for his investigation of the relationship between language and thought, a relationship which he came to conceive of as "correlative" rather than as mechanistically determined.

expressions that refer directly to what we call "time," or to past, present, or future, or to enduring or lasting, or to motion as kinematic rather than dynamic (i.e. as a continuous translation in space and time rather than as an exhibition of dynamic effort in a certain process), or that even refer to space in such a way as to exclude that element of extension or existence that we call time, and so by implication leave a residue that could be referred to as time. Hence, the Hopi language contains no reference to "time," either explicit or implicit.

At the same time, the Hopi language is capable of accounting for and describing correctly, in a pragmatic or operational sense, all observable phenomena of the universe. Hence, I find it gratuitous to assume that Hopi thinking contains any such notion as the supposed intuitively felt flowing of time, or that the intuition of a Hopi gives him this as one of its data. Just as it is possible to have any number of geometries other than the Euclidean which give an equally perfect account of space configurations, so it is possible to have descriptions of the universe, all equally valid, that do not contain our familiar contrasts of time and space. The relativity viewpoint of modern physics is one such view, conceived in mathematical terms, and the Hopi Weltanschauung is another and quite different one, nonmathematical and linguistic.

Thus, the Hopi language and culture conceals a METAPHYSICS, such as our so-called naïve view of space and time does, or as the relativity theory does; yet it is a different metaphysics from either. In order to describe the structure of the universe according to the Hopi, it is necessary to attempt—insofar as it is possible—to make explicit this metaphysics, properly describable only in the Hopi language, by means of an approximation expressed in our own language, somewhat inadequately it is true, yet by availing ourselves of such concepts as we have worked up into relative consonance with the system underlying the Hopi view of the universe.

In this Hopi view, time disappears and space is altered, so that it is no longer the homogeneous and instantaneous timeless space of our supposed intuition or of classical Newtonian mechanics. At the same time, new concepts and abstractions flow into the picture, taking up the task of describing the universe without reference to such time or space—abstractions for which our language lacks adequate terms. These abstractions, by approximations of which we attempt to reconstruct for ourselves the metaphysics of the Hopi, will undoubtedly appear to us as psychological or even mystical in character. They are ideas which we are accustomed to consider as part and parcel either of so-called animistic or vitalistic beliefs, or of those transcendental unifications of experience and intuitions of things unseen that are felt by the consciousness of the mystic, or which are given out in mystical and (or) so-called occult systems of thought. These abstractions are definitely given either explicitly in words—psychological or metaphysical terms—in the Hopi language, or, even more, are implicit in the very structure and grammar of that language, as well as being observable in Hopi culture and behavior. They are not, so far as I can consciously avoid it, projections of other systems upon the Hopi language and culture made by me in my attempt at an objective analysis. Yet, if MYSTICAL be perchance a term of abuse in the eyes of a modern Western scientist, it must be emphasized that these underlying abstractions and postulates of the Hopian metaphysics are, from a detached viewpoint, equally (or to the Hopi, more) justified pragmatically and experientially, as compared to the flowing time and static space of our own metaphysics, which are *au fond* equally mystical. The Hopi postulates equally account for all phenomena and their interrelations, and lend themselves even better to the integration of Hopi culture in all its phases.

The metaphysics underlying our own language, thinking, and modern culture (I speak not of the recent and quite different relativity metaphysics of modern science) imposes upon the universe two grand COSMIC FORMS, space and time; static three-dimensional infinite space, and kinetic one-dimensional uniformly and perpetually flowing time—two utterly separate and unconnected aspects of reality (according to this familiar way of thinking). The flowing realm of time is, in turn, the subject of a threefold division: past, present, and future.

The Hopi metaphysics also has its cosmic forms comparable to these in scale and scope. What are they? It imposes upon the universe two grand cosmic forms, which as a first approximation in terminology we may call MANIFESTED and MANIFESTING (or, UNMANIFEST) or, again, OBJECTIVE and SUBJECTIVE. The objective or manifested comprises all that is or has been accessible to the senses, the historical physical universe, in fact, with no attempt to distinguish between present and past, but excluding everything that we call future. The subjective or manifesting comprises all that we call future, BUT NOT MERELY THIS; it includes equally and indistinguishably all that we call mental—everything that appears or exists in the mind, or, as the Hopi would prefer to say, in the HEART, not only the heart of man, but the heart of animals, plants, and things, and behind and within all the forms and appearances of nature in the heart of nature, and by an implication and extension which has been felt by more than one anthropologist, yet would hardly ever be spoken of by a Hopi himself, so charged is the idea with religious and magical awesomeness, in the very heart of the Cosmos, itself.[1] The subjective realm (subjective from our viewpoint, but intensely real and quivering with life, power, and potency to the Hopi) embraces not only our FUTURE, much of which the Hopi regards as more or less predestined in essence if not in exact form, but also all mentality, intellection, and emotion, the essence and typical form of which is the striving of purposeful desire, intelligent in character, toward manifestation—a manifestation which is much resisted and delayed, but in some form or other is inevitable. It is the realm of expectancy, of desire and purpose, of vitalizing life, of efficient causes, of thought thinking itself out from an inner realm (the Hopian HEART) into manifestation. It is in a dynamic state, yet not a state of motion—it is not advancing toward us out of a future, but ALREADY WITH US in vital and mental form, and its dynamism is at work in the field of eventuating or manifesting, i.e. evolving without motion from the subjective by degrees to a result which is the objective. In translating into English, the Hopi will say that these entities in process of causation "will come" or that they—the Hopi—"will come to" them, but, in their own language, there are no verbs corresponding to our "come" and "go" that mean simple and abstract motion, our purely kinematic concept. The words in this case translated "come" refer to the process of eventuating without calling it motion—they are "eventuates to here" (*pew'i*) or "eventuates from it" (*angqö*) or "arrived" (*pitu*, pl. *öki*) which refers only to the terminal manifestation, the actual arrival at a given point, not to any motion preceding it.

This realm of the subjective or of the process of manifestation, as distinguished from the objective, the result of this universal process, includes also—on its border but still pertaining to its own realm—an aspect of existence that we include in our present time. It is that which is beginning to emerge into manifestation; that is, something which is beginning to be done, like going to sleep or starting to write, but is not yet in full operation. This can be and usually is referred to by the same verb form (the EXPECTIVE form in my terminology of Hopi grammar) that refers to our future, or to wishing, wanting, intending, etc. Thus, this nearer edge of the subjective cuts across and includes a part of our present time, viz. the moment of inception, but most of our present belongs in the Hopi scheme to the objective realm and so is indistinguishable from our past. There is also a verb form, the INCEPTIVE which refers to this EDGE of emergent manifestation in the reverse way—as belonging to the objective, as the edge at which objectivity is attained; this is used to indicate beginning or starting, and in most cases there is no difference apparent in the translation from the similar use of the expective. But, at certain crucial points, significant and fundamental differences appear. The inceptive, referring to the objective and result side, and not like the expective to the subjective and causal side, implies the ending of the work of causation in the same breath that it states the beginning of manifestation. If the verb has a suffix which answers somewhat to our passive, but really means that causation impinges upon a subject to effect a certain result—i.e. "the food is being eaten," then addition of the INCEPTIVE suffix in such a way as to refer to the basic action produces a meaning of causal cessation. The basic action is in the inceptive state; hence whatever causation is behind it is ceasing; the causation explicitly referred to by the causal suffix is hence such as WE would call past time, and the verb includes this and the incepting and the decausating of the final state (a state of partial or total eatenness) in one statement. The translation is "it stops getting eaten." Without knowing the underlying Hopian metaphysics, it would be impossible to understand how the same suffix may denote starting or stopping.

If we were to approximate our metaphysical terminology more closely to Hopian terms, we should probably speak of the subjective realm as the realm of HOPE or HOPING. Every language contains terms that have come to attain cosmic scope of reference, that crystallize in themselves the basic postulates of an unformulated philosophy, in which is couched the thought of a people, a culture, a civilization, even of an era. Such are our words "reality, substance, matter, cause," and as we have seen "space, time, past, present, future." Such a term in Hopi is the word most often translated "hope"—*tunátya*—"it is in the action of hoping, it hopes, it is hoped for, it thinks or is thought of with hope," etc. Most metaphysical words in Hopi are verbs, not nouns as in European languages. The verb *tunátya* contains in its idea of hope something of our words "thought," "desire," and "cause," which sometimes must be used to translate it. The word is really a term which crystallizes the Hopi philosophy of the universe in respect to its grand dualism of objective and subjective; it is the Hopi term for SUBJECTIVE. It refers to the state of the subjective, unmanifest, vital and causal aspect of the Cosmos, and the fermenting activity toward fruition and manifestation with which it seethes—an action of HOPING; i.e. mental-causal activity, which is forever pressing upon and into the manifested realm. As anyone acquainted with Hopi society knows, the Hopi see this burgeoning activity in the growing of plants, the forming of clouds and their condensation in rain, the careful planning out of the communal activities of agriculture and architecture, and in all human hoping, wishing, striving, and taking thought; and as most especially concentrated in prayer, the constant hopeful praying of the Hopi community, assisted by their exoteric communal ceremonies and their secret, esoteric rituals in the underground kivas—prayer which conducts the pressure of the collective Hopi thought and will out of the subjective into the objective. The inceptive form of *tunátya*, which is *tunátyava*, does not mean "begins to hope," but rather "comes true, being hoped for." Why it must logically have this meaning will be clear from what has already been said. The inceptive denotes the first appearance of the objective, but the basic meaning of *tunátya* is subjective activity or force; the inceptive is then the terminus of such activity. It might then be said that *tunátya* "coming true" is the Hopi term for objective, as contrasted with subjective, the two terms being simply two different inflectional nuances of the same verbal root, as the two cosmic forms are the two aspects of one reality.

As far as space is concerned, the subjective is a mental realm, a realm of no space in the objective sense, but it seems to be symbolically related to the vertical dimension and its poles the zenith and the underground, as well as to the "heart" of things, which corresponds to our word "inner" in the metaphorical sense. Corresponding to each point in the objective world is such a vertical and vitally INNER axis which is what we call the wellspring of the future. But to the Hopi there is no temporal future; there is nothing in the subjective state corresponding to the sequences and successions conjoined with distances and changing physical configurations that we find in the objective state. From each subjective axis, which may be thought of as more or less vertical and like the growth-axis of a plant, extends the objective realm in every physical direction, though these directions are typified more especially by the horizontal plane and its four cardinal points. The objective is the great cosmic form of extension; it takes in all the strictly extensional aspects of existence, and it includes all intervals and distances, all seriations and numbers. Its DISTANCE includes what we call time in the sense of the temporal relation between events which have already happened. The Hopi conceive time and motion in the objective realm in a purely operational sense—a matter of the complexity and magnitude of operations connecting events—so that the element of time is not separated from whatever element of space enters into the operations. Two events in the past occurred a long "time" apart (the Hopi language has no word quite equivalent to our time) when many periodic physical motions have occurred between them in such a way as to traverse much distance or accumulate magnitude of physical display in other ways. The Hopi metaphysics does not raise the question whether the things in a distant village exist at the same present moment as those in one's own village, for it is frankly pragmatic on this score and says that any events in the distant village can be compared to any events in one's own village only by an interval of magnitude that has both time and space forms in it. Events at a distance from the observer can only be known objectively when they are "past" (i.e. posited in the objective) and the more distant, the more past (the more worked upon from the subjective side). Hopi, with its preference for verbs, as contrasted to our own liking for nouns, perpetually turns our propositions about things into propositions about events. What happens at a distant village, if actual (objective) and not a conjecture (subjective) can be known "here" only later. If it does not happen "at this place," it does not happen "at this time"; it happens at "that" place and at "that" time. Both the "here" happening and the "there" happening are in the objective, corresponding in general to our past, but the there happening is the more objectively distant, meaning, from our standpoint, that it is further away in the past just as it is further away from us in space than the here happening.

As the objective realm displaying its characteristic attribute of extension stretches away from the observer toward that unfathomable remoteness which is both far away in space and long past in time, there comes a point where extension in detail ceases to be knowable and is lost in the vast distance, and where the subjective, creeping behind the scenes as it were, merges into the objective, so that at this inconceivable distance from the observer—from all observers—there is an all-encircling end and beginning of things where it might be said that existence, itself, swallows up the objective and the subjective. The borderland of this realm is as much subjective as objective. It is the abysm of antiquity, the time and place told about in the myths, which is known only subjectively or mentally—the Hopi realize and even express in their grammar that the things told in myths or stories do not have the same kind of reality or validity as things of the present day, the things of practical concern. As for the far distances of the sky and stars, what is known and said about them is supposititious, inferential—hence, in a way subjective—reached more through the inner vertical axis and the pole of the zenith than through the objective distances and the objective processes of vision and locomotion. So the dim past of myths is that corresponding distance on earth (rather than in the heavens) which is reached subjectively as myth through the vertical axis of reality via the pole of the nadir—hence it is placed BELOW the present surface of the earth, though this does not mean that the nadir-land of the origin myths is a hole or cavern as we should understand it. It is *Palátkwapi* "At the Red Mountains," a land like our present earth, but to which our earth bears the relation of a distant sky—and similarly the sky of our earth is penetrated by the heroes of tales, who find another earthlike realm above it.

It may now be seen how the Hopi do not need to use terms that refer to space or time as such. Such terms in our language are recast into expressions of extension, operation, and cyclic process provided they refer to the solid objective realm. They are recast into expressions of subjectivity if they refer to the subjective realm—the future, the psychic-mental, the mythical period, and the invisibly distant and conjectural generally. Thus, the Hopi language gets along perfectly without tenses for its verbs.

Note

1. This idea is sometimes alluded to as the "spirit of the Breath" (*hikwsu*) and as the "Mighty Something" (*ʔaʔne himu*), although these terms may have lower and less cosmic though always awesome connotations.

9

Linguistic Reflection of Wintu Thought

Dorothy Lee

A basic tenet of the Wintu language, expressed both in nominal and verbal categories, is that reality—ultimate truth—exists irrespective of man. Man's experience actualizes this reality, but does not otherwise affect its being. Outside man's experience, this reality is unbounded, undifferentiated, timeless.

In fact, if "existence" and "being" are seen as referring to history, to the here and now, then this reality cannot be said to exist, and the Wintu certainly do not assert its existence or being. Yet I must apply these terms to it, since I have to use the English language. Man believes it but does not know it. He refers to it in his speech but does not assert it; he leaves it untouched by his senses, inviolate. Within his experience, the reality assumes tem-

From Dorothy Lee, *Freedom and Culture* (Homewood, Ill.: Prentice-Hall, 1959); originally published in *International Journal of American Linguistics* 10 (1944). Copyright © 1959 by Dorothy Lee; reprinted by permission of Prentice-Hall, Inc. The Wintu once occupied most of the valley of the Sacramento River in California. Dorothy Lee, who first came to them in the 1920s, is Greek by birth; she has taught her philosophically oriented anthropology at colleges throughout the United States.

porality and limits. As it impinges upon his consciousness he imposes temporary shape upon it. Out of the undifferentiated qualities and essences of the given reality, he individuates and particularizes, impressing himself diffidently and transiently, performing acts of will with circumspection. Matter and relationships, essence, quality are all given. The Wintu actualizes a given design endowing it with temporality and form through his experience. But he neither creates nor changes; the design remains immutable.

The given as undifferentiated content is implicit in the nominal categories of the Wintu. Nouns—except for kinship terms, which are classified with pronouns—all make reference primarily to generic substance. To the Wintu, the given is not a series of particulars, to be classed into universals. The given is unpartitioned mass; a part of this the Wintu delimits into a particular individual. The particular then exists, not in nature, but in the consciousness of the speaker. What to us is a class, a plurality of particulars, is to him a mass or a quality or an attribute. These concepts are one for the Wintu; the word for *red,* for example, is the same as for *redness* or *red-mass.* Plurality, on the other hand, is not derived from the singular and is of slight interest to him. He has no nominal plural form, and when he does use a plural word, such as *men,* he uses a root which is completely different from the singular word; *man* is wita but *men* is gis.

To someone brought up in the Indo-European tradition, this is a position hard to understand. We know that the plural is derived from the singular. It is logical and natural for our grammars to start with the singular form of a noun or a verb, and then go on to the plural. When we are faced with words like group or herd or flock, we call them, as a matter of course, collective plurals. Words like sheep or deer, which make no morphological distinction between singular and plural, are explained on the basis of historical accident or the mechanics of enunciation. But to the Wintu it is natural to speak of deer or salmon without distinction of number; to him a flock is a whole, not a collection of singular individuals. To us, the distinction of number is so important that we cannot mention an object unless we also simultaneously indicate whether it is singular or plural; and if we speak of it in the present tense, the verb we use must echo this number. And the Greek had to do more than this; if he had to make a statement such as *the third man who entered was old and blind,* the words *third, who entered, was, old* and *blind,* though referring to nonquantitative concepts, all had to reiterate the singularity of the man. The Wintu, on the other hand, indicates number only if he, the speaker, chooses to do so. In such a case he can qualify his noun with a word such as *many* or *one;* or he can express plurality of object or subject through special forms of the verb.

The care which we bestow on the distinction of number is lavished by the Wintu on the distinction between particular and generic. But here is a further difference. Whereas we find number already present in substance itself, the Wintu imposes particularity upon substance. We *must* use a plural when we are confronted by plural objects; the Wintu *chooses* to use a particularizing form. It is true that for certain nouns, such as those referring to live people and animals, the Wintu uses a particularizing form almost always; that for substances which we also regard as generic, such as fire and sand and wood, he almost always uses a generic form. But these are merely habitual modes of speaking from which he can and does deviate.

His distinction, then, is subjective. He starts from *whiteness* or *white* (hayi) a quality, and derives from this, as an observer, the particular—the *white one* (hayit). With the use of derivative suffixes, he delimits a part of the mass. We take the word for *deer* for example. In the instances I give, I shall use only the objective case, nop for the generic, and the nopum for the particular. A hunter went out but saw no *deer,* nop; another killed a *deer,* nopum. A woman carried *deer,* nop, to her mother; a hunter brought home *deer,* nopum. Now the woman's deer was cut in pieces and carried, a formless mass, in her back-basket; but the man carried his two deer slung whole from his shoulder. Some brothers were about to eat venison; they called, "Old man, come and eat *venison,* (nop)." The old man replied, "You can eat that stinking *venison,* (nopum) yourselves." The brothers saw it just as deer meat; to the old man it was the flesh of a particular deer, one which had been killed near human habitation, fed on human offal.

I have recorded two versions of the same tale, told respectively by a man and a woman. The man refers to a man's weapons and implements in the particular; the woman mentions them all as generic. The use of the word sem (se) is illuminating in this connection. As generic, sem, it means *hand* or *both hands* of one person, the fingers merged in one mass; spread out the hand, and now you have delimited parts of the hand: semum, *fingers*.

For the Wintu, then, essence or quality is generic and found in nature; it is permanent and remains unaffected by man. Form is imposed by man, through act of will. But the impress man makes is temporary. The deer stands out as an individual only at the moment of man's speech; as soon as he ceases speaking, the deer merges into deerness.

The concept of the immutability of essence and the transiency of form, of the fleeting significance of delimitation, is reflected in Wintu mythology. Matter was always there; the creator, *He who is above,* a vague being, was really a Former. People do not *come into being* as I say in my faulty literal translation of the myths; they *grow out of the ground;* they always existed. Dawn and daylight, fire and obsidian have always been in existence, hoarded; they are finally stolen and given a new role. In the myths, various characters *form* men out of materials which are already present; Coyote, for example, changes sticks into men. Throughout, form is shifting and relatively unimportant.

The characters, Coyote, Buzzard, Grizzly Bear, etc., are bewilderingly men and animals in their attributes, never assuming stable form. Even this semi-defined form may be changed with ease; Grosbeak is steamed faultily, for example, and turns into a grasshopper. The Wintu speak of these characters in English as *Coyote, Loon,* not *a coyote.* We have assumed that by this they mean a proper name. But it is probable that they refer to something undelimited, as we, for example, distinguish between fire and a fire. These characters die and reappear in another myth without explanation. They become eventually the coyotes and grizzly bears we know, but not through a process of generation. They are a prototype, a genus, a quality which, however, is not rigidly differentiated from other qualities.

The premise of primacy of the whole finds expression in the Wintu concept of himself as originally one, not a sum of limbs or members. When I asked for a word for the body I was given the term *the whole person*. The Wintu does not say *my head aches;* he says *I head ache*. He does not say *my hands are hot;* he says *I hands am hot*. He does not say *my leg,* except extremely rarely and for good reason, such as that his leg has been severed from his body. The clothes he wears are part of this whole. A Wintu girl does not say *her dress was striped* but *she was dress striped*. In dealing with the whole, the various aspects referred to are generic; only when particularization is necessary as a device to distinguish toes or fingers from feet and hands is it used. But when the leg is not part of the whole, when the subject is cutting out the heart of a victim, then particularization is used, since the activity is seen from the point of view of the subject. And when a woman is ironing her dress, which is not part of her body any more, she refers to it as something separate: *my dress*.

In his verbal phrase, the Wintu shows himself again humble in the face of immutable reality, but not paralyzed into inactivity. Here again he is faced with being which is, irrespective of himself, and which he must accept without question. A limited part of this comes within his ken; his consciousness, cognition, and sensation act as a limiting and formalizing element upon the formless reality. Of this delimited part he speaks completely in terms of the bounds of his own person. He uses a stem, derived from the primary root, which means *I know,* or *this is within experience*.

The definitive suffixes (in parentheses below) which he uses with this convey, in every case, the particular source of his information, the particular aspect of himself through which he has become cognizant of what he states. The material he presents has become known to him through his eyes,—"the child is playing (-be) in the sand"; or through his other senses—"this is sour (-nte)" or "he is yelling (-nte)"; or through his logic—"he is hungry (-el; he must be hungry since he has had no food for two days)"; or through the action of logic upon the circumstantial evidence of the senses—"a doe went by with two fawns (-re; I see their tracks)"; or through his acceptance of hearsay evidence—

"they fought long (-ke; someone told me)." In this category of experience, the future is stated in terms of intention or desire or attempt. This is a future which depends on an act of will and is not stated with certainty. This is the aspect of experience with which the unreflective among us concern themselves exclusively; as one of my students asked: "And what is left outside?"

Outside is the reality which is beyond personal cognition, a reality which is accepted in faith. For this, the Wintu uses the primary form of the verb. Alone this stem forms a command; yoqu means *wash!* (*you must wash*), a reference to given necessity. With the aid of different suffixes, this stem may refer to a timeless state, as when setting given conditions for a certain activity; or to what we call the passive, when the individual does not participate as a free agent. In general, it refers to the not-experienced and not-known. To this stem is appended the non-assertive -mina, and the resulting verbal form contains, then, potentially both positive and negative alternatives simultaneously. With the proper auxiliaries, this may either be used to negate, or to ask a question requiring a yes-or-no answer; or in phrases implying ignorance; but it can never assert the known. And when a Wintu gives a negative command, he uses this form again; he does not say "don't chop" but *may it remain* (bedi) *unactualized-chop* (kopmina).

To this not-experienced, timeless, necessary reality, the Wintu refers chiefly in terms of natural necessity; by means of one suffix, -les, (a nominal form of -le) he refers to a future that must be realized, to a probability which is at the same time potential, necessary and inevitable. Words modified by this suffix, are translated by the Wintu variously with the aid of *may,* or *might,* or *would,* or *must,* or *can* or *shall.* Another reference to this reality is made with the aid of the unmodified -le. This suffix can be used with personal suffixes, to indicate a future of certainty, in the realization of which the subject does not participate as a free agent. It is a future so certain, that this form, also, is sometimes translated with *must;* for example, "You, too, shall die." Without personal endings, the -le ties together two events or states of being in inevitable sequence, with no reference to specific time. The sequence may be translated by the Wintu with the aid of the purposive *so as to,* or *to* or with *about to,* but there is no subjective purpose involved; or the word *before* may be used in the translation.

Now the -le refers to a succession of events in nature, and to an inevitable sequence. But here the Wintu can act of his own free will and decide on one of the members of the sequence. He can interpolate an act of choice and thus bring about a desired sequence. Or the subject can intercept an undesirable sequence, by changing the first unit. The same stem is used for this, but a different suffix -ken (second person), which the Wintu translates either as *so that you should not,* or *you might* or *don't;* that is, the suffix warns of the pending sequence, and implies: avoid it. For example, a man shouts to his daughter who is standing on a ladder, *Be careful, you might fall off* or *don't fall off* (talken). Someone instructs two boys: sight carefully when you shoot, *so as not to miss,* or *you might miss,* or *don't miss* (manaken). And a woman, who hears that a rattlesnake has been seen near the water, says, "Let me not go swimming; I *might get stung* (toptcukida)." Pia ihkedi (*he might do it himself,* or *don't let him do it*) is, according to my informant, equivalent to saying, "you'd better do it yourself." So the role of the Wintu in the future is not creative, but can be formative, i.e., it is either negative, or takes the form of an interpolation between necessary events. Here, again the act of will exists, but appears limited to a choice between actualizing and refraining from actualizing.

It is impossible to tell to what extent the reluctance to penetrate beyond external form is active in the formation of words. If the Wintu offers me an English word in translation for a Wintu one, I rarely have any way of knowing what exactly the word means to him. When he says that watca is to *weep,* for example, is he, like me, thinking of the whole kinesthetic activity with all its emotional implications, or is he merely concerned with the sound of weeping, as I think he is? Whenever I find a group of words derived from the same root, I can clearly see that they point to a preoccupation with form alone. I find in my glossary a word for *to shave the head* (poyoqteluna) for example. There is no reason to question the English rendering till I examine the root from which it is derived. I find other derivatives from this root. One means: *to pull off a scab;*

another *to have a damp forehead*. If there is to be a common meaning the first is not concerned with the activity of prying off a scab, or with the sensation of the skin; it refers only to the glistening skin exposed. Neither is the second concerned with the sensation of dampness, but, again, merely with the appearance of the skin. So, though the Wintu uses *to shave the head* as the equivalent to poyoqteluna, I am concerned rather with the activity of cutting itself, with the feel of the scalp, the complete removal of hair, whereas the Wintu refers only to the way the end result appears to the observer; his word means *to make one's own scalp glisten*.

I have recorded a word which applies to the pounding of non-brittle objects. I have translated it as *to pound to a pulp*. I have passed judgment as to what happens to the consistency of the buckeye when I pound it. But the Wintu is merely making a statement as to the external form of the pounded mass; from this word tira, he derives his word for terus, *tick*.

The same insistence upon outward form alone has influenced the naming of White traits. Where I say *he plays the piano*, the Wintu says *he makes a braying noise*. I name the automobile after its locomotion, an essential aspect of its being. But the Wintu in his preoccupation with form alone, finds no incongruity in classifying the automobile with the turtle as: *that which looks like an inverted pot in motion*.

Especially illustrative of this attitude are the words tlitiq and -lila, which the Wintu uses in situations where we would have used *make, create, manufacture;* or, more colloquially, *fix*. But these English equivalents are far from the meaning of the Wintu words: -lila, which I have often translated as *manufacture,* actually means *to turn into, to transform;* that is, to change one form into another. And tlitiq does not mean *make;* it means *to work on*. Our *make* often implies creation, the tlitiq finds matter, assumes its presence. *Make* presupposes an act of aggression, the imposition of self upon matter; tlitiq also involves an act of will but one which is restrained and spends itself on the surface.

This respect for the inviolability of the given finds further expression in the conception of the relationship between self and other. Two Wintu suffixes, which in English are rendered as coercive, reflect this attitude. One of these is -il or -wil, used to make a verb transitive, when the object is particular. For example, tipa means *to cross* (a river or ridge); tepuwil means *to take across* (a child, beads, weapons, etc.). But the -il may also mean *to do with;* so that tepuwil may mean *to go across with.* There is the term bewil which means *to possess something particular;* but it also means *to be with.* The initiative is with the subject in both cases; but there is no act of aggression; there is a coordinate relationship. The word sukil, applied to a chief, I have translated as *to rule;* but the word means *to stand with.* We would say, at best, that the suffix has the two meanings at the same time; but the Wintu makes no distinction between the two concepts, except when he has to use a language which reflects a habit of thought that regards this distinction as natural.

Another suffix which, like the -il, deals with the relationship of self and other, is -ma. This sometimes appears as a causative; for example, ba means *to eat* and bama means *to feed,* that is, *to give to eat, to make eat.* Pira means *to swallow;* peruma *to fish with bait.* But like the -il this too implies a coordinate relationship, and one of great intimacy between self and other; for example a chief tells his people (with the coming of the Whites) *you shall hunger—* biralebosken, *your children shall hunger*—biramalebosken (literally *children you shall hunger in respect of*). The relatives of a pubescent girl -bahlas—are referred to as bahlmas (*they were pubescent in respect of*). A man says, koyumada ilam; kuya is *to be ill;* the man says in effect *I am ill in respect to my child.* I use *in respect to* for an other which is not entirely separated from the self, and with which the self is intimately concerned. What we express as an act of force, is here expressed in terms of continuity between self and other.

I have avoided advisedly the use of the term identification here. This term implies an original delimitation and separation. It is the nearest that our social scientists, starting from delimitation, can come to unity. But if the Wintu starts with an original oneness, we must speak, not of identification, but of a premise of continuity.

We find this premise underlying, not only linguistic categories, but his thought and behavior throughout. It is basic to the

Wintu attitude toward society, for example. It explains why kinship terms are classified, not with the substantives, but with the pronouns such as *this;* why the special possessives used with them, such as the net, in nettan *my father,* are really pronouns of participation, to be used also with aspects of one's identity as, for example, my act, my intention, my future death. To us, in the words of Ralph Linton, "society has as its foundation an aggregate of individuals." For the Wintu, the individual is a delimited part of society; it is society that is basic, not a plurality of individuals. Again, this premise of the primacy of the unpartitioned whole gives a valid basis to beliefs such as that a man will lose his hunting luck if he goes on a hunt while his wife is menstruating. Where formal distinctions are derivative and transitory, a man is at one with his wife in a way which is difficult if not impossible for us to appreciate.

There is further the Wintu premise of a reality beyond his delimiting experience. His experience is that of a reality as shaped by his perception and conceptualization. Beyond it is the timeless design to which his experience has given temporality. He believes in it, and he taps it through his ritual acts and his magic, seeking luck to reinforce and validate his experiential skills and knowledge, to endow his acts with effectiveness. A hunter must have both skill and luck; but skill is the more limited. An unskilled hunter who has luck, can still hit a deer by rare chance, but a skilled hunter without luck can never do so. The myths contain examples of hunters who, having lost their luck, can never kill a deer again. Now knowledge and skill are phrased agentively and experientially; but luck is phrased passively or in terms of non-actualized reality. The hunter who has lost his luck does not say *I cannot kill deer any more,* but *Deer don't want to die for me.*

The natural, reached through luck, is impersonal; it cannot be known or sensed, and it is never addressed; but not so the supernatural. It can be felt or seen; it is personal. It is within experience. Such experience can be questioned and proof of it is often offered; the doctoring shaman produces as evidence the fish he has extracted from a patient, the missile of some supernatural being. Klutchie, a shaman, offers his knowledge of a coast language as proof that, during a protracted trance of which he has no memory, he was carried by a spirit to the West Coast. But natural necessity is beyond question, and demands no proof. It is only implied; there is no name for it. The supernatural is named and can be spoken of. Toward the supernatural the Wintu performs acts of will. The shaman, speaking to the spirit he controls, will command and demand. But the man who dives deep into a sacred pool to seek luck, will say *May it happen that I win at gambling*. His request is non-agentive and impersonal; he does not address nature, neither does he command.

Recurring through all this is the attitude of humility and respect toward reality, toward nature and society. I cannot find an adequate English term to apply to a habit of thought which is so alien to our culture. We are aggressive toward reality. We say, This is bread; we do not say like the Wintu, *I call this bread,* or *I feel* or *taste* or *see it to be bread*. The Wintu never says starkly *this is;* if he speaks of reality which is not within his own restricting experience, he does not affirm it, he only implies it. If he speaks of his experience, he does not express it as categorically true. Our attitude toward nature is colored by a desire to control and exploit. The Wintu relationship with nature is one of intimacy and mutual courtesy. He kills a deer only when he needs it for his livelihood, and utilizes every part of it, hoofs and marrow and hide and sinew and flesh. Waste is abhorrent to him, not because he believes in the intrinsic virtue of thrift, but because the deer had died for him. A man too old to fend for himself prays:

> . . . I cannot go up to the mountains in the west to you, deer;
> I cannot kill you and bring you home . . .
> You, water, I can never dip you up and fetch you home again . . .
> You who are wood, you wood, I cannot carry you home on my
>   shoulder.

This is not the speech of one who has plucked the fruits of nature by brute force; it is the speech of a friend.

10

Ojibwa Ontology, Behavior, and World View

A. Irving Hallowell

It is, I believe, a fact that future investigations will thoroughly confirm, that the Indian does not make the separation into personal as contrasted with impersonal, corporeal with impersonal, in our sense at all. What he seems to be interested in is the question of existence, of reality; and everything that is perceived by the sense, thought of, felt and dreamt of, exists.

PAUL RADIN

Introduction

It has become increasingly apparent in recent years that the potential significance of the data collected by cultural anthropologists far transcends in interest the level of simple, objective, ethnographic description of the peoples they have studied. New per-

From Stanley Diamond, ed., *Culture in History: Essays in Honor of Paul Radin* (New York: Columbia University Press, 1960). Reprinted by permission of the author and publisher. Hallowell did anthropological field work primarily among the Saulteaux branch of the Northern Ojibwa, on the Berens River in Manitoba.

spectives have arisen; fresh interpretations of old data have been offered; investigation and analysis have been pointed in novel
directions. The study of culture and personality, national character
and the special attention now being paid to values are illustrations
that come to mind. Robert Redfield's concept of world view, "that
outlook upon the universe that is characteristic of a people," which
emphasizes a perspective that is not equivalent to the study of
religion in the conventional sense, is a further example.

> "World view" [he says] differs from culture, ethos, mode of
> thought, and national character. It is the picture the members of a
> society have of the properties and characters upon their stage of
> action. While "national character" refers to the way these people
> look to the outsider looking in on them, "world view" refers to
> the way the world looks to that people looking out. Of all that is
> connoted by "culture," "world view" attends especially to the
> way a man, in a particular society, sees himself in relation to all
> else. It is the properties of existence as distinguished from and
> related to the self. It is, in short, a man's idea of the universe. It
> is that organization of ideas which answers to a man the ques-
> tions: Where am I? Among what do I move? What are my rela-
> tions to these things? . . . Self is the axis of "world view." [1]

In an essay entitled "The Self and Its Behavioral Environment," I have pointed out that self-identification and culturally
constituted notions of the nature of the self are essential to the
operation of all human societies and that a functional corollary is
the cognitive orientation of the self to a world of objects other than
self. Since the nature of these objects is likewise culturally constituted, a unified phenomenal field of thought, values, and action
which is integral with the kind of world view that characterizes a
society is provided for its members. The behavioral environment of
the self thus becomes structured in terms of a diversified world of
objects other than self, "discriminated, classified, and conceptualized with respect to attributes which are culturally constituted
and symbolically mediated through language. Object orientation
likewise provides the ground for an intelligible interpretation of
events in the behavioral environment on the basis of traditional as-

sumptions regarding the nature and attributes of the objects involved and implicit or explicit dogmas regarding the 'causes' of events.'' [2] Human beings in whatever culture are provided with cognitive orientation in a cosmos; there is ''order'' and ''reason'' rather than chaos. There are basic premises and principles implied, even if these do not happen to be consciously formulated and articulated by the people themselves. We are confronted with the philosophical implications of their thought, the nature of the world of being as they conceive it. If we pursue the problem deeply enough we soon come face to face with a relatively unexplored territory—ethno-metaphysics. Can we penetrate this realm in other cultures? What kind of evidence is at our disposal? The forms of speech as Benjamin Whorf and the neo-Humboldtians have thought? [3] The manifest content of myth? Observed behavior and attitudes? And what order of reliability can our inferences have? The problem is a complex and difficult one, but this should not preclude its exploration.

In this paper I have assembled evidence, chiefly from my own field work on a branch of the Northern Ojibwa,[4] which supports the inference that in the metaphysics of being found among these Indians, the action of persons provides the major key to their world view.

While in all cultures ''persons'' comprise one of the major classes of objects to which the self must become oriented, this category of being is by no means limited to *human* beings. In Western culture, as in others, ''supernatural'' beings are recognized as persons, although belonging, at the same time, to an other than human category.[5] But in the social sciences and psychology, persons and human beings are categorically identified. This identification is inherent in the concept of ''society'' and ''social relations.'' In Warren's *Dictionary of Psychology* person is defined as ''a human organism regarded as having distinctive characteristics and social relations.'' The same identification is implicit in the conceptualization and investigation of social organization by anthropologists. Yet this obviously involves a radical abstraction if, from the standpoint of the people being studied, the concept of person is not, in fact, synonymous with human being but transcends it. The significance of the abstraction only becomes apparent when we stop to consider the perspective adopted. The study of social organization, defined as human relations of a certain kind, is perfectly intelligible as an objective approach to the study of this subject in any culture. But if, in the world view of a people, persons as a class include entities other than human beings, then our objective approach is not adequate for presenting an accurate description of "the way a man, in a particular society, sees himself in relation to all else." A different perspective is required for this purpose. It may be argued, in fact, that a thoroughgoing "objective" approach to the study of cultures cannot be achieved solely by projecting upon those cultures categorical abstractions derived from Western thought. For, in a broad sense, the latter are a reflection of *our* cultural subjectivity. A higher order of objectivity may be sought by adopting a perspective which includes an analysis of the outlook of the people themselves as a complementary procedure. It is in a world view perspective, too, that we can likewise obtain the best insight into how cultures function as wholes.

The significance of these differences in perspective may be illustrated in the case of the Ojibwa by the manner in which the kinship term "grandfather" is used. It is not only applied to human persons but to spiritual beings who are persons of a category other than human. In fact, when the collective plural "our grandfathers" is used, the reference is primarily to persons of this latter class. Thus if we study Ojibwa social organization in the usual manner, we take account of only one set of grandfathers. When we study their religion we discover other grandfathers. But if we adopt a world view perspective no dichotomization appears. In this perspective grandfather is a term applicable to certain "person objects," without any distinction between human persons and those of an other-than-human class. Futhermore, both sets of grandfathers can be said to be functionally as well as terminologically equivalent in certain respects. The other-than-human grandfathers are sources of power to human beings through the "blessings" they bestow, i.e., a sharing of their power which enhances the "power" of human beings. A child is always given a name by an old man, i.e., a terminological grandfather. It is a matter of indifference whether he is a blood relative or not. This name carries with it a special blessing because it has reference to a dream of the human grandfather in which he obtained power from one or more of the other-than-human grandfathers. In other words, the relation between a human child and a human grandfather is functionally patterned in the same way as the relation between human beings and grandfathers of an other-than-human class. And, just as the latter type of grandfather may impose personal taboos as a condition of a blessing, in the same way a human grandfather may impose a taboo on a "grandchild" he has named.

Another direct linguistic clue to the inclusiveness of the person category in Ojibwa thinking is the term *wíndígo*. Baraga defines it in his *Dictionary* as "fabulous giant that lives on human flesh; a man that eats human flesh, cannibal." From the Ojibwa standpoint all *wíndígowak* are conceptually unified as terrifying, anthropomorphic beings who, since they threaten one's very existence, must be killed. The central theme of a rich body of anecdotal material shows how this threat was met in particular instances. It ranges from cases in which it was necessary to kill the closest of kin because it was thought an individual was becoming a *wíndígo*, through accounts of heroic fights between human beings and these fabulous giant monsters, to a first-hand report of a personal encounter with one of them.[6]

The more deeply we penetrate the world view of the Ojibwa the more apparent it is that social relations between human beings (*änícinábek*) and other-than-human persons are of cardinal significance. These relations are correlative with their more comprehensive categorization of persons. Recognition must be given to the culturally constituted meaning of "social" and "social relations" if we are to understand the nature of the Ojibwa world and the living entities in it.[7]

Linguistic Categories and Cognitive Orientation

Any discussion of persons in the world view of the Ojibwa must take cognizance of the well known fact that the grammatical structure of the language of these people, like all their Algonkian relatives, formally expresses a distinction between "animate" and "inanimate" nouns. These particular labels, of course, were imposed upon Algonkian languages by Europeans; [8] it appeared to outsiders that the Algonkian differentiation of objects approximated the animate-inanimate dichotomy of Western thought. Superficially this seems to be the case. Yet a closer examination indicates that, as in the gender categories of other languages, the distinction in some cases appears to be arbitrary, if not extremely puzzling, from the standpoint of common sense or in a naturalistic frame of reference. Thus substantives for some, but not all—trees, sun-moon (*gízis*), thunder, stones, and objects of material culture like kettle and pipe—are classified as animate.

If we wish to understand the cognitive orientation of the Ojibwa, there is an ethno-linguistic problem to be considered: What is the meaning of animate in Ojibwa thinking? Are such generic properties of objects as responsiveness to outer stimulation—sentience, mobility, self-movement, or even reproduction—primary characteristics attributed to all objects of the animate class irrespective of their categories as physical objects in our thinking? Is there evidence to substantiate such properties of objects independent of their formal linguistic classification? It must not be forgotten that no Ojibwa is consciously aware of, or can abstractly articulate the animate-inanimate category of his language, despite the fact that this dichotomy is implicit in his speech. Consequently, the grammatical distinction as such does not emerge as a subject for reflective thought or bear the kind of relation to individual thinking that would be present if there were some formulated dogma about the generic properties of these two classes of objects.

Commenting on the analogous grammatical categories of the Central Algonkian languages with reference to linguistic and non-linguistic orders of meaning, Greenberg writes: "Since all persons and animals are in Class I (animate), we have at least one ethnoseme, but most of the other meanings can be defined only by a linguiseme." In Greenberg's opinion, "unless the actual behavior of Algonquian speakers shows some mode of conduct common to all these instances such that, given this information, we could predict the membership of Class I, we must resort to purely linguistic characterization.'' [9]

In the case of the Ojibwa, I believe that when evidence from beliefs, attitudes, conduct, and linguistic characterization are all considered together the psychological basis for their unified cognitive outlook can be appreciated, even when there is a radical departure from the framework of our thinking. In certain instances, behavioral predictions can be made. Behavior, however, is a function of a complex set of factors—including actual experience. More important than the linguistic classification of objects is the kind of vital functions attributed to them in the belief system and the conditions under which these functions are observed or tested in experience. This accounts, I think, for the fact that what we view as material, inanimate objects—such as shells and stones—are placed in an animate category along with persons which have no physical existence in our world view. The shells, for example, called *mígis* on account of the manner in which they function in the Midewiwin, could not be linguistically categorized as inanimate. Thunder, as we shall see, is not only reified as an animate entity, but has the attributes of a person and may be referred to as such. An inanimate categorization would be unthinkable from the Ojibwa point of view. When Greenberg refers to persons as clearly members of the animate grammatical category he is, by implication, identifying person and human being. Since in the Ojibwa universe there are many kinds of reified person-objects which are other than human but have the same ontological status, these, of course, fall into the same ethnoseme as human beings and into the animate linguistic class.

Since stones are grammatically animate, I once asked an old man: Are *all* the stones we see about us here alive? He reflected a long while and then replied, ''No! But *some* are.'' This qualified answer made a lasting impression on me. And it is thoroughly consistent with other data that indicate that the Ojibwa are not animists in the sense that they dogmatically attribute living souls to inanimate objects such as stones. The hypothesis which suggests itself to me is that the allocation of stones to an animate grammatical category is part of a culturally constituted cognitive ''set.'' It does not involve a consciously formulated theory about the nature of stones. It leaves a door open that our orientation on dogmatic grounds keeps shut tight. Whereas we should never expect a stone to manifest animate properties of any kind under any circumstances, the Ojibwa recognize, *a priori,* potentialities for animation in certain classes of objects under certain circumstances.[10] The Ojibwa do not perceive stones, in general, as animate, any more than we do. The crucial test is experience. Is there any personal testimony available? In answer to this question we can say that it is asserted by informants that stones have been seen to move, that some stones manifest other animate properties, and, as we shall see, Flint is represented as a living personage in their mythology.

The old man to whom I addressed the general question about the animate character of stones was the same informant who told me that during a Midewiwin ceremony, when his father was the leader of it, he had seen a "big round stone move." He said his father got up and walked around the path once or twice. Coming back to his place he began to sing. The stone began to move "following the trail of the old man around the tent, rolling over and over, I saw it happen several times and others saw it also." [11] The animate behavior of a stone under these circumstances was considered to be a demonstration of magic power on the part of the Midé. It was not a voluntary act initiated by the stone considered as a living entity. Associated with the Midewiwin in the past there were other types of large boulders with animate properties. My friend Chief Berens had one of these, but it no longer possessed these attributes. It had contours that suggested eyes and mouth. When Yellow Legs, Chief Berens's great-grandfather, was a leader of the Midewiwin he used to tap this stone with a new knife. It would then open its mouth, Yellow Legs would insert his fingers and take out a small leather sack with medicine in it. Mixing some of this medicine with water, he would pass the decoction around. A small sip was taken by those present.[12]

If, then, stones are not only grammatically animate, but, in particular cases, have been observed to manifest animate properties, such as movement in space and opening of a mouth, why should they not on occasion be conceived as possessing animate properties of a higher order? The actualization of this possibility is illustrated by the following anecdote:

A white trader, digging in his potato patch, unearthed a large stone similar to the one just referred to. He sent for John Duck, an Indian who was the leader of the *wábano,* a contemporary ceremony that is held in a structure something like that used for the Midewiwin. The trader called his attention to the stone, saying that it must belong to his pavilion. John Duck did not seem pleased at this. He bent down and spoke to the boulder in a low voice, inquiring whether it had ever been in his pavilion. According to John the stone replied in the negative.

It is obvious that John Duck spontaneously structured the situation in terms that are intelligible within the context of Ojibwa language and culture. Speaking to a stone dramatizes the depth of the categorical difference in cognitive orientation between the Ojibwa and ourselves. I regret that my field notes contain no information about the use of direct verbal address in the other cases mentioned. But it may well have taken place. In the anecdote describing John Duck's behavior, however, his use of speech as a mode of communication raises the animate status of the boulder to the level of social interaction common to human beings. Simply as a matter of observation we can say that the stone was treated *as if* it were a "person," not a "thing," without inferring that objects of this class are, for the Ojibwa, necessarily conceptualized as persons.

Further exploration might be made of the relations between Ojibwa thinking, observation, and behavior and their grammatical classification of objects but enough has been said, I hope, to indicate that not only animate properties but even "person" attributes may be projected upon objects which to us clearly belong to a physical inanimate category.

The "Persons" of Ojibwa Mythology

The Ojibwa distinguish two general types of traditional oral narratives: 1. "News or tidings" (*täbắtcamowin*), i.e., anecdotes, or stories, referring to events in the lives of human beings (*änícin-*

ábek). In content, narratives of this class range from everyday occurrences, through more exceptional experiences, to those which
verge on the legendary. (The anecdotes already referred to, although informal, may be said to belong to this general class.)
2. Myths (*ätíso'kanak*),[13] i.e., sacred stories, which are not only
traditional and formalized; their narration is seasonally restricted
and is somewhat ritualized. The significant thing about these stories
is that the characters in them are regarded as living entities who
have existed from time immemorial. While there is genesis through
birth and temporary or permanent form-shifting through transformation, there is no outright creation. Whether human or animal in
form or name, the major characters in the myths behave like people, though many of their activities are depicted in a spatio-tem-
poral framework of cosmic, rather than mundane, dimensions.
There is "social interaction" among them and between them and
änícinábek.

A striking fact furnishes a direct linguistic cue to the attitude
of the Ojibwa towards these personages. When they use the term
ätíso'kanak, they are not referring to what I have called a "body of
narratives." The term refers to what we would call the characters in
these stories; to the Ojibwa they are living persons of an other-than-
human class. As William Jones said many years ago, "Myths are
thought of as conscious beings, with powers of thought and action." [14] A synonym for this class of persons is "our grandfathers."

The *ätíso'kanak,* or our grandfathers, are never "talked
about" casually by the Ojibwa. But when the myths are narrated on
long winter nights, the occasion is a kind of invocation: "Our
grandfathers" like it and often come to listen to what is being said.
In ancient times one of these entities (*Wísekedjak*) is reputed to
have said to the others: "We'll try to make everything to suit the
änícinábek as long as any of them exist, so that they will never
forget us and will always talk about us."

It is clear, therefore, that to the Ojibwa, their "talk" about
these entities, although expressed in formal narrative, is not about
fictitious characters. On the contrary, what we call myth is accepted
by them as a true account of events in the past lives of living "per-

sons.'' [15] It is for this reason that narratives of this class are significant for an understanding of the manner in which their phenomenal field is culturally structured and cognitively apprehended. As David Bidney has pointed out, ''The concept of 'myth' is relative to one's accepted beliefs and convictions, so that what is gospel truth for the believer is sheer 'myth' and 'fiction' for the non-believer or skeptic. . . . Myths and magical tales and practices are accepted precisely because pre-scientific folk do not consider them as merely 'myths' or 'magic,' since once the distinction between myth and science is consciously accepted, the acquired critical insight precludes the belief in and acceptance of magic and myth.'' [16] When taken at their face value, myths provide a reliable source of prime value for making inferences about Ojibwa world outlook. They offer basic data about unarticulated, unformalized, and unanalyzed concepts regarding which informants cannot be expected to generalize. From this point of view, myths are broadly analogous to the concrete material of the texts on which the linguist depends for his derivation, by analysis and abstraction, of the grammatical categories and principles of a language.

In formal definitions of myth (e.g., *Concise Oxford Dictionary* and Warren's *Dictionary of Psychology*) the subject matter of such narrative often has been said to involve not only fictitious characters but supernatural persons. This latter appellation, if applied to the Ojibwa characters, is completely misleading, if for no other reason than the fact that the concept of supernatural presupposes a concept of the natural. The latter is not present in Ojibwa thought. It is unfortunate that the natural-supernatural dichotomy has been so persistently invoked by many anthropologists in describing the outlook of peoples in cultures other than our own. Linguists learned long ago that it was impossible to write grammars of the languages of nonliterate peoples by using as a framework Indo-European speech forms. Lovejoy has pointed out that ''The sacred word 'nature' is probably the most equivocal in the vocabulary of the European peoples . . .'' [17] and the natural-supernatural antithesis has had its own complex history in Western thought. [18]

To the Ojibwa, for example, *gízis* (day luminary, the sun) is not a natural object in our sense at all. Not only does their conception differ; the sun is a person of the other-than-human class. But more important still is the absence of the notion of the ordered regularity in movement that is inherent in our scientific outlook. The Ojibwa entertain no reasonable certainty that, in accordance with natural law, the sun will rise day after day. In fact, *Tcakábec,* a mythical personage, once set a snare in the trail of the sun and caught it. Darkness continued until a mouse was sent by human beings to release the sun and provide daylight again. And in another story (not a myth) it is recounted how two old men at dawn vied with each other in influencing the sun's movements.

> The first old man said to his companion: "It is about sunrise now and there is a clear sky. You tell the sun to rise at once." So the other old man said to the sun: "My grandfather, come up quickly." As soon as he had said this the sun came up into the sky like a shot. "Now you try something," he said to his companion. "See if you can send it down." So the other man said to the sun: "My grandfather, put your face down again." When he said this the sun went down again. "I have more power than you," he said to the other old man, "The sun never goes down once it comes up."

We may infer that, to the Ojibwa, any regularity in the movements of the sun is of the same order as the habitual activities of human beings. There are certain expectations, of course, but, on occasion, there may be temporary deviations in behavior "caused" by other persons. Above all, any concept of *impersonal* "natural" forces is totally foreign to Ojibwa thought.

Since their cognitive orientation is culturally constituted and thus given a psychological "set," we cannot assume that objects, like the sun, are perceived as natural objects in our sense. If this were so, the anecdote about the old men could not be accepted as an actual event involving a case of "social interaction" between human beings and an other-than-human person. Consequently, it would be an error to say that the Ojibwa "personify" natural objects. This would imply that, at some point, the sun was first perceived as an inanimate, material thing. There is, of course, no evidence for this. The same conclusion applies over the whole area of their cognitive orientation towards the objects of their world.

The Four Winds and Flint, for instance, are quintuplets. They were born of a mother (unnamed) who, while given human characteristics, lived in the very distant past. As will be more apparent later, this character, like others in the myths, may have anthropomorphic characteristics without being conceived as a human being. In the context she, like the others, is an *ätíso'kan*. The Winds were born first, then Flint "jumped out," tearing her to pieces. This, of course, is a direct allusion to his inanimate, stony properties. Later he was penalized for his hurried exit. He fought with *Misábos* (Great Hare) and pieces were chipped off his body and his size reduced. "Those pieces broken from your body may be of some use to human beings some day," *Misábos* said to him. "But you will not be any larger so long as the earth shall last. You'll never harm anyone again."

Against the background of this "historic" event, it would be strange indeed if flint were allocated to an inanimate grammatical category. There is a special term for each of the four winds that are differentiated, but no plural for wind. They are all animate beings, whose "homes" define the four directions.

The conceptual reification of Flint, the Winds and the Sun as other-than-human persons exemplifies a world view in which a natural-supernatural dichotomy has no place. And the representation of these beings as characters in true stories reinforces their reality by means of a cultural device which at the same time depicts their vital roles in interaction with other persons as integral forces in the functioning of a unified cosmos.

Anthropomorphic Traits and Other-than-Human Persons

In action and motivations the characters in the myths are indistinguishable from human persons. In this respect, human and other-than-human persons may be set off, in life as well as in myth, from animate beings such as ordinary animals (*awésiak*, pl.) and objects belonging to the inanimate grammatical category. But, at the same time, it must be noted that persons of the other-than-human class do not always present a human appearance in the myths. Consequently, we may ask: What constant attributes do unify the concept of person? What is the essential meaningful core of the concept of person in Ojibwa thinking? It can be stated at once that anthropomorphic traits in outward appearance are not the crucial attributes.

It is true that some extremely prominent characters in the myths are given explicit human form. *Wísekedjak* and *Tcakábec* are examples. Besides this they have distinctive characteristics of their own. The former has an exceptionally long penis and the latter is very small in size, yet extremely powerful. There are no equivalent female figures. By comparison, Flint and the Winds have human attributes by implication; they were born of a "woman" as human beings are born; they speak, and so on. On the other hand, the High God of the Ojibwa, a very remote figure who does not appear in the mythology at all, but is spoken of as a person, is not even given sexual characteristics. This is possible because there is no sex gender in Ojibwa speech. Consequently an animate being of the person category may function in their thinking without having explicitly sexual or other anthropomorphic characteristics. Entities seen in dreams (*pawáganak*) are "persons"; whether they have anthropomorphic attributes or not is incidental. Other entities of the person category, whose anthropomorphic character is undefined or ambiguous, are what have been called the masters or owners of animals or plant species. Besides these, certain curing procedures and conjuring are said to have other-than-human personal entities as patrons.

If we now examine the cognitive orientation of the Ojibwa toward the Thunder Birds it will become apparent why anthropomorphism is not a constant feature of the Ojibwa concept of person. These beings likewise demonstrate the autonomous nature of Ojibwa reification. For we find here a creative synthesis of objective naturalistic observation integrated with the subjectivity of dream experiences and traditional mythical narrative which, assuming the character of a living image, is neither the personification of a natural phenomenon nor an altogether animal-like or human-like being. Yet it is impossible to deny that, in the universe of the Ojibwa, Thunder Birds are persons.

My Ojibwa friends, I discovered, were as puzzled by the white man's conception of thunder and lightning as natural phenomena as they were by the idea that the earth is round and not flat. I was pressed on more than one occasion to explain thunder and lightning, but I doubt whether my somewhat feeble efforts made much sense to them. Of one thing I am sure: My explanations left their own beliefs completely unshaken. This is not strange when we consider that, even in our naturalistic frame of reference, thunder and lightning as perceived do not exhibit the lifeless properties of inanimate objects. On the contrary, it has been said that thunder and lightning are among the natural phenomena which exhibit some of the properties of "person objects." [19] Underlying the Ojibwa view there may be a level of naïve perceptual experience that should be taken into account. But their actual construct departs from this level in a most explicit direction: Why is an avian image central in their conception of a being whose manifestations are thunder and lightning? Among the Ojibwa with whom I worked, the linguistic stem for bird is the same as that for Thunder Bird (*pinésī;* pl. *pinésīwak*). Besides this, the avian characteristics of Thunder Birds are still more explicit. Conceptually they are grouped with the hawks, of which there are several natural species in their habitat.

What is particularly interesting is that the avian nature of the Thunder Birds does not rest solely on an arbitrary image. Phenomenally, thunder does exhibit "behavioral" characteristics that are analogous to avian phenomena in this region.[20] According to meteorological observations, the average number of days with thunder begins with one in April, increases to a total of five in midsummer (July) and then declines to one in October. And if a bird calendar is consulted, the facts show that species wintering in the south begin to appear in April and disappear for the most part not later than October, being, of course, a familiar sight during the summer months. The avian character of the Thunder Birds can be rationalized to some degree with reference to natural facts and their observation.

But the evidence for the existence of Thunder Birds does not rest only on the association of the occurrence of thunder with the migration of the summer birds projected into an avian image. When I visited the Ojibwa an Indian was living who, when a boy of twelve or so, saw *pinésí* with his own eyes. During a severe thunderstorm he ran out of his tent and there on the rocks lay a strange bird. He ran back to call his parents, but when they arrived the bird had disappeared. He was sure it was a Thunder Bird, but his elders were skeptical because it is almost unheard of to see *pinésí* in such a fashion. But the matter was clinched and the boy's account accepted when a man who had *dreamed* of *pinésí* verified the boy's description. It will be apparent later why a dream experience was decisive. It should be added at this point, however, that many Indians say they have seen the nests of the Thunder Birds; these are usually described as collections of large stones in the form of shallow bowls located in high and inaccessible parts of the country.

If we now turn to the myths, we find that one of them deals in considerable detail with Thunder Birds. Ten unmarried brothers live together. The oldest is called *Mätcíkīwis*. A mysterious housekeeper cuts wood and builds a fire for them which they find burning when they return from a long day's hunt, but she never appears in person. One day the youngest brother discovers and marries her. *Mätcíkīwis* is jealous and kills her. She would have revived if her husband had not broken a taboo she imposed. It turns out, however, that she is not actually a human being but a Thunder Bird and, thus, one of the *ätíso'kanak* and immortal. She flies away to the land above this earth inhabited by the Thunder Birds. Her husband, after many difficulties, follows her there. He finds himself brother-in-law to beings who are the "masters" of the duck hawks, sparrow hawks, and other species of this category of birds he has known on earth. He cannot relish the food eaten, since what the Thunder Birds call beaver are to him like the frogs and snakes on this earth (a genuinely naturalistic touch since the sparrow hawk, for example, feeds on batrachians and reptiles). He goes hunting gigantic snakes with his male Thunder Bird relatives. Snakes of this class also exist on this earth, and the Thunder Birds are their inveterate enemies. (When there is lightning and thunder this is the prey the Thunder Birds are after.) One day the great Thunder Bird says to his son-in-law, "I know you are getting lonely; you must want to see your people. I'll let you go back to earth now. You have nine brothers at home and I have nine girls left. You can take them with you as wives for your brothers. I'll be related to the people on earth now and I'll be merciful towards them. I'll not hurt any of them if I can possibly help it." So he tells his daughters to get ready. There is a big dance that night and the next morning the whole party starts off. When they come to the edge of Thunder Bird land the lad's wife says to him, "Sit on my back. Hang on tight to my neck and keep your eyes shut." Then the thunder crashes and the young man knows that they are off through the air. Having reached this earth they make their way to the brothers' camp. The Thunder Bird women, who have become transformed into human form, are enthusiastically received. There is another celebration and the nine brothers marry the nine sisters of their youngest brother's wife.

This is the end of the myth but a few comments are necessary. It is obvious that the Thunder Birds are conceived to act like human beings. They hunt and talk and dance. But the analogy can be pressed further. Their social organization and kinship terminology are precisely the same as the Ojibwa. The marriage of a series of female siblings (classificatory or otherwise) to a series of male siblings often occurs among the Ojibwa themselves. This is, in fact, considered a kind of ideal pattern. In one case that I know of six blood brothers were married to a sorority of six sisters. There is a conceptual continuity, therefore, between the social life of human beings and that of the Thunder Birds which is independent of the avian form given to the latter. But we must infer from the myth that this avian form is not constant. Appearance cannot then be taken as a permanent and distinguishable trait of the Thunder Birds. They are capable of metamorphosis, hence, the human attributes with which they are endowed transcend a human outward form. Their conceptualization as persons is not associated with a permanent human form any more than it is associated with a birdlike form. And the fact that they belong to the category of *ätíso'kanak* is no barrier to their descending to earth and mating with human beings. I was told of a woman who claimed that North Wind was the father of one of her children. My informant said he did not believe this;

nevertheless, he thought it would have been accepted as a possibility in the past.[21] We can only infer that in the universe of the Ojibwa the conception of person as a living, functioning social being is not only one which transcends the notion of person in the naturalistic sense; it likewise transcends a human appearance as a constant attribute of this category of being.

The relevance of such a concept to actual behavior may be illustrated by one simple anecdote. An informant told me that many years before he was sitting in a tent one summer afternoon during a storm, together with an old man and his wife. There was one clap of thunder after another. Suddenly the old man turned to his wife and asked, "Did you hear what was said?" "No," she replied, "I didn't catch it." My informant, an acculturated Indian, told me he did not at first know what the old man and his wife referred to. It was, of course, the thunder. The old man thought that one of the Thunder Birds had said something to him. He was reacting to this sound in the same way as he would respond to a human being, whose words he did not understand. The casualness of the remark and even the trivial character of the anecdote demonstrate the psychological depth of the "social relations" with other-than-human beings that becomes explicit in the behavior of the Ojibwa as a consequence of the cognitive set induced by their culture.

Metamorphosis as an Attribute of Persons

The conceptualization in myth and belief of Thunder Birds as animate beings who, while maintaining their identity, may change their outward appearance and exhibit either an avian or a human form exemplifies an attribute of "persons" which, although unarticulated abstractly, is basic in the cognitive orientation of the Ojibwa.

Metamorphosis occurs with considerable frequency in the myths where other-than-human persons change their form. *Wisekedjak,* whose primary characteristics are anthropomorphic, becomes transformed and flies with the geese in one story, assumes the form of a snake in another, and once turns himself into a stump.

Men marry "animal" wives who are not "really" animals. And *Míkīnäk,* the Great Turtle, marries a human being. It is only by breaking a taboo that his wife discovers she is married to a being who is able to assume the form of a handsome young man.

The senselessness and ambiguities which may puzzle the outsider when reading these myths are resolved when it is understood that, to the Ojibwa, persons of this class are capable of metamorphosis by their very nature. Outward appearance is only an incidental attribute of being. And the names by which some of these entities are commonly known, even if they identify the character as an animal, do not imply unchangeableness in form.

Stith Thompson has pointed out that the possibility of transformation is a "commonplace assumption in folk tales everywhere. Many of such motifs are frankly fictitious, but a large number represent persistent beliefs and living tradition." [22] The case of the Ojibwa is in the latter category. The world of myth is not categorically distinct from the world as experienced by human beings in everyday life. In the latter, as well as the former, no sharp lines can be drawn dividing living beings of the animate class because metamorphosis is possible. In outward manifestation neither animal nor human characteristics define categorical differences in the core of being. And, even aside from metamorphosis, we find that in everyday life interaction with nonhuman entities of the animate class is only intelligible on the assumption that they possess some of the attributes of persons.

So far as animals are concerned, when bears were sought out in their dens in the spring they were addressed, asked to come out so that they could be killed, and an apology was offered to them.[23] The following encounter with a bear, related to me by a pagan Ojibwa named Birchstick, shows what happened in this case when an animal was treated as a person:

> One spring when I was out hunting I went up a little creek where I knew suckers were spawning. Before I came to the rapids I saw fresh bear tracks. I walked along the edge of the creek and when I reached the rapids I saw a bear coming towards me, along the same trail I was following. I stepped behind a tree and when the animal was about thirty yards from me I fired. I missed and

before I could reload the bear made straight for me. He seemed mad, so I never moved. I just waited there by the tree. As soon as he came close to me and rose up on his hind feet, I put the butt end of my gun against his heart and held him there. I remembered what my father used to tell me when I was a boy. He said that a bear always understands what you tell him. The bear began to bite the stock of the gun. He even put his paws upon it something like a man would do if he were going to shoot. Still holding him off as well as I could I said to the bear, "If you want to live, go away," and he let go the gun and walked off. I didn't bother the bear anymore.[24]

These instances suffice to demonstrate that, at the level of individual behavior, the interaction of the Ojibwa with certain kinds of plants and animals in everyday life is so structured culturally that individuals act as if they were dealing with persons who both understand what is being said to them and have volitional capacities as well. From the standpoint of perceptual experience if we only take account of autochthonous factors in Birchstick's encounter with the bear his behavior appears idiosyncratic and is not fully explained. On the other hand, if we invoke Ojibwa concepts of the nature of animate beings, his behavior becomes intelligible to us. We can understand the determining factors in his definition of the situation, and the functional relations between perception and conduct are meaningful. This Indian was not confronted with an animal with objective ursine properties, but rather with an animate being who had ursine attributes and *also* person attributes. These, we may infer, were perceived as an integral whole. I am sure, however, that in narrating this episode to another Indian, he would not have referred to what his father had told him about bears. That was for my benefit!

Since bears, then, are assumed to possess person attributes, it is not surprising to find that there is a very old, widespread, and persistent belief that sorcerers may become transformed into bears in order better to pursue their nefarious work.[25] Consequently some of the best documentation of the metamorphosis of human beings into animals comes from anecdotal material referring to cases of this sort. Even contemporary, acculturated Ojibwa have a term for this. They all know what a "bearwalk" is, and Dorson's recent collection of folk traditions, including those of the Indian populations of the Upper Peninsula of Michigan, bears the title *Bloodstoppers and Bearwalkers*. One of Dorson's informants gave him this account of what he had seen:

> When I was a kid, 'bout seventeen, before they build the highway, there was just an old tote road from Bark River to Harris. There was three of us, one a couple years older, coming back from Bark River at nighttime. We saw a flash coming from behind us. The older fellow said, "It's a bearwalk, let's get it. I'll stand on the other side of the road (it was just a wagon rut) and you stand on this side." We stood there and waited. I saw it 'bout fifty feet away from us—close as your car is now. It looked like a bear, but every time he breathe you could see a fire gust. My chum he fall over in a faint. That brave feller on the other side, he faint. When the bear walk, all the ground wave, like when you walk on soft mud or on moss. He was goin' where he was goin'.[26]

It is clear from this example, and others that might be added, that the Indian and his companions did not perceive an ordinary bear. But in another anecdote given by Dorson, which is not told in the first person, it is said that an Indian "grabbed hold of the bear and it wasn't there—it was the old woman. She had buckskin bags all over her, tied on to her body, and she had a bearskin hide on." [27] I also have been told that the "bearwalk" is dressed up in a bearskin. All such statements, of course, imply a skeptical attitude towards metamorphosis. They are rationalizations advanced by individuals who are attempting to reconcile Ojibwa beliefs and observation with the disbelief encountered in their relations with the whites.

An old-fashioned informant of mine told me how he had once fallen sick, and, although he took various kinds of medicine these did him no good. Because of this, and for other reasons, he believed he had been bewitched by a certain man. Then he noticed that a bear kept coming to his camp almost every night after dark. This is most unusual because wild animals do not ordinarily come anywhere near a human habitation. On one occasion the bear would have entered his wigwam if he had not been warned in a dream. His anxiety increased because he knew, of course, that sorcerers often transformed themselves into bears. So when the bear appeared one night he got up, went outdoors, and shouted to the animal that he knew what it was trying to do. He threatened retaliation in kind if the bear ever returned. The animal ran off and never came back.

In this case there are psychological parallels to Birchstick's encounter with a bear: In both cases the bear is directly addressed as a person might be, and it is only through a knowledge of the cultural background that it is possible fully to understand the behavior of the individuals involved. In the present case, however, we can definitely say that the animal was perceived as a human being in the form of a bear; the Indian was threatening a human person with retaliation, not an animal.

A question that I have discussed in *Culture and Experience* in connection with another bearwalk anecdote, also arises in this case.[28] Briefly, the Ojibwa believe that a human being consists of a vital part, or *soul,* which, under certain circumstances may become detached from the body, so that it is not necessary to assume that the body part, in all cases, literally undergoes transformation into an animal form. The body of the sorcerer may remain in his wigwam while his soul journeys elsewhere and appears to another person in the form of an animal.

This interpretation is supported by an account which an informant gave me of a visit his deceased grandchild had paid him. One day he was traveling in a canoe across a lake. He had put up an improvised mast and used a blanket for a sail. A little bird alighted on the mast. This was a most unusual thing for a bird to do. He was convinced that it was not a bird but his dead grandchild. The child, of course, had left her body behind in a grave, nevertheless she visited him in animal form.

Thus, both living and dead human beings may assume the form of animals. So far as appearance is concerned, there is no hard and fast line that can be drawn between an animal form and a human form because metamorphosis is possible. In perceptual experience what looks like a bear may sometimes *be* an animal and, on other occasions, a human being. What persists and gives continuity to being is the vital part, or soul. Dorson goes to the heart of the matter when he stresses the fact that the whole socialization process in Ojibwa culture "impresses the young with the concepts of transformation and of 'power,' malign or benevolent, human or demonic. These concepts underlie the entire Indian mythology, and make sensible the otherwise childish stories of culture heroes, animal husbands, friendly thunders, and malicious serpents. The bear-walk idea fits at once into this dream world—literally a dream world, for Ojibwa go to school in dreams." [29]

We must conclude, I believe, that the capacity for metamorphosis is one of the features which links human beings with the other-than-human persons in their behavioral environment. It is one of the generic properties manifested by beings of the person class. But is it a ubiquitous capacity of all members of this class equally? I do not think so. Metamorphosis to the Ojibwa mind is an earmark of power. Within the category of persons there is a graduation of power. Other-than-human persons occupy the top rank in the power hierarchy of animate beings. Human beings do not differ from them in kind, but in power. Hence, it is taken for granted that all the *ätíso'kanak* can assume a variety of forms. In the case of human beings, while the potentiality for metamorphosis exists and may even be experienced, any outward manifestation is inextricably associated with unusual power, for good or evil. And power of this degree can only be acquired by human beings through the help of other-than-human persons. Sorcerers can transform themselves only because they have acquired a high order of power from this source.

Powerful men, in the Ojibwa sense, are also those who can make inanimate objects behave as if they were animate. The *Midé* who made a stone roll over and over has been mentioned earlier. Other examples, such as the animation of a string of wooden beads, or animal skins, could be cited.[30] Such individuals also have been observed to transform one object into another, such as charcoal into bullets and ashes into gunpowder, or a handful of goose feathers into birds or insects.[31] In these manifestations, too, they are elevated to the same level of power as that displayed by other-than-human persons. We can, in fact, find comparable episodes in the myths.

The notion of animate being itself does not presume a capacity for manifesting the highest level of power any more than it implies person-attributes in every case. Power manifestations vary within the animate class of being as does the possession of person-attributes. A human being may possess little, if any, more power than a mole. No one would have been more surprised than Birchstick if the bear he faced had suddenly become human in form. On the other hand, the spiritual "masters" of the various species of animals are inherently powerful and, quite generally, they possess the power of metamorphosis. These entities, like the *átíso'kanak,* are among the sources from which human beings may seek to enhance their own power. My Ojibwa friends often cautioned me against judging by appearances. A poor forlorn Indian dressed in rags might have great power; a smiling, amiable woman, or a pleasant old man, might be a sorcerer.[32] You never can tell until a situation arises in which their power for good or ill becomes manifest. I have since concluded that the advice given me in a common sense fashion provides one of the major clues to a generalized attitude towards the objects of their behavioral environment—particularly people. It makes them cautious and suspicious in interpersonal relations of all kinds. The possibility of metamorphosis must be one of the determining factors in this attitude; it is a concrete manifestation of the deceptiveness of appearances. What looks like an animal, without great power, may be a transformed person with evil intent. Even in dream experiences, where a human being comes into direct contact with other-than-human persons, it is possible to be deceived. Caution is necessary in "social" relations with all classes of persons.

Dreams, Metamorphosis, and the Self

The Ojibwa are a dream-conscious people. For an understanding of their cognitive orientation it is as necessary to appreciate their attitude towards dreams as it is to understand their attitude towards the characters in the myths. For them, there is an inner connection which is as integral to their outlook as it is foreign to ours.

The basic assumption which links the *ätíso'kanak* with dreams is this: Self-related experience of the most personal and vital kind includes what is seen, heard, and felt in dreams. Although there is no lack of discrimination between the experiences of the self when awake and when dreaming, both sets of experiences are equally self-related. Dream experiences function integrally with other re-called memory images in so far as these, too, enter the field of self-awareness. When we think autobiographically we only include events that happened to us when awake; the Ojibwa include remem-bered events that have occurred in dreams. And, far from being of subordinate importance, such experiences are for them often of more vital importance than the events of daily waking life. Why is this so? Because it is in dreams that the individual comes into direct communication with the *ätíso'kanak,* the powerful persons of the other-than-human class.

In the long winter evenings, as I have said, the *ätíso'kanak* are talked about; the past events in their lives are recalled again and again by *änícinábek.* When a conjuring performance occurs, the voices of some of the same beings are heard issuing from within the conjuring lodge. Here is actual perceptual experience of the "grandfathers" during a waking state. In dreams, the same other-than-human persons are both "seen" and "heard." They address human beings as "grandchild." These "dream visitors" (i.e., *pa-wáganak*) interact with the dreamer much as human persons do. But, on account of the nature of these beings there are differences, too. It is in the context of this face-to-face personal interaction of the self with the grandfathers (i.e., synonymously *ätíso'kanak, pa-wáganak*) that human beings receive important revelations that are the source of assistance to them in the daily round of life, and, be-sides this, of blessings that enable them to exercise exceptional powers of various kinds.

But dream experiences are not ordinarily recounted save under special circumstances. There is a taboo against this, just as there is a taboo against myth narration except in the proper seasonal context. The consequence is that we know relatively little about the manifest content of dreams. All our data come from acculturated Ojibwa. We do know enough to say, however, that the Ojibwa recognize quite as much as we do that dream experiences are often qualitatively different from our waking experiences. This fact, moreover, is turned to positive account. Since their dream visitors are other-than-human persons possessing great power, it is to be expected that the experiences of the self in interaction with them will differ from those with human beings in daily life. Besides this, another assumption must be taken into account: When a human being is asleep and dreaming his *òtcatcákwin* (vital part, soul), which is the core of the self, may become detached from the body (*mīyó*). Viewed by another human being, a person's body may be easily located and observed in space. But his vital part may be somewhere else. Thus, the self has greater mobility in space and even in time while sleeping. This is another illustration of the deceptiveness of appearances. The body of a sorcerer may be within sight in a wigwam, while "he" may be bearwalking. Yet the space in which the self is mobile is continuous with the earthly and cosmic space of waking life. A dream of one of my informants documents this specifically. After having a dream in which he met some (mythical) anthropomorphic beings (*mémengwécīwak*) who live in rocky escarpments and are famous for their medicine, he told me that he had later identified precisely the rocky place he had visited and entered in his dream. Thus the behavioral environment of the self is all of a piece. This is why experiences undergone when awake or asleep can be interpreted as experiences of self. Memory images, as recalled, become integrated with a sense of self-continuity in time and space.

Metamorphosis may be *experienced* by the self in dreams. One example will suffice to illustrate this. The dreamer in this case had been paddled out to an island by his father to undergo his puberty fast. For several nights he dreamed of an anthropomorphic figure. Finally, this being said, "Grandchild, I think you are strong enough now to go with me." Then the *pawágan* began dancing and as he danced he turned into what looked like a golden eagle. (This being must be understood as the "master" of this species.) Glancing down at his own body as he sat there on a rock, the boy noticed it was covered with feathers. The "eagle" spread its wings and flew off to the south. The boy then spread his wings and followed.

Here we find the instability of outward form in both human and other-than-human persons succinctly dramatized. Individuals of both categories undergo metamorphosis. In later life the boy will recall how he first saw the master of the golden eagles in his anthropomorphic guise, followed by his transformation into avian form; at the same time he will recall his own metamorphosis into a bird. But this experience, considered in context, does not imply that subsequently the boy can transform himself into a golden eagle at will. He might or might not be sufficiently "blessed." The dream itself does not inform us about this.

This example, besides showing how dream experiences may reinforce the belief in metamorphosis, illustrates an additional point: the *pawáganak,* whenever "seen," are always experienced as appearing in a specific form. They have a bodily aspect, whether human-like, animal-like, or ambiguous. But this is not their most persistent, enduring and vital attribute any more than in the case of human beings. We must conclude that all animate beings of the person class are unified conceptually in Ojibwa thinking because they have a similar structure—an inner vital part that is enduring and an outward form which can change. Vital personal attributes such as sentience, volition, memory, speech are not dependent upon outward appearance but upon the inner vital essence of being. If this be true, human beings and other-than-human persons are alike in another way. The human self does not die; it continues its existence in another place, after the body is buried in the grave. In this way *änícinábek* are as immortal as *ätíso'kanak.* This may be why we find human beings associated with the latter in the myths where it is sometimes difficult for an outsider to distinguish between them.

Thus the world of personal relations in which the Ojibwa live is a world in which vital social relations transcend those which are maintained with human beings. Their culturally constituted cognitive orientation prepares the individual for life in this world and for a life after death. The self-image that he acquires makes intelligible the nature of other selves. Speaking as an Ojibwa, one might say: all other persons—human or other than human—are structured the same as I am. There is a vital part which is enduring and an outward appearance that may be transformed under certain conditions. All other "persons," too, have such attributes as self-awareness and understanding. I can talk with them. Like myself, they have personal identity, autonomy, and volition. I cannot always predict exactly how they will act, although most of the time their behavior meets my expectations. In relation to myself, other "persons" vary in power. Many of them have more power than I have, but some have less. They may be friendly and help me when I need them but, at the same time, I have to be prepared for hostile acts, too. I must be cautious in my relations with other "persons" because appearances may be deceptive.

The Psychological Unity of the Ojibwa World

Although not formally abstracted and articulated philosophically, the nature of persons is the focal point of Ojibwa ontology and the key to the psychological unity and dynamics of their world outlook. This aspect of their metaphysics of being permeates the content of their cognitive processes: perceiving, remembering, imagining, conceiving, judging, and reasoning. Nor can the motivation of much of their conduct be thoroughly understood without taking into account the relation of their central values and goals to the awareness they have of the existence of other-than-human, as well as human, persons in their world. Persons, in fact, are so inextricably associated with notions of causality that, in order to understand their appraisal of events and the kind of behavior demanded in situations as they define them, we are confronted over and over again with the roles of persons as *loci* of causality in the dynamics of their universe. For the Ojibwa make no cardinal use of any concept of impersonal forces as major determinants of events. In the context of my exposition the meaning of the term *manitu,* which has become so generally known, may be considered as a synonym for a person of the other-than-human class (grandfather, *ätíso'kan,*

A mnemonic pictograph for a Midewi-win song: "When the waters are calm and the fog rises, I will now and then appear." The circle represents the sky, filled with moisture, and from it there emerges the face of a *manitu*. Engraving on birch bark, from Bulletin 45 of the Bureau of American Ethnology, p. 64.

pawágan). Among the Ojibwa I worked with, it is now quite generally confined to the God of Christianity, when combined with an augmentative prefix (*k'tci manītu*). There is no evidence to suggest, however, that the term ever did connote an impersonal, magical, or supernatural force.[33]

In an essay on the "Religion of the North American Indians" published over forty years ago, Radin asserted that "from an examination of the data customarily relied upon as proof and from individual data obtained, there is nothing to justify the postulation of a belief in a universal force in North America. Magical power as an 'essence' existing apart and separate from a definite spirit, is, we believe, an unjustified assumption, an abstraction created by investigators."[34] This opinion, at the time, was advanced in opposition to the one expressed by those who, stimulated by the writings of R. R. Marett in particular, interpreted the term *manitu* among the Algonkians (W. Jones), *orenda* among the Iroquois (Hewitt) and *wakanda* among the Siouan peoples (Fletcher) as having reference to a belief in a magical force of some kind. But Radin pointed out that in his own field work among both the Winnebago and the Ojibwa the terms in question "always referred to definite spirits, not necessarily definite in shape. If at a vapor-bath the steam is regarded as *wakanda* or *manitu*, it is because it is a spirit transformed into steam for the time being; if an arrow is possessed of specific virtues, it is because a spirit has either transformed himself into the arrow or because he is temporarily dwelling in it; and finally, if tobacco is offered to a peculiarly-shaped object it is because either this object belongs to a spirit, or a spirit is residing in it." *Manitu,* he said, in addition to its substantive usage may have such connotations as sacred, strange, remarkable or powerful without "having the slightest suggestion of inherent power, but having the ordinary sense of these adjectives." [35]

With respect to the Ojibwa conception of causality, all my own observations suggest that a culturally constituted psychological set operates which inevitably directs the reasoning of individuals towards an explanation of events in personalistic terms. *Who* did it, *who* is responsible, is always the crucial question to be answered. Personalistic explanation of past events is found in the myths. It was *Wísekedjak* who, through the exercise of his personal power, expanded the tiny bit of mud retrieved by Muskrat from the depths of the inundating waters of the great deluge into the inhabitable island-earth of Ojibwa cosmography. Personalistic explanation is central in theories of disease causation. Illness may be due to sorcery; the victim, in turn, may be responsible because he has offended the sorcerer—even unwittingly. Besides this, I may be responsible for my own illness, even without the intervention of a sorcerer. I may have committed some wrongful act in the past, which is the cause of my sickness. My child's illness, too, may be the consequence of my past transgressions or those of my wife.[36] The personalistic theory of causation even emerges today among acculturated Ojibwa. In 1940, when a severe forest fire broke out at the mouth of the Berens River, no Indian would believe that lightning or any impersonal or accidental determinants were involved. *Somebody* must have been responsible. The German spy theory soon became popular. "Evidence" began to accumulate; strangers had been seen in the bush, and so on. The personalistic type of explanation satisfies the Ojibwa because it is rooted in a basic metaphysical assumption; its terms are ultimate and incapable of further analysis within the framework of their cognitive orientation and experience.

Since the dynamics of events in the Ojibwa universe find their most ready explanation in a personalistic theory of causation, the qualitative aspects of interpersonal relations become affectively charged with a characteristic sensitivity.[37] The psychological importance of the range and depth of this sensitive area may be over-looked if the inclusiveness of the concept of person and social relations that is inherent in their outlook is not borne in mind. The reason for this becomes apparent when we consider the pragmatic relations between behavior, values, and the role of persons in their world view.

The central goal of life for the Ojibwa is expressed by the term *pīmädäzīwin,* life in the fullest sense, life in the sense of longevity, health and freedom from misfortune. This goal cannot be achieved without the effective help and cooperation of *both* human and other-than-human persons, as well as by one's own personal efforts. The help of other-than-human "grandfathers" is particularly important for men. This is why all Ojibwa boys, in aboriginal days, were motivated to undergo the so-called puberty fast or "dreaming" experience. This was the means by which it was possible to enter into direct social interaction with persons of the other-than-human class for the first time. It was the opportunity of a lifetime. Every special aptitude, all a man's subsequent successes and the explanation of many of his failures, hinged upon the help of the guardian spirits he obtained at this time, rather than upon his own native endowments or the help of his fellow *änícinábek.* If a boy received blessings during his puberty fast and, as a man, could call upon the help of other-than-human persons when he needed them he was well prepared for meeting the vicissitudes of life. Among other things, he could defend himself against the hostile actions of human persons which might threaten him and thus interfere with the achievement of *pīmädäzīwin.* The grandfather of one of my informants said to him: "you will have a long and good life if you dream well." The help of human beings, however, was also vital, especially the services of those who had acquired the kind of power which permitted them to exercise effective curative functions in cases of illness. At the same time there were moral responsibilities which had to be assumed by an individual if he strove for *pīmädäzīwin.* It was as essential to maintain approved standards of personal and social conduct as it was to obtain power from the "grandfathers" because, in the nature of things, one's own conduct, as well as that of other "persons," was always a potential threat to the achievement of *pīmådäzīwin*. Thus we find that the same values are implied throughout the entire range of social interaction that characterizes the Ojibwa world; the same standards which apply to mutual obligations between human beings are likewise implied in the reciprocal relations between human and other-than-human persons. In his relations with the grandfathers the individual does not expect to receive a blessing for nothing. It is not a free gift; on his part there are obligations to be met. There is a principle of reciprocity implied. There is a general taboo imposed upon the human being which forbids him to recount his dream experiences in full detail, except under certain circumstances. Specific taboos may likewise be imposed upon the suppliant. If these taboos are violated he will lose his power; he can no longer count on the help of his grandfathers.

The same principle of mutual obligations applies in other spheres of life. The Ojibwa are hunters and food gatherers. Since the various species of animals on which they depend for a living are believed to be under the control of "masters" or "owners" who belong to the category of other-than-human persons, the hunter must always be careful to treat the animals he kills for food or fur in the proper manner. It may be necessary, for example, to throw their bones in the water or to perform a ritual in the case of bears. Otherwise, he will offend the masters and be threatened with starvation because no animals will be made available to him. Cruelty to animals is likewise an offense that will provoke the same kind of retaliation. And, according to one anecdote, a man suffered illness because he tortured a fabulous *wíndīgo* after killing him. A moral distinction is drawn between the kind of conduct demanded by the primary necessities of securing a livelihood, or defending onself against aggression, and unnecessary acts of cruelty. The moral values implied document the consistency of the principle of mutual obligations which is inherent in all interactions with persons throughout the Ojibwa world.

One of the prime values of Ojibwa culture is exemplified by the great stress laid upon sharing what one has with others. A balance, a sense of proportion must be maintained in all interpersonal relations and activities. Hoarding, or any manifestation of greed, is discountenanced. The central importance of this moral value in their world outlook is illustrated by the fact that other-than-human persons share their power with human beings. This is only a particular instance of the obligations which human beings feel towards one another. A man's catch of fish or meat is distributed among his kin. Human grandfathers share the power acquired in their dreams from other-than-human persons with their classificatory grandchildren. An informant whose wife had borrowed his pipe for the morning asked to borrow one of mine while we worked together. When my friend Chief Berens once fell ill he could not explain it. Then he recalled that he had overlooked one man when he had passed around a bottle of whiskey. He believed this man was offended and had bewitched him. Since there was no objective evidence of this, it illustrates the extreme sensitivity of an individual to the principle of sharing, operating through feelings of guilt. I was once told about the puberty fast of a boy who was not satisfied with his initial blessing. He demanded that he dream of all the leaves of all the trees in the world so that absolutely nothing would be hidden from him. This was considered greedy and, while the *pawágan* who appeared in his dream granted his desire, the boy was told that "as soon as the leaves start to fall you'll get sick and when all the leaves drop to the ground that is the end of your life." And this is what happened.[38] Overfasting is as greedy as hoarding. It violates a basic moral value and is subject to a punitive sanction. The unity of the Ojibwa outlook is likewise apparent here.

The entire psychological field in which they live and act is not only unified through their conception of the nature and role of persons in their universe, but by the sanctioned moral values which guide the relations of persons. It is within this web of social relations that the individual strives for *pīmádäzīwin*.

Notes

1. Redfield 1952,* p. 30; cf. *African Worlds*.

2. Hallowell 1955, p. 91. For a more extended discussion of the culturally constituted behavioral environment of man see *ibid.*, pp. 86–89 and note 33. The term "self" is not used as a synonym for ego in the psychoanalytic sense. See *ibid.*, p. 80.

3. See Basilius 1952, Carroll in Whorf, 1956, Hoijer, 1954, Feuer, 1953.

4. Hallowell 1955, chap. 5.

5. Bruno de Jésus-Marie 1952, p. xvii: "The studies which make up this book fall into two main groups, of which the first deals with the theological Satan. Here the analysis of exegesis, of philosophy, of theology, treat of the devil under his aspect of a personal being whose history—his fall, his desire for vengeance—can be written as such." One of the most startling characteristics of the devil ". . . is his agelessness" (p. 4). He is immune to "injury, to pain, to sickness, to death. . . . Like God, and unlike man, he has no body. There are in him, then, no parts to be dismembered, no possibilities of corruption and decay, no threat of a separation of parts that will result in death. He is incorruptible, immune to the vagaries, the pains the limitations of the flesh, immortal" (p. 5). "Angels have no bodies, yet they have appeared to men in physical form, have talked with them, journeyed the roads with them fulfilling all the pleasant tasks of companionship" (p. 6).

6. Hallowell 1934b, pp. 7–9; 1936, pp. 1308–9; 1951, pp. 182–83; 1955, pp. 256–58.

7. Kelsen 1943, chapter 2, discusses the "social" or "personalistic interpretation of nature" which he considers the nucleus of what has been called animism.

8. In a prefatory note to *Ojibwa Texts,* Part I, Jones says (p. xiii) that " 'Being' or 'creature' would be a general rendering of the animate while 'thing' would express the inanimate." Cf. Schoolcraft's pioneer analysis of the animate and inanimate categories in Ojibwa speech, pp. 171–72.

9. Greenberg 1954, pp. 15–16.

10. I believe that Jenness grossly overgeneralizes when he says (p. 21): "To the Ojibwa . . . all objects have life. . . ." If this were true, their *inanimate* grammatical category would indeed be puzzling.

Within the more sophisticated framework of modern biological thought, the Ojibwa attitude is not altogether naïve. N. W. Pirie points out (pp. 184–85) that the words "life" and "living" have been borrowed by science from lay usage and are no longer serviceable. "Life is not a thing, a philosophical entity: it is an attitude of mind towards what is being observed."

11. Field notes. From this same Indian I obtained a smoothly rounded pebble, about two inches long and one and a half inches broad, which his father had given him. He told me that I had better keep it enclosed in a tin box or it might "go." Another man, Ketegas, gave me an account of the circumstances under which he obtained a stone with animate properties and of great medicinal value. This stone was egg shaped. It had some dark amorphous markings on it which he interpreted as representing his three children and himself. "You may not think this stone is alive," he said, "but it is. I can make it move." (He did not demonstrate this to me.) He went on to say that on two occasions he had loaned the stone to sick people to keep during the night. Both times he found it in his pocket in the morning. Ketegas kept it in a little leather case he had made for it.

12. Yellow Legs had obtained information about this remarkable stone in a dream. Its precise location was revealed to him. He sent two other Indians to get it. These men, following directions, found the stone on Birch Island, located in the

middle of Lake Winnipeg, some thirty miles south of the mouth of the Berens River.

13. Cognate forms are found in Chamberlain's compilation of Cree and Ojibwa "literary" terms.

14. Jones, *Texts,* Part II, p. 574*n*.

15. The attitude manifested is by no means peculiar to the Ojibwa. Almost half a century ago Swanton remarked that "one of the most widespread errors, and one of those most unfortunate for folk-lore and comparative mythology, is the off-hand classification of myth with fiction. . . ." On the contrary, as he says, "It is safe to say that most of the myths found spread over considerable areas were regarded by the tribes among which they were collected as narratives of real occurrences."

16. Bidney 1953, p. 166. [What Bidney calls "critical insight" might better be called an erroneous application of the "calculative" mind to a "contemplative" matter; see the introduction—eds.]

17. Lovejoy and Boas 1935, p. 12; Lovejoy 1948, p. 69.

18. See, e.g., Collingwood 1945, also the remarks in Randall 1944, pp. 355–56. With respect to the applicability of the natural-supernatural dichotomy to primitive cultures see Van Der Leeuw 1938, pp. 544–45; Kelsen 1943, p. 44; Bidney 1953, p. 166.

19. Krech and Crutchfield 1948 write (p. 10): "clouds and storms and winds are excellent examples of objects in the psychological field that carry the perceived properties of mobility, capriciousness, causation, power of threat and reward."

20. Cf. Hallowell 1934a.

21. Actually, this was probably a rationalization of mother-son incest. But the woman never was punished by sickness, nor did she confess. Since the violation of the incest prohibition is reputed to be followed by dire consequences, the absence of both may have operated to support the possibility of her claim when considered in the context of the Ojibwa world view.

22. Thompson 1946, p. 258.

23. Hallowell 1926.

24. Hallowell 1934a, p. 397.

25. Sorcerers may assume the form of other animals as well. Peter Jones, a converted Ojibwa, who became famous as a preacher and author says that "they can turn themselves into bears, wolves, foxes, owls, bats, and snakes. . . . Several of our people have informed me that they have seen and heard witches in the shape of these animals, especially the bear and the fox. They say that when a witch in the shape of a bear is being chased all at once she will run around a tree or hill, so as to be lost sight of for a time by her pursuers, and then, instead of seeing a bear they behold an old woman walking quietly along or digging up roots, and looking as innocent as a lamb" (Jones 1861, pp. 145–46).

26. Dorson 1952, p. 30.

27. *Ibid.,* p. 29. This rationalization dates back over a century. John Tanner, an Indianized white man who was captured as a boy in the late eighteenth century and lived with the Ottawa and Ojibwa many years, refers to it. So does Peter Jones.

28. Hallowell 1955, pp. 176–77.

29. Dorson 1952, p. 31.

30. Hoffman 1891, pp. 205–6.

31. Unpublished field notes.

32. See Hallowell 1955, Chapter 15.

33. Cf. Skinner 1915, p. 261. Cooper 1933 (p. 75) writes: "The Manitu was clearly personal in the minds of my informants, and not identified with impersonal supernatural force. In fact, nowhere among the Albany River Otchipwe, among the Eastern Cree, or among the Montagnais have I been able thus far to find the word Manitu used to denote such force in connection with the Supreme Being belief, with conjuring, or with any other phase of magico-religious culture. *Manitu,* so far as I can discover, always denotes a supernatural personal being. . . . The word *Manitu* is, my informants say, not used to denote magical or conjuring power among the coastal Cree, nor so I was told in 1927, among the Fort Hope Otchipwe of the upper Albany River."

34. Radin 1914a, p. 350.

35. *Ibid.,* pp. 349–50.

36. "Because a person does bad things, that is where sickness starts," is the way one of my informants phrased it. For a fuller discussion of the relations between unsanctioned sexual behavior and disease, see Hallowell 1955, pp. 294–95; 303–4. For case material, see Hallowell 1939.

37. Cf. Hallowell 1955, p. 305.

38. Radin 1927, p. 177, points out that "throughout the area inhabited by the woodland tribes of Canada and the United States, overfasting entails death." Jones, *Texts,* Part II, pp. 307–11, gives two cases of overfasting. In one of them the bones of the boy were later found by his father.

* Dates refer to works in Reference section below.

References

African Worlds: Studies in the Cosmological Ideas and Social Values of African Peoples. 1954. Published for the International African Institute. London, Oxford University Press.

Baraga, R. R. Bishop. 1878. A Theoretical and Practical Grammar of the Otchipwe Language. Montreal, Beauchemin and Valois.

Baraga, R. R. Bishop. 1880. A Dictionary of the Otchipwe Language Explained in English. Montreal, Beauchemin and Valois.

Basilius, H. 1952. "Neo-Humboldtian Ethnolinguistics," *Word,* Vol. 8.

Bidney, David. 1953. Theoretical Anthropology. New York, Columbia University Press.

Bruno de Jésus-Marie, père, ed. 1952. Satan. New York, Sheed and Ward.

Chamberlain, A. F. 1906. "Cree and Ojibwa Literary Terms," *Journal of American Folklore,* 19:346–47.

Collingwood, R. G. 1945. The Idea of Nature. Oxford, Clarendon Press.

Cooper, John M. 1933. "The Northern Algonquian Supreme Being," *Primitive Man*, 6:41–112.

Dorson, Richard M. 1952. Bloodstoppers and Bearwalkers: Folk Traditions of the Upper Peninsula. Cambridge, Mass., Harvard University Press.

Feuer, Lewis S. 1953. "Sociological Aspects of the Relation between Language and Philosophy," *Philosophy of Science*, 20:85–100.

Fletcher, Alice C. 1910. "Wakonda," in *Handbook of American Indians*. Washington, D.C.: Bureau of American Ethnology, Bull. 30.

Greenberg, Joseph H. 1954. "Concerning Inferences from Linguistic to Nonlinguistic Data," in *Language in Culture*, ed. by Harry Hoijer. (Chicago University "Comparative Studies in Cultures and Civilizations.") Chicago, University of Chicago Press.

Hallowell, A. Irving. 1926. "Bear Ceremonialism in the Northern Hemisphere," *American Anthropologist*, 28:1–175.

——— 1934a. "Some Empirical Aspects of Northern Saulteaux Religion," *American Anthropologist*, 36:389–404.

——— 1934b. "Culture and Mental Disorder," *Journal of Abnormal and Social Psychology*, 29:1–9.

——— 1936. "Psychic Stresses and Culture Patterns," *American Journal of Psychiatry*, 92:1291–1310.

——— 1939. "Sin, Sex and Sickness in Saulteaux Belief," *British Journal of Medical Psychology*, 18:191–97.

———1951. "Cultural Factors in the Structuralization of Perception," in John H. Rohver and Muzafer Sherif, *Social Psychology at the Crossroads*. New York, Harper.

——— 1955. Culture and Experience. Philadelphia, University of Penna. Press.

Hewitt, J. N. B. 1902. "Orenda and a Definition of Religion," *American Anthropologist*, 4:33–46.

Hoffman, W. J. 1891. The Mide'wiwin or "Grand Medicine Society" of the Ojibwa. Washington, D.C., Bureau of American Ethnology 7th Annual Report.

Hoijer, Harry, ed. 1954. Language in Culture. Memoir 79, American Anthropological Association.

Jenness, Diamond. 1935. The Ojibwa Indians of Parry Island, their social and religious life. Ottawa, Canada Department of Mines, National Museum of Canada Bull. 78, Anthropological Series 12.

Jones, Peter. 1861. History of the Ojibway Indians. London.

Jones, William. 1905. "The Algonkin Manitu," *Journal of American Folklore*, 18:183–90.

——— Ojibwa Texts. (Publications of the American Ethnological Society, Vol. 7, Parts I and II.) Leyden: 1917; New York: 1919.

Kelsen, Hans. 1943. Society and Nature: A Sociological Inquiry. Chicago, University of Chicago Press.

Krech, David, and Richard S. Crutchfield. 1948. Theory and Problems of Social Psychology. New York, McGraw-Hill.

Lovejoy, Arthur O. 1948. Essays in the History of Ideas. Baltimore, Johns Hopkins Press.

Lovejoy, Arthur O., and George Boas. 1935. Primitivism and Related Ideas in Antiquity. Baltimore, Johns Hopkins Press. Vol. I of A Documentary History of Primitivism and Related Ideas.

Pirie, N. W. 1937. "The Meaninglessness of the Terms 'Life' and 'Living,' " in Perspectives in Biochemistry, ed. by J. Needham and D. Green. New York, Macmillan.

Radin, Paul. 1914a. "Religion of the North American Indians," Journal of American Folklore, 27:335–73.

———— 1914b. Some Aspects of Puberty Fasting among the Ojibwa. Geological Survey of Canada, Department of Mines, Museum Bull. No. 2, Anthropological Series, No. 2, pp. 1–10.

———— 1927. Primitive Man as Philosopher. New York, D. Appleton & Co.

Randall, John Herman, Jr. 1944. "The Nature of Naturalism," in Naturalism and the Human Spirit, ed. by H. Krikorian. New York, Columbia University Press.

Redfield, Robert. 1952. "The Primitive World View," Proceedings of the American Philosophical Society, 96:30–36.

Schoolcraft, Henry R. 1834. Narrative of an Expedition through the Upper Mississippi to Itasca Lake, the Actual Source of the River. . . . New York, Harper.

Skinner, Alanson. 1915. "The Menomini Word 'Häwätûk,' " Journal of American Folklore, 28:258–61.

Swanton, John R. 1910. "Some practical aspects of the study of myths," Journal of American Folklore, 23:1–7.

Tanner, John. 1830. Narrative of the Captivity and Adventures of John Tanner, ed. by E. James.

Thompson, Stith. 1946. The Folktale. New York, Dryden Press.

Van Der Leeuw, G. 1938. Religion in Essence and Manifestation. London, Allen and Unwin.

Whorf, Benjamin Lee. 1956. Language Thought and Reality: Selected Writings of Benjamin L. Whorf, ed. with an introduction by J. B. Carroll; Foreword by Stuart Chase. New York, Wiley.

11

The Tewa World View

Alfonso Ortiz

According to the Tewa, life began for them, as for other Pueblo Indians, in a world below this one. This primordial home, called *Sipofene,* was located somewhere far to the north, beneath a lake. Men, gods and animals lived together at this time, and man could still communicate with animals. Illness and death were also unknown in this underworld home. The world above—this world—was also known to exist, but it was *ochu,* "green" or "unripe." It was also shrouded in mist and the ground was soft, so people could not walk on it.

In time the ground hardened, so the Tewa left their home underneath the lake to live in this world. The transition from this mythical time before emergence to the present or historical time—or the transition from one world to another—is explained by the Tewa concept of *seh t'a,* a term which has several symbolic referents. Literally translated, *seh t'a* means "dry food," as when the

---

This paper was presented at the 1966 meeting of the American Anthropological Association; it is printed here with the permission of the author. The Tewa occupy six villages near Santa Fe, New Mexico. Professor Ortiz, himself a Tewa, now teaches anthropology at the University of New Mexico; he is President of the Association on American Indian Affairs, Inc.

origin myth compares the world before emergence to green or unripe food. When referring to time it means "hardened matter," a reference to the hardening of the earth upon the people's emergence from the lake. The term also embodies a sacred-profane distinction because what occurred in the lake, prior to emergence, is sacred. What has been occurring since is profane, because evil, illness and death were introduced only after emergence.

Let us return to the literal meaning of *seh t'a,* by way of indicating how the Tewa view existence. There are six levels or categories of being recognized, as Figure 1 illustrates. They are levels in the sense that they are discrete and hierarchical. However, they are also cultural categories in the sense that they divide and classify *all* of Tewa social and supernatural existence.

Those of the first or lowest category are called, appropriately, "Dry Food People." These are the common Tewa who serve in no official capacity in the political or ritual system. The common Tewa are also called *Whe t'owa* (Weed or Trash People) and *Na'yi wha t'owa* (Dust Dragging People), both terms intended to clearly differentiate them from the other categories. Level 2 indicates the *T'owa é,* or simply, "persons." They are political officials and constitute the core of the political organization of the Tewa. Category 3 represents the *Pat'owa* or Made People. They are called such because their offices were made or instituted in the underworld before emergence. These include the two moiety societies, the medicine men, the *Kwiřana* or cold clowns, the *K'ossa* or warm clowns, and the Hunt, Scalp and Women's societies. They consti-

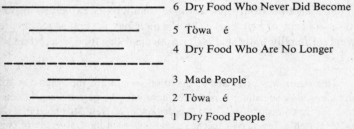

Figure 1. Tewa levels of being.

tute a hierarchy of eight discrete but functionally interrelated orga-
nizations.

The next three categories may be regarded as supernatural
counterparts of the first three. The "Dry Food Who Are No
Longer" are the souls of the Dry Food People; that is to say, when
a person of Category 1 dies, he becomes a spirit of Category 4.
Category 5 represents the supernatural counterparts of Category 2.
This category consists of the six pairs of male spirits who were sent
out to explore the world before emergence. They are commonly
known in the literature as "Twin War Gods." The Tewa term,
which simply means "persons," is used here because the *T'owa é*
are neither gods, nor are they twins, in Tewa thought. Nor are their
human representatives (Category 2) war captains, war chiefs or outside chiefs, as they have been called for so long. Category 6, the
"Dry Food Who Never Did Become," includes all of the deities
recognized by the Tewa, and who were present before emergence.
In other words, these deities never became *seh t'a* or dry food; they
did not walk on the earth after it hardened. A whole host of spirits
belong to this category, which is the Tewa counterpart to the more
familiar *Kachina* of the Hopi. Like the Hopi *Kachinas* they are
represented by masked impersonators in ritual. The Made People
join these deities after death.

Let us now turn to Figure 2, which presents the principal reference points in the Tewa world as a series of tetrads or structures of
four parts. It may be regarded as a counterpart, in the physical
world, to Figure 1. The color indicated is associated with each cardinal direction, and the arrows indicate the directional circuit,
which proceeds anti-sunwise and which always begins with north.
Taking the outermost tetrad first (A, B, C, D), the world of the
Tewa is bound by four sacred mountains. These mountains were
seen by the first four pairs of *T'owa é* as they were sent out to
explore the world in the origin myth.

Approximately sixty miles to the north of San Juan, New
Mexico is *Tse Shu Pín* (Hazy or Shimmering Mountain); *Tsikomo*
(Obsidian-covered Mountain) is about fifteen miles to the west; *Oku
Pín* (Turtle Mountain) is about eighty miles to the south, and *Ku*

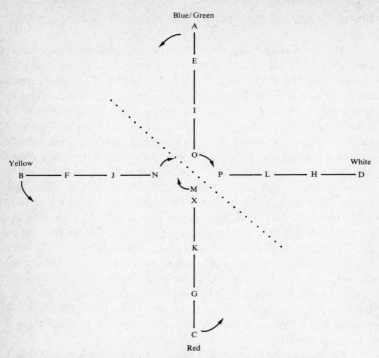

Figure 2. Principal reference points in the Tewa world.

Sehn Pín (Stone Man Mountain) is about twenty miles to the east. The northern mountain appears on topographic maps as Conjilon Peak; the second by its Tewa name, the third as Sandia Crest, just northeast of present day Albuquerque, and the last as Truchas Peak. The point to naming and locating them is to give proof of their objective existence, and to give some indication of the conceptual range of the Tewa world. It is about 140 miles north to south, and thirty-five miles east to west.

These mountains are understood by the Tewa as endowed with sacredness in several ways. First, a lake or pond is associated with each, and within this body of water live the "Dry Food Who Never Did Become," of the appropriate directional color. Secondly, there is a *nan sipu* or earth navel on top of each mountain, and within these live the *T'owa é* who stand watch over the Tewa world. The color classification is again replicated. The *T'owa é* are distinguished from the spirits of Category 6 because they emerged with the people—or, more properly, led the way out—in the origin myth. Consequently, they are associated with the earth navels, which are represented by shrines, rather than with the lakes or ponds.

The next tetrad (E,F,G,H) represents the sacred *Tsin* or flat-topped hills created by the *T'owa é* of the directions. The northern hill is *T'ema Yoh,* located just above the small Spanish-speaking village of La Madera. A few miles to the southwest is *T'oma Yoh;* *Tun Yoh* is between San Ildefonso and Santa Clara Pueblos to the south, while *Tsi Mayoh* is near the Spanish-speaking village, Chimayó, which is named after it, east of San Juan. Each of these hills is sacred because it is particularly dark and foreboding; each has a cave and/or labyrinths running through it. All are believed to be inhabited by *Tsaveyoh,* the masked supernatural whippers who are impersonated by the *T'owa é* and who constitute one of the Pueblo universals, being found in some manifestation from Taos in the east, to Hopi in the west.[1] The *T'owa é* of each directional color are also believed to watch over the Pueblo from these hills. In other words, the *T'owa é* are both of the mountains and of the hills.

The third tetrad represents the principal shrines of the directions. First in the directional circuit is *Than Powa* "Sun-water-wind," represented by a pile of large stones at the northern edge of the village. At the western edge of the village is *A'we Kwiyoh* or Spider Woman, represented by a single stone; to the south is *Nu Enu* or Ash Youth, also represented by a single stone. Approximately one mile east of the village is a low hill with a pile of stones on top; this is *Ti tan he i'* "Large Marked Rise," the shrine of the east. Collectively these shrines are known as *Xayeh t'a pingeh* "Souls-Dwelling Middle Places." Souls belong to a larger category of spirits and man-associated objects called *xayeh,* which also includes fossilized bone, sea shells, tools, weapons, and other objects rescued from ruins; in essence, all objects which have been used by people are endowed with sacredness because they are associated with the souls and with the sacred past.

Three of the shrines are located in the middle of refuse dumps. This follows from the ancient Pueblo practice of burying the dead near the village, and then leaving a rock or pile of stones to mark the spot. Thus one informant told me: "Long ago we buried the dead there and left a pile of stones. Every pile of stones you see shows where the *xayeh* live, for the dead have become *xayeh*." E. C. Parsons presents photographs and drawings of the northern shrine and notes that informants told her the shrines were on all four sides.[2] Regrettably, she did not also note that the shrines constituted a portion of a complex and meaningful system of classification.

The final tetrad represents the *bu pingeh* or dance plazas within the village. Even the village itself is conceptualized as consisting of four parts, or four houseblocks. In any case, all public rituals must be performed at least four times, in each of the dance areas. Nor do the tetrads end here, for there are other circuits within this circuit; in some rituals the participants must face each of the four directions, and even the accompanying songs are divided into four parts. The circuit here (M,N,O,P) is seen as proceeding from the south plaza to the west, then north, and finally east; in other words north and south are reversed, and the circuit becomes clockwise. This is one instance in which the directional circuit, to which they relentlessly adhere in thought, prayer and ritual behavior, is broken. The Tewa explain this discrepancy as follows. Long ago all of the houses of San Juan were grouped around the south plaza; this was the only plaza. As the pueblo grew to the north, east and west, other dance areas were set aside in each direction. The available information from the mid-nineteenth century, consisting of photographs, church records, and the location of the church itself, tends to justify this claim, at least to the extent that there were no houses facing what are now the west and east plazas. Toward the end of the nineteenth century the north plaza was already in existence, as an undated photograph of San Juan published in Winship [3] demonstrates.

A more important form of proof is provided by point X on Figure 2. It represents the *Nang echu kwi nang sipu pingeh,* or "Earth mother earth navel middle place." This is the sacred center of the village, and the ring of stones representing it is on the south plaza. Ritual dances and other performances must continue to be initiated here, as the Tewa explain it, because this is the center.

Figures 1 and 2 may now be put together, keeping in mind that Categories 1, 2 and 3 become 4, 5 and 6, respectively, in the supernatural realm. By so doing we note that Category 6 on Figure 1 is represented by the four sacred mountains of Figure 2; Category 5 is represented by the sacred mesas, and Category 4 by the shrines near the village. To go one step further, we may now draw the six categories of existence as the Tewa see them; as six differentiated but continuous levels, proceeding outward from the village in each direction:

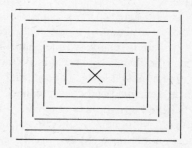

Let X represent the earth navel, or sacred center once again. Now, since the outermost points on Figure 2 contain earth navels (like that of the middle place) as well as representing the dwelling places of the most sacred beings of the Tewa world, and since the sacred center itself is located in the geographical center of the village, we have no simple spatial opposition between a sacred and a profane. The points at both spatial extremes are sacred, and it would be fruitless to argue about which is the more so.

In justification of the foregoing interpretation of the Tewa system of classification let me add, first, that six levels of being are recognized because *all six* of them are sometimes represented on the ground. Secondly, one of my informants showed he understood the underlying dialectic of Figure 2 by a remark which may be translated as follows:

> Remember that the words and the method of delivery of all prayers and speeches are the same; only the places mentioned are different. If you are a "Made" person you always pray to and invoke the authority of the mountains, and the "Dry Food Who Never Did Become." If you are a *T'owa é* you always mention the mesas and the *T'owa é*. . . .

Now that we have noted how human and spiritual existence is classified into six levels, and how these levels relate to the Tewa classification of horizontal space, let us return to the vertical classification, or the notion of cosmic levels. Unlike most of the other Pueblos, the Tewa do not believe in multiple underworld levels. Rather, as we have noted above, and as J. P. Harrington recorded more than half a century ago [4] there is a single Tewa underworld.

The world above, on the other hand, is also regarded as being like the middle, but there is relatively little concern with it; most of spiritual existence is attributed to the world below, and all human existence occurs on the middle level. The celestial bodies, the more prominent of which are named and conceptualized as anthropomorphic deities, are believed to live there much as do the beings of the other levels. But as a sub-system of classification in its own right, the above is almost undeveloped. Moreover, these deities may pass from one world level to another, or more specifically, from the upper to the lower level. Let us consider the sun and the moon, the most prominent of the celestial deities, by way of illustration. To quote from Harrington's *Ethnogeography of the Tewa:*

> The sun and moon pass daily from east to west over trails which run above the great waters of the sky. They see and know as do Indians here on earth. When they set they pass through a lake to the underworld and travel all night to the east, where they emerge through a lake and start on their trails again.[5]

Harrington goes on to note: "The sun is said to walk through the sky clothed in white deerskin and ornamented with many fine beads.

Elsewhere he adds that "The Tewa believe that the sun has a house in the east, and has a wife." [6]

The four sacred mountains illustrate the point in another way. While the nearby lakes serve as entrances to the below, the mountains themselves are regarded as the points at which the above, the middle and the below come closest to intersecting in each cardinal direction. Thus the deities of the lakes ascend to the sky from the mountaintops to make thunder and rain, and they descend back onto the mountains and into the lakes when their work is done.

In these and other ways, the three cosmic levels are resolved, or brought together. There are three levels, but there is also passage from one to another. We may thus view the Tewa conception of vertical space as triadic; as involving a union of three levels.

We have also noted that at death the souls of each of the human categories pass into the underworld, and are localized, as it were, in the lakes, mountains, hills and shrines. What this means is that the living can communicate with the spirits at these various points; they are points of entry into the underworld. Moreover, members of one category ordinarily do not visit the sacred points associated with the spiritual counterparts of another category. Thus Dry Food People, or common Tewa, visit the shrines, while Made People visit the lakes and earth navels on the distant mountaintops. To state it another way, the Dry Food person appeals to the ancestral souls in times of crisis, while the Made person appeals to the high deities in the lakes, on behalf of everyone in the village.

The *T'owa é,* on the other hand, are associated not only with the hills, but with the mountains as well. Analytically speaking, they seem to be an ambiguous category. This comes about partly because they are recruited from among the Dry Food People, and serve the Made People for terms of one year. Their classic function is to watch over the village from the sacred hills, but they also accompany the Made People to the mountains whenever the latter go to the lakes or earth navels. The *T'owa é* are an intermediary group, not only in the hierarchical sense, but in the sense that they are close to each of the other categories while being not quite either. Consequently their role as mediators in the society is reflected in the fact that they are also assigned a middle place in the spiritual and physical world. Because of this fact they must remain analytically somewhat vague.

To turn to another problem, while the spirits of each direction are localized at particular points within the sacred world of the Tewa, they do not remain there. As the Tewa explain it, just as Dry Food People, *T'owa é* and Made People live together in this world, so also do the various categories of spirit live together in the underworld. Since the underworld is like this one, the spirits may move freely within it. In this way the elaborate conceptual and spatial distinctions of Figure 2 lose some of their imposing characteristics. In the end, these physical points are only points of reference, reflecting in the physical world the undeniable fact that there are differences between the three social, or human categories of existence.

A further implication of this overall system of classification is that while the system, as a system, exists in just the way we have outlined it, whenever the spirits themselves are impersonated in ritual, they reflect the divisions found in the society. The principal social division is that into winter and summer moieties, as previous writers on the Tewa have pointed out. Consequently, whenever the deities of the lakes are impersonated they come either from the north as cold winter gods, from the south as warm summer gods, or from the west between seasons as mediators between the other two groups. The winter gods visit the village during the fall and winter, while the summer gods visit during the spring and summer. Rituals involving the former are sponsored by the winter moiety, and only members of the moiety may impersonate the winter gods, while only members of the summer moiety may sponsor and impersonate the summer gods. The group of deities which mediate between the moieties is discussed in detail in *The Tewa World*.[7]

Similarly, the *T'owa é,* whenever they act in an official capacity, always do so in pairs, one representing each moiety. Whenever the *T'owa é* impersonate the *Tsaveyoh,* or masked supernatural whippers, they also do so in pairs, one for each moiety. Only the souls are not impersonated in ritual, but at death each Tewa soul is believed to be met at the edge of the village by the ancestral souls, and thereafter guided into the afterworld by them.

To extend the argument to its logical conclusion, north and east and the associated spirits and colors are attributed to the winter moiety, while south and west and the corresponding spirits and colors are attributed to the summer moiety. This is the meaning of the dotted line separating the two sets of directions on Figure 2. In this way physical space and the various categories of being are reduced to a series of dyads. Everything in the sacred world of the Tewa is attributed to one or the other of the moieties. While we cannot here go into the precise ways in which all of these transformations come about, we have some indication of just how it is done. The examples could be multiplied, but what they would tell us, briefly, is that the system of thought is not always the system of action. There is not a one-to-one correlation between the way the Tewa perceive their world, and the way they behave at any given time. The system, as a conceptual system, exists, but when any portion of its spiritual component is brought to life, as it were, it reflects the basic social division: the moieties, or groups based upon the moieties.

Notes

1. Elsie Clews Parsons, *Social Organization of the Tewa of New Mexico,* American Anthropological Association Memoir 36, p. 270 (1929).

2. *Ibid.,* pp. 238, 244.

3. George P. Winship, The Coronado Expedition, 1540–42. 14th Annual Report, Bureau of American Ethnology (1896). Washington.

4. John P. Harrington, Ethnogeography of the Tewa. 29th Annual Report, Bureau of American Ethnology, p. 51 (1916). Washington.

5. *Ibid.,* p. 46.

6. *Ibid.,* p. 47.

7. Alfonso Ortiz, *The Tewa World.* Chicago: University of Chicago Press (1969).

12

The Inner Eye of Shamanism and Totemism

Robin Ridington and Tonia Ridington

Lévi-Strauss has shown us that totemism is not an institution but a way of thought. For this if for nothing else we should be eternally grateful. But knowing the dialectical structure of totemic thought alone is incomplete without a knowledge of its meaning. Totemic symbols are not merely syllogistic but refer to a systematic

From Robin Ridington and Tonia Ridington, "The Inner Eye of Shamanism and Totemism," *History of Religions* (An International Journal for Comparative Historical Studies) 10, no. 1 (August 1970). Reprinted with the permission of the University of Chicago Press and the authors. The Ridingtons note: "Our only role has been to put the words of this essay together. To the extent that they fall short of representing the way things are we accept responsibility and ask for your patience. The ideas we have attempted to communicate belong to everyone. In particular we have learned with and from David Jongeward, Susan Reid, and Sandra Slind, members of a seminar on myth at the University of British Columbia. The Beaver Indians and their shaman, Charlie Yahey, are, of course, our real teachers. We have been learning from them since 1964. The works of Mircea Eliade have also been immensely important in preparing the path." The Beaver Indians are in northeastern British Columbia and northern Alberta.

conceptualization of natural, psychic, and cultural reality that in mythically oriented traditions can best be called a cosmic structure (a term I have borrowed from a paper by Susan Reid on the meaning of Kwakiutl ceremonialism).[1]

Mythical cosmologies are not the attempts of savages to explain in fantasy where empirical knowledge of reality is absent, but are rather the opposite—statements in allegorical form about knowledge of the interrelations between what we would call natural (objective), psychic (psychological), and cultural (learned adaptational) aspects of reality. Myth and science are polar opposites, not because one is wrong and the other right, but because myth portrays reality as it is experienced while science postulates a reality that is thought to exist but can never be experienced. Myth unveils what is known to be true, while science experiments to build realities that are thought not to be untrue. Myths through their symbols allow men to enter directly and experientially into the realm of meaningful reality, and totemism is a form of symbolic communication that categorically associates human experience with its objects. Totemic symbols are good to experience as well as good to think. That they are sometimes, but not always, good to eat is simply to say that there are other experiences than eating. The eagle is not only a symbol of high as opposed to low; it is also a bird. The Hidatsa who go eagle hunting, to refer to an example of totemic classification used by Lévi-Strauss,[2] undergo an experience of great power. The eagles that they lure from the sky and capture by hand are more than convenient abstractions. They, and through them the hunter, are participants in the cosmic structure of meaningful experience. There is more meaning to eagle hunting than its formal intellectual structure.

Mythic and totemic systems reveal to men a cosmic structure that synthesizes and organizes their individual and collective experiences. They do not ''give meaning'' to life but rather disclose the meaning that is its intrinsic property. The cosmic structure most often if not universally associated with myth and totem can be loosely described as shamanic. The essential axes of this structure are the four cardinal points and a central vertical axis passing through their point of intersection that connects the three worlds of sky, earth, and underworld. The structure is that of a mandala whose center leads to a break in space and time [3] that generates upper and lower supernatural worlds. They exist in a dimension apprehended through inner experience. The North-South and East-West axes encompass the manifest world of ordinary reality (see Carlos Castaneda for discussion of ordinary and nonordinary reality) [4] and their point of intersection is the entrance to the supernatural upper and underworlds. The central vertical axis that connects the three worlds is variously symbolized as the world pole, the tree of life, the sacred mountain, the central house pole, Jacob's ladder, and even the church steeple.[5]

Shamanism is usually described as a magical flight into a supernatural realm. But what do we really mean when we speak of supernatural realms? Surely we do not still believe that savages imagine nonexistent worlds because of their poor understanding of physical reality. The real meaning of the supernatural must be symbolic and the shamanic flight an inner journey into a realm of experience for which the symbols stand. The three worlds of a shamanic cosmology are not geographical places but internal states of being represented by a geometric analogy. The shaman does not really fly up or down, but inside to the meaning of things. Shamanism is a magical flight into a hidden, internal, experiential dimension in which time, space, and distance as we know them, as well as the distinction between subject and object, merge into a unity. In fact, shamanism so defined is a universal human experience even though it tends to be institutionalized only in small-scale "savage" societies.

As Lévi-Strauss has brilliantly shown, the geometrical axes of shamanic cosmology can be used as the basis of endless elegant structural oppositions, mediations, and syntheses. The point I wish to illustrate is that the mental structure of totemism is simply a framework for the cosmic structure of shamanism. Totemism is an intellectual abstraction of one element from the universe of shamanic meaning. I do not mean to attempt an exhaustive cross-cultural exercise in scientific validation of this point (although Eliade's monumental book on shamanism has laid much of the groundwork), but would rather illustrate it with a single example from my own field experience among a shamanic and totemic people, the Beaver Indians of northeastern British Columbia.

Beaver Cosmic Structure [6]

The Beaver myth of creation begins with the creator God, *Yagesatí* (that which is motionless in heaven), who draws a cross upon the primeval waters. It is this cross that fixes the middle earth and determines its qualities. Horizontally the cross defines the cardinal points or quarters of the earth: East, South, West, and North. Vertically its center is to become the link between the upper and underworlds. (Fig. 1 is a Beaver drawing of their cosmos, showing the cross and the roads leading into the supernatural realms at its center. Fig. 2 is the authors' conceptualization of the qualities symbolically associated with the four quarters. The following discussion explicates the symbolism of these structural diagrams.)

Figure 1. Design of Beaver shaman's drum showing the world of the four quarters and the two inner supernatural worlds.

Each direction is defined by a color, a time of day, a season, a sex, and a quality. The East is red, dawn, spring, birth, male, and benevolent. The South is yellow, noon, summer, infancy, female, and benevolent. The West is red, dusk, fall, female, and dangerous. The North is white, night, winter, male, and dangerous. The sequence of the directions embodies the sequence of the day, of the seasons which make up the year, and the stages of life which make up the youth of man. The East is the place where the sun comes out "from behind the mountains," bringing the beginning of day—the dawn, which is red in color. It is the time of day of the beginning of warmth. By noon the sun has moved in an arc southward, and at its zenith it marks the South. It is bright yellow and warm. The West is the place where the sun "goes behind the mountains" at dusk, burning red. It is the beginning of the cold time of day. The North is the place where the moon is at its zenith in the night, when the sun has disappeared from earthly view. The white moon is the shadow or soul of the sun. The night is the time of cold when the shadows or souls of dead people roam the earth and can see. Thus the cross that *Yagesatī* drew on the waters set in motion the succession of the days.

At the same time it set in motion the succession of the seasons. The East is the bringer of spring, of the beginning of warmth, of the resurrection of the plants and the animals; for the place where the sun comes out from behind the mountains is also the place through which *Yagesatī* sends down the souls of animals (moose, caribou, deer, and so on) which are born in the spring. The East wind which blows in the spring melts the ice and snow. It is brought back by the ducks and geese when they return from the South in spring. The South is the height of warmth which nourishes the plants, and hence the animals, and makes them grow. The South wind is warm, and when it blows in winter it suddenly gets warm, and the ice and snow disappear for a day or two. The West is the beginning of cold which kills the plants. The place where the sun "goes behind the mountains" is also the place through which the souls of animals which have been killed go back to heaven. The West and fall is the time and place of death. The West wind brings thunder and lightning, tumult and downpours. It is brought by

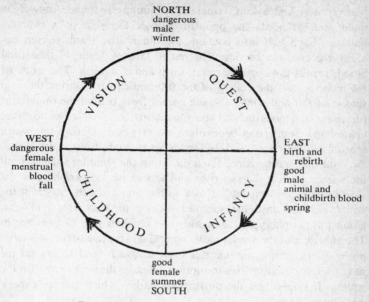

Figure 2. Some Beaver totemic associations.

Thunderbird to destroy Snake. Fall is also the mating season for the animals. The North is the time of cold, when white snow and ice cover the dead leaves of fall. It is dangerous on the physical plane because the cold itself is killing and it is the hardest season in which to stay alive. The North wind is fierce and cold and brought by the underworld icebreaker monster.

The Beavers see the succession of the four seasons associated with the four quarters as "two years," the cold half made up of fall and winter and the warm half made up of spring and summer. The warm half is benevolent, made of a long day and a short night; the cold half is dangerous, made of a long night and a short day. Each half is made up of a male and a female season, which implies a union and an issue which keeps the cycle turning round. The male and female seasons of the two halves are also of unequal lengths: the cold half has a short female part (fall) and a long male part (winter), male outweighs female; the warm half has a short male part (spring) and a long female part (summer), female outweighs male, and so needs the opposite half of the year as a counter-balance. Each half also contains the other. The warm season has night; the cold season day. The red of fall, of death, of menstrual blood, recalls the opposite red of birth and childbirth. The white of the moon recalls the yellow of the full-bodied sun. During the cold season of fall and winter the sun comes from behind the mountains (or rises) and goes behind the mountains (or sets) close together toward the South, the benevolent warm place. During the warm season the sun rises and sets farther apart; more toward the North, the cold, dangerous zone. Each day from the summer solstice until the winter solstice the sun rises and sets along the periphery of the world one "chicken step" closer to the South. Each day from the winter solstice until the summer solstice the sun rises and sets, along the periphery of the world, one chicken step farther North. The sunrise and the sunset move up and down the eastern and western quarters, reminding one that each season is tending toward the next. All this *Yagesatī* set in motion when he drew the cross on the waters. It symbolizes the dimensions within which Beaver experience takes place.

At the same time the four quarters set in motion the sequence of stages of human development. The East symbolizes human birth, since the soul of the unborn child comes through the mountains at the same place as the sun and the souls of animals. The red of the East is also the blood of childbirth, and of killed animals, which is distinguished from the blood of menstruation. Although it is woman who gives birth, the East is male because the generative impulse is seen as male. Men as hunters give animals new life when they kill them.

The South, the noontime, the summer of childhood, the Beavers identify with the period when the child is nursing, from birth until the birth of the next child when he is about two or three. On the human plane the warmth of the South is the warmth of the protecting mother, whose milk makes the child grow as the sun nourishes plants and animals. It is a period when the mother, a female, is important and benevolent. In Freudian terms, this would be the oral stage.

Then, as the child continues on in the cycle of life, his perception of his mother changes. She ceases to be the warm and nurturing female when she weans the child. This is the fall or sunset of the child's youth when the mother is seen as harmful and even killing. It is the season of the child's life when he first becomes aware of the power of sex and, being unready for it, sees it as a destructive force. During the rutting season the moose reinforce this image, for they go crazy and charge humans. The most negative aspects of a woman's sexuality come to the forefront. The red of the West is not only the sunset, but menstrual blood which kills. Indeed the mountains of the West, through which the sun goes down, are the body of a giant woman ("finish-people-between-the-legs") who, in the beginning of the world, used to lure people between her legs as she lay supine upon the ground. People would think they were walking in a valley between two long mountain ridges until they came to the juncture of the mountain ridges in the cave of her vagina and realized that they were trapped. *Usakindji*, the culture hero, killed the giant woman by throwing a huge rock into her vagina, and the West wind, which had lived in her womb, leaped up into the sky where it is today. But still the place of the West and this stage of a child's life remain dangerous and female. In Freudian terms this is a special sort of Oedipal stage.

After the initial shock of realization that the summer season of childhood is transformed into the horror of the nightfall stage, the child passes into the night, northern, winter stage of his life. As the fallen leaves of autumn are covered with snow, so the upheaval of the autumn of the child's life is submerged by the wisdom of the white-haired men. This is the time when the sages teach the child the myths of *Yagesati* and *Usakindji*, and so prepare him to attempt a vision quest. It is a dangerous period because it is the period of the recovery from the symbolic death of fall, and the cure is not always easy. It is dangerous too because psychic forces mobilized in the child are like the North wind, severe, chilling, and even killing. To a certain extend it corresponds to the latency stage in Freud's outline of youth.

As the winter season of the year passes, and spring returns, so does the winter of a child's youth pass. He has gone full circle. For life is not a straight line but a circle, an all-encompassing circle through which the child has passed and through which he will pass again and again, each day, each season, with each wife and each of his children. For each sunrise symbolizes all at once the rebirth of the sun, of the day, of warmth, of human and plant and animal life, of spring; as noontime recalls warmth and growth, early childhood and summer; as sunset stands for death, menstruation, fire, destructive sex, and fall; and as night recalls the North, the cold, the difficult and dangerous. Each day each person relives the cycle of life. But after a child has passed through the four quarters of his life once, his direction is toward the center.

The center of the axis which *Yagesatī* drew upon the water is the point where all the specific attributes of the four directions meet. The male and female, warm and cold, benevolent and harmful oppositions of the North-South, East-West axes are joined into one whole at the center. By having passed through the cycle of the four directions, the child is prepared to enter the center which is more than the coming together of all the earthly qualities, for these qualities themselves come down from the upper world and up from the underworld through this point. From this point they radiate out upon the surface of the earth, each to its appointed place. The center is the focal point of another axis as well, which fixes the cross on the earth. This is the axis which goes from the upper world through the center of the earth to the underworld. This is the axis of transcendence which is attained through the vision quest and which constitutes the real rebirth of man. When *Yagesatī* drew the cross upon the water he also fixed the upright pole and hence the structure of the whole cosmos which is symbolized by the number seven. The seven is made up of the four directions; East, South, West, and North; the center; the zenith in heaven; and the nadir in the underworld.

The Vision Quest

The central experience to which Beaver symbols relate is found in the vision quest. Between weaning and puberty both boys and girls seek supernatural power from animal friends. This power is referred to as *mə yine,* literally, "its song," after the songs that are the cries of giant prototypical animals represented in myth. In the myths, the giant animals talk and live in camps like men. They are hunters and their prey are humans until a culture hero, the first shaman, transforms them into their present form. The cries and powers of these giant animals are the source of the supernatural power sought in the vision quest.

In their vision quests, children actually live for a time apart from the world of men. They become, in effect, practicing ethologists, able to understand the behaviour and communications of animals and accepted by the animals because of their understanding and lack of fear. At the time of his vision quests, the Beaver's understanding is that of a child, immediate and participatory. It is a stage of developing independence, or rather, of transferring dependence from parents to animal protectors and thus identifying himself with the objects of his livelihood. It is a learning experience more than an initiation since he does not yet fully know the symbolic significance of his separation. Power can only be acquired between weaning and puberty, a time in which organic ties with the mother have been severed and sexual ties with a wife have not yet begun. The vision quest represents a developmental stage between the families of orientation and procreation. During this stage he symbolically moves from the western to the northern phase of his maturation.

Manifestly the vision quest takes place on the horizontal plane, the real world formed by the intersection of the North-South and East-West axes. The animals are real animals that exist in the "ordinary" dimensions of space and time. But experience also takes place on another inner axis and dimension, that of meaning. This dimension is cosmically symbolized as the point of intersection of the two horizontal axes, the center of the mandala, the "axis mundi" or break in space that is a point of entry into the empyrean upper sky world and the lower subterranean underworld. This dimension and its worlds is the inner realm in which experience encounters meaning. It is the dimension of mythic time and cosmic space that is the beginning and the end of experience.

Initiation for the Beaver comes when he is ready to accept full understanding of the meaning of his vision quest. When he has become an adult, taken on the responsibilities of parenthood, and shown that animals will give themselves to him in order that he may in turn give them to his fellowmen, the Beaver is ready for initiation. It is his progression from North to East and his completion of the first cycle of his life. His initiation is a rebirth or a reentry into the domain of his birth. As he is himself reborn, he is now able to give others life as a hunter, provider, and parent. Initiation comes through the experience of dreaming, and in his dream he sees himself going through his vision quest but in the perspective of knowledge of its cosmic significance. In these dreams he experiences, for the first time, the meaning of what happened to him as a child in terms of a shamanic cosmic structure. He has entered the center of the mandala and seen that the child, who was and is himself, became a god, an animal, a mythical supernatural being. The dreams reveal that his life in the bush was actually an entry into the dimension of mythic time and cosmic space. His communication with animals on this world took him into the internal world in which the myths of creation still exist and the giant animals that are the "boss" of the species are still alive. Spatially the inner dimension of meaning is symbolized by the upper and lower worlds inhabited, respectively, by the giant forms of the game animals and birds, and the other, underworld animals. In anthropological terms, these dreamings constitute his totemic initiation and his entry into a shamanic cosmology. The myths in which giant animals had powers over humans exist not in the distant past, but in the experience of every Beaver Indian. The upper and underworlds to which they were sent by the culture hero, the first man to acquire power, are not geographical places but states of being that may be experienced.

Although the childhood experience of living with animals makes a person the recipient of their powers, complete knowledge of its meaning and uses comes only when he has completed a full life cycle; from receiving life from his parents to giving life to his children. Through the dreaming, an inner flight to the center of the childhood experience, the center of the mandala, the point of entry into the upper and lower cosmic realms, the initiate learns the taboos of his power and is instructed about the collection of a medicine bundle. These taboos that must be observed by others in his presence and his medicine bundle that hangs above where he sleeps are the external symbols of his internal transformation or initiation.

The dreaming flight that is the completion of a child's vision quest and his entry into a system of totemic symbolization is also the prototypical shamanic experience. This is not to say that every Beaver is a shaman, for they distinguish between the initiatory dreaming as an expected encounter with the world of myth, and the shamanic flight of a man who has "died," been initiated not by animals but by a society of shamans in heaven, and returned to earth.

Beaver Shamanism

There are two levels of power symbolized by two kinds of songs. The vision quest animal power is *mə-yine,* the gift of an animal to a man. Shamans' songs are *ahata-yine,* "god songs," the gifts of the creative power itself. To know the powers of animals one must join one's life to theirs, but to know the powers of creation one must die and be re-created. *Mə-yine* are the songs of animals that stand for their essential qualities in the mythic dimension. *Ahata-yine* are songs given to men who have died and been re-created through their experience of the power of creation. Men with animal power sleep facing East because they know that to kill an animal is to give it new life and be given life by it; but shamans with *ahata-yine* sleep facing West because they have died and learned the road to heaven. Men with *mə-yine* dream to bring the shadows of animals from heaven to earth, while shamans dream to guide the shadows of men along the path to heaven. In both cases men dream to the places they have experienced and along the paths they have been initiated into.

Just as every animal species and natural property has a "boss" that exists in cosmic space and the mythic time out of time, the human species, too, has its boss which is the androgynous creative force behind all things. The totemism of the Beaver vision quest is a journey into the inner realm of meaning within experience; an encounter with the boss of an animal species. Its logical extension is the shamanic experience; through death and rebirth, an encounter with the boss of the human species, *Yagesatī*. It is not that their creator god is anthropomorphic, but that they see creation totemically as the beginning and end of all human experience. Few people became shamans, and it is a calling that comes upon a man rather than being sought. Although *mǝ-yine* power is possessed by every normal adult, it is a guarded secret used to defend oneself and friends from enemies and to provide them with food and fortune, and *ahata-yine,* although known by only a few dreamers, are sung publicly for the benefit of all people.

Mǝ-yine power may be used both for good and evil depending on the qualities of its possessor. A bad man may use his power selfishly but his misuse of it will always harm himself more than his victim. If a person uses his power to kill another, he sends the victim directly to heaven but takes upon himself all the burdens that weighed down that person's shadow. The selfish use of power is totemically associated with misfortune, while the sharing of power brings the things that men desire. Good human qualities are best symbolized by the conjunction of events that bring men fortune, while bad human qualities symbolize what to us would be inexplicable bad luck. Their totemism seizes upon more than the intellectual symbols available in the world of nature. It also associates destructive and constructive human states with natural states that destroy and enhance the lives of men.

Again, Beaver shamanism is an extension of their system of totemism. While *mǝ-yine* is covert and potentially destructive in the hands of bad men, *ahata-yine* is public and only capable of human benefit. The true shaman who has experienced the road to heaven and brought back the songs of creation can only use his powers to bring men closer to knowledge of themselves and their environment. *Ahata-yine* are the basis of public ceremonials usually presided over by the shaman. Unlike *mǝ-yine* which can only be sung by their recipients in times of personal crisis, the songs brought back by a shaman are public property and are sung and remembered after his death. The Beavers dance to *ahata-yine,* going clockwise, or as they say, "like the sun" around a fire. The songs and dances symbolize the cycle of creation, transformation and re-creation through which men, animals, and indeed all things pass. Beaver ceremonials are "dancing to heaven." Through the dances and songs, the experience of the shaman is transmitted to his people, and during the ceremonials he often speaks of his dreams and prophesies.

Every Beaver Indian has, through his vision quest, entered into the inner dimension of mythical meaning, but only the shaman has followed this path to its beginning and end. Ordinary men must know that to take the lives of animals is to give them another form of life (hence their sleeping to the East), but it is the shaman alone who knows, through his own experience, the meaning of human life and death. His sharing of this knowledge is the basis of Beaver ceremonial life, a form of ritual that unites the life cycles of animals with those of men. Thus, the totemic experience that is entered into in the vision quest is completed in the death and return of the shaman. The mythic time and cosmic space that every adult Beaver knows is but the beginning of the road to heaven that has been explored by the shaman in whose footsteps he hopes to follow.

Every Beaver has transcended objective reality to grasp, through the symbols of his culture, its subjective meaning, but the shaman has followed this *axis mundi,* the center of the mandala, to its furthest extreme. Hence his flight is symbolized by the highest-flying bird, the swan, who in flight makes the sign of the cross and who is the only bird capable of flying to heaven and returning alive. We shall end this brief discussion of Beaver belief with the identification of shaman with swan, and by pointing out that the swan is the beginning of their mythic symbolization, for the myth of the culture hero that is the prototype of both the vision quest and shamanic flights tells the story of a boy named Swan who becomes the first man to discover the road to heaven.

To summarize a paper that has taken much for granted and has led the reader onto a path only poorly understood by the writers is a difficult task. In terms of anthropological theory we have argued that the symbols of totemic thought are also, and more significantly, those of shamanic cosmology. But in terms of a more general human experience, we have tried to show that the Beaver way of knowledge is simply one culture's symbolization of a dimension of meaning that is open to all men. Although our culture has forgotten its myths and has replaced them with scientific truths that are outside of experience, the enquiry of anthropology into a realm of meaning understood by mythic peoples may help us rediscover an inner reality that has probably never been wholly lost. Just as the Beaver initiation gives symbolic meaning to the naïve experiences of childhood, an excursion into their minds may lead us back and forward into the mental states of our individual childhood and cultural old age.

Notes

1. Susan Reid, "A Methodological Inquiry into the Nature of Kwakiutl Ceremonialism" (unpublished manuscript, Department of Anthropology, University of British Columbia, 1969).

2. Claude Lévi-Strauss, *The Savage Mind* (Chicago: University of Chicago Press, 1966), p. 50.

3. See Mircea Eliade, *The Sacred and the Profane* (New York: Harcourt, Brace & World, 1957), and *Shamanism: Archaic Techniques of Ecstasy,* Bollingen Series, no. 76 (New York, 1964).

4. Carlos Castaneda, *The Teachings of Don Juan* (Berkeley: University of California Press, 1968).

5. For a detailed description of shamanic cosmology, see Eliade, *Shamanism,* chap. 8.

6. Based on Beaver myths, stories, shamanic texts, and unpublished field notes compiled between 1964 and 1968.

13

Oglala Metaphysics

*Sword, Finger, One-Star, and Tyon,
through J. R. Walker*

Wakan

by Sword

Wakan means very many things. The Lakota understands what
it means from the things that are considered *wakan;* yet sometimes
its meaning must be explained to him. It is something that is hard
to understand. Thus *wasica wakan,* means a white man medicine-
man; but a Lakota medicineman is called *pejuta wacasa. Wicasa
wakan* is the term for a Lakota priest of the old religion. The white
people call our *wicasa wakan,* medicineman, which is a mistake.
Again, they say a *wicasa wakan* is making medicine when he is
performing ceremonies. This is also a mistake. The Lakota call a
thing a medicine only when it is used to cure the sick or the
wounded, the proper term being *pejuta.* When a priest uses any ob-

From J. R. Walker, *The Sun Dance and Other Ceremonies of the
Teton Dakota.* Anthropological Papers of the American Museum of Natural
History 16, pt. 1 (1917). Walker, a physician, lived among the Oglala (a
division of the Teton Sioux) for many years; he befriended Sword, Finger,
One-Star, Tyon, and other shamans and was initiated into their practices.
For an interpretation of some of the concepts presented here, see the
chapter following this one.

ject in performing a ceremony that object becomes endowed with a spirit, not exactly a spirit, but something like one, the priests call it *tonwan* or *ton*. Now anything that thus acquires *ton* is *wakan*, because it is the power of the spirit or quality that has been put into it. A *wicasa wakan* has the power of the *wakan* beings.

The roots of certain plants are *wakan* because they are poisonous. Likewise some reptiles are *wakan* because if they bite they would kill. Again, some birds are *wakan* because they do very strange things and some animals are *wakan* because the *wakan* beings make them so. In other words anything may be *wakan* if a *wakan* spirit goes into it. Thus a crazy man is *wakan* because the bad spirit has gone into him.

Again, if a person does something that cannot be understood, that is also *wakan*. Drinks that make one drunk are *wakan* because they make one crazy.

Every object in the world has a spirit and that spirit is *wakan*. Thus the spirit of the tree or things of that kind, while not like the spirit of man, are also *wakan*.

Wakan comes from the *wakan* beings. These *wakan* beings are greater than mankind in the same way that mankind is greater than

A *wicasa wakan,* a man with the power of the *wakan* beings. The wavy lines, which mean *wakan,* are based on the gesture for *wakan,* in which the right hand, with fingers pointing upward and palm facing the speaker, describes an upward-reaching helix, starting at the forehead. Part of a hide painting, from the 10th Annual Report of the Bureau of American Ethnology, p. 463.

animals. They are never born and never die. They can do many things that mankind cannot do. Mankind can pray to the *wakan* beings for help. There are many of these beings but all are of four kinds. The word *Wakan Tanka* means all of the *wakan* beings because they are all as if one. *Wakan Tanka Kin* signifies the chief or leading *Wakan* being, which is the Sun. However, the most powerful of the *Wakan* beings is *Nagi Tanka,* the Great Spirit who is also *Taku Skanskan; Taku Skanskan* signifies the Blue, in other words, the Sky.

Iya is a *Wakan Tanka,* but he is an evil *Wakan Tanka.* Mankind is permitted to pray to the *Wakan* beings. If their prayer is directed to all the good *Wakan* beings they should pray to *Wakan Tanka;* but if the prayer is offered only to one of these beings, then the one addressed should be named.

Wakan Tanka is pleased with music. He likes to hear the drums and the rattles. When any of the *Wakan* beings hear the drum and the rattles they always give attention. He is also fond of the smoke of sweetgrass and evil *Wakan* beings are afraid of the smoke of sage. All of the *Wakan,* both the good and evil, are pleased with the smoke of the pipe.

The *Wicasa Wakan* or priests, speak for all the *Wakan* beings. *Wakan Tanka* gives them the power that makes them *Wakan* and by which they can put *ton* into anything. Eash priest has an object for himself into which *ton* has been put. This is called a *Wasicun.* A *Wasicun* is one of the *Wakan* beings. It is the least of them, but if its *ton* is from a powerful being it may be more powerful than many of the *Wakan* beings. This *Wasicun* is what the priests do their work with, but the white people call it the medicine bag, which is a mistake, for there are no medicines in it. A medicine bag is a bag that doctors have their medicines in. If a man has a *Wasicun* he may pray to it, for it is the same as the *Wakan* being whose *ton* (*wan*) is in it.

The earth and the rock and the mountains pertain to the chief *Wakan.* We do not see the real earth and the rock, but only their *tonwanpi.*

When a Lakota prays to *Wakan Tanka* he prays to the earth and to the rock and all the other good *Wakan* beings. If a man wishes to do evil things he may pray to the evil *Wakan.*

Wakan Tanka

by Sword

When *Wakan Tanka* wishes one of mankind to do something he makes his wishes known either in a vision or through a shaman. . . . The shaman addresses *Wakan Tanka* as *Tobtob Kin*. This is part of the secret language of the shamans. . . . *Tobtob Kin* are four times four gods while *Tob Kin* is only the four winds. The four winds is a god and is the *akicita* or messenger of all the other gods. The four times four are: *Wikan* and *Hanwikan; Taku Skanskan* and *Tatekan* and *Tob Kin* and *Yumnikan; Makakan* and *Wohpe; Inyankan* and *Wakinyan; Tatankakan; Hunonpakan; Wanagi; Waniya; Nagila;* and *Wasicunpi*. These are the names of the good Gods as they are known to the people.

Wakan Tanka is like sixteen different persons; but each person is *kan*. Therefore, they are all only the same as one. . . . All the God persons have *ton*. *Ton* is the power to do supernatural things. . . . Half of the good Gods are *ton ton* (have physical properties) and half are *ton ton sni* (have no physical properties). Half of those who are *ton ton* are *ton ton yan* (visible), and half of those who are *ton ton sni* are *ton ton yan sni* (invisible). All the other Gods are visible or invisible as they choose to be. . . . All the evil Gods are visible or invisible as they choose to be. . . . The invisible Gods never appear in a vision except to a shaman. . . . Except for the Sun dance, the ceremonies for the visible and the invisible Gods differ. The Sun dance is a ceremony the same as if *Wikan* were both visible and invisible. This is because *Wi* is the chief of the Gods. . . .

Skan

by Finger

I heard you exclaim when a meteorite fell and heard you address the people immediately afterwards. Then I saw you burning sweet-grass. Will you tell me why you did this?

You are a white man's medicineman and you want to know

the mysteries of the Lakota. Why do you want to know these things?

The old Indians who know these things will soon be dead and gone and as the younger Indians do not know them they will be lost. I wish to write them so they will be preserved and your people can read them in years to come. Will you tell them to me?

My father was a shaman and he taught me the mysteries of the shamans and I will tell them to you. What is it you want to know?

When the meteor fell you cried in a loud voice, "*Wohpa. Wohpe-e-e-e.*" Why did you do this?

Because that is *wakan*.

What is *wohpa*?

It is what you saw. It is one of the stars falling.

What causes the stars to fall?

Taku Skanskan.

Why does *Taku Skanskan* cause the stars to fall?

Because he causes everything that falls to fall and he causes everything to move that moves.

When you move what is it that causes you to move?

Skan.

If an arrow is shot from a bow what causes it to move through the air?

Skan.

What causes a stone to fall to the ground when I drop it?

Skan.

If I lift a stone from the ground what causes the movement?

Skan. He gives you power to lift the stone and it is he that causes all movement of any kind.

Has the bow anything to do with the movement of an arrow shot from it?

Taku Skanskan gives the spirit to the bow and he causes it to send the arrow from it.

What causes smoke to go upward?

Taku Skanskan.

What causes water to flow in a river?

Skan.

What causes the clouds to move over the world?

Skan.

Are *Taku Skan* and *Skan* one and the same?

Yes. When the people speak to him, they say *Taku Skanskan.* When a shaman speaks of him, he says *Skan. Skan* belongs to the *wakan* speech used by the shamans.

Is *Skan, Wakan Tanka?*

Yes.

Is he *Wakan Tanka Kin?*

No. That is *Wi,* the Sun.

Are *Wi* and *Skan* one and the same?

No. *Wi* is *Wakan Tanka Kin* and Skan is *Nagi Tanka,* the Great Spirit.

Are they both *Wakan Tanka?*

Yes.

Are there any other wakan that are *Wakan Tanka?*

Yes. *Inyan,* the Rock and *Maka,* the Earth.

Are there any others?

Yes. *Wi Han,* the Moon; *Tate,* the Wind; *Wakinyan,* the Winged; and *Wohpe,* the Beautiful Woman.

Are there any others that are *Wakan Tanka?*

No.

Then there are eight *Wakan Tanka,* are there?

No, there is but one.

You have named eight and say there is but one. How can this be?

That is right. I have named eight. There are four, *Wi, Skan, Inyan,* and *Maka.* These are the *Wakan Tanka.*

You named four others, the Moon, the Wind, the Winged, and the Beautiful Woman and said they were *Wakan Tanka,* did you not?

Yes. But these four are the same as the *Wakan Tanka.* The Sun and the Moon are the same, the *Skan* and the Wind are the same, the Rock and the Winged are the same, and the Earth and the Beautiful Woman are the same. These eight are only one. The shamans know how this is, but the people do not know. It is *wakan* (a mystery).

Did the *Wakan Tanka* always exist?

Yes. The Rock is the oldest. He is grandfather of all things.
Which is the next oldest?

The Earth. She is grandmother of all things.

Which is next oldest?

Skan. He gives life and motion to all things.

Which is the next oldest after *Skan?*

The Sun. But he is above all things and above all *Wakan Tanka*.

Lakota have told me that the Sun and *Taku Skanskan* are one and the same. Is that true?

No. Many of the people believe that it is so, but the shamans know that it is not so. The Sun is in the sky only half the time and *Skan* is there all the time.

Lakota have told me the *Skan* is the sky. Is that so?

Yes. *Skan* is a Spirit and all that mankind can see of him is the blue of the sky. But he is everywhere.

Do you pray to *Wakan Tanka?*

Yes, very often.

To which of the eight you have named do you pray?

When I pray I smoke the pipe and burn (sweetgrass) and *Wohpe* carries my prayer to the *Wakan Tanka*. If the prayer is about things of great importance, it is carried to the Sun; if about my health or my strength it goes to *Skan;* if about my implements, to *Inyan;* if about food or clothing and such things, to the Earth.

Are such prayers ever carried to the Moon, or the Wind, or the Winged, or to *Wohpe?*

They may be carried to the Moon and to the Wind; but this is the same as if to the Sun or *Skan*. Lakota do not pray to the Winged. They defy him. They do not pray to *Wohpe*, for she carries all prayers. The Lakota may pray to any *Wakan*, but if to a *Wakan* that is below *Wakan Tanka*, such must be named in the prayer and it will be carried to the one named.

You say *wohpa* is a falling star. Is *Wohpe* in any way related to a falling star?

She first came like a falling star.

Where did she come from?

From the stars.

What are the stars?

Waniya.

What are *waniya?*

They are ghosts. *Skan* takes from the stars a ghost and gives it to each babe at the time of its birth and when the babe dies the ghost returns to the stars.

Is *Wohpe* a ghost?

She is *Wakan Tanka.* A ghost is *Wakan,* but it is not *Wakan Tanka.*

Has a Lakota ever seen *Wohpe?*

Yes. When she gave the pipe to the Lakota she was in their camp for many days.

How did she appear at that time?

Like a very beautiful young woman. For this reason the people speak of her as the Beautiful Woman. The people do not speak of her as *Wohpe.* Only the shamans call her that.

Lakota have told me that her *ton* is in the pipe and in the smoke of the sweetgrass. Is that true?

It was a shaman who told you that. When the people say *ton* they mean something that comes from a living thing, such as the birth of anything or the discharge from a wound or a sore or the growth from a seed. Only shamans speak of the *ton* of the *Wakan.* Such *ton* is *wakan* and the shamans only know about it. The people are afraid to talk of such *ton* because it is *wakan.* The people smoke the pipe and burn sweet grass because *Wohpe* will do no harm to anyone.

You say the Rock is the grandfather of all things and the Earth the grandmother of all things. Are the Rock and the Earth as a man and wife?

Some shamans think they are, and some think they are not.

Who were the father and mother of all things?

The *Wakan* have no father or mother. Anything that has a birth will have a death. The *Wakan* were not born and they will not die.

Is anything about a Lakota *wakan?*

Yes. The spirit, the ghost, and the *sicun.*

Do these die?

No. They are *wakan.*

What becomes of them when the body dies?

The spirit goes to the spirit world, the ghost goes to where *Skan* got it, and the *sicun* returns to the *Wakan* it belongs to.

What is the *sicun?*

It is the *ton* of a *Wakan*. *Skan* gives it at the time of the birth.

What are its functions?

It remains with the body during life, to guard it from danger and help it in a *wakan* manner.

How does the spirit get to the spirit world?

It goes on the spirit trail.

Where is the spirit trail?

It can be seen in the sky at night. It is a white trail across the sky.

Is it made of stars?

No. It is like the clouds, so that nothing but *Wakan* can travel on it. No man knows where it begins or where it ends. The Wind alone knows where it begins. It moves about. Sometimes it is in one direction and sometimes in another.

How does the ghost go to the place where *Skan* got it?

The ghost is like smoke and it goes upward until it arrives at the stars.

What becomes of the body when it dies?

It rots and becomes nothing.

Sicun

by Sword

The word *sicun* is from the sacred language of the shamans. It signifies the spirit of a man. This spirit is given to him at birth to guard him against the evil spirits and at death it conducts him to the land of the spirits, but does not go there itself. In the course of his life a man my choose other *sicun*. He may choose as many as he wishes but such *sicun* do not accompany him after death; if he has led an evil life no *sicun* will accompany him.

A shaman should direct a person in the choice of his *sicun*. When the Lakota chooses a *sicun* such is the *ton* of a *Wakan* or it may be the *ton* of anything. When one chooses a *sicun* he should give a feast and have a shaman to conduct the ceremony, for no one can have the knowledge necessary to conduct his own ceremony unless he has learned it in a vision. One's *sicun* may be in any object as in a weapon or even in things to gamble with or in a medicine. But the *sicun* that a man receives at birth is never found in anything but his body. This *sicun* is like one's shadow.

No one ever had the *ton* of the Sun for a *sicun,* for the Sun will not be a *sicun* for anyone. On the other hand, the *ton* of the Sky, while a very powerful *sicun,* may be secured through old and wise shamans. The *sicun* of the earth is the next most powerful and next in rank is the *sicun* of the rock. The *sicuns* of the bear and the buffalo are often chosen, but that of the bear more frequently. A shaman's *Wakan* bag is his *sicun* and all *sicun* are considered *wakan.* A doctor's medicine is his *sicun* and the implements used by a shaman in any ceremony aré the *sicun* of that shaman. Implements that are in such *sicun* will not be appropriate in a ceremony. A person may lend his *sicun* to another. The term *wasicun* is applied to any object used as a *sicun* or it may represent anything which is *wakan.* If a ceremony by which one gets a *wasicun* is performed in the most acceptable manner that *wasicun* will be the same in essence as the *wakan* thing it represents. An evil man cannot secure a good *sicun,* but may secure an evil one. If the ceremony be performed, a *sicun* is secured. Then that *sicun* must do as it is directed to do by the one who chooses it; but the chooser must know the songs that belong to it.

Sicun

by One-Star

A *sicun* is like a spirit. It is the *ton-ton sni,* that is, it is immortal and cannot die. A Lakota may have many many *sicunpi,* but he always has one. It is *wakan,* that is, it is like *Wakan Tanka.* It may be the spirit of anything. A shaman puts the spirit in a *sicun.* The bear taught the shamans how to do this. A Lakota should know the songs and if he sings them his *sicun* will do as he wishes.

One *sicun* may be more powerful than another. The *sicun* may be of the Great Spirit. If it is opposed by the *sicun* of herbs it is the most powerful. The *sicun* of a good spirit is more powerful than the *sicun* of a bad spirit. The power of sweetgrass is always the spirit of the spirit that is with the south wind. This is always pleasing to the good spirits. The bad spirits do not like the smoke of the sweetgrass. The smoke of sage will drive bad spirits away. A medicineman knows the songs of his medicines and they are his *sicun*. The *sicun* that has the power of the spirit should be colored. Red is the color of the sun; blue, the color of the moving spirit; green the color of the spirit of the earth; and yellow is the color of the spirit of the rock. These colors are also for other spirits. Blue is the color of the wind; red is the color of all spirits. The colors are the same for the friends of the great spirits. Black is the color of the bad spirits. A man who paints red is pleasing to the spirits. A *sicun* is a man's spirit. A man's real spirit is different from his *sicun* spirit. *Ni* is also like a spirit. It is a man's breath. It is the spirit of smoke. It is the spirit of steam. It is the spirit of the sweatlodge. It purifies the body. The bear taught these things to the shamans.

The Number Four

by Tyon

In former times the Lakota grouped all their activities by fours. This was because they recognized four directions: the west, the north, the east, and the south; four divisions of time: the day, the night, the moon, and the year; four parts in everything that grows from the ground: the roots, the stem, the leaves, and the fruit; four kinds of things that breathe: those that crawl, those that fly, those that walk on four legs, and those that walk on two legs; four things above the world: the sun, the moon, the sky, and the stars; four kinds of gods: the great, the associates of the great, the gods below them, and the spiritkind; four periods of human life: babyhood, childhood, adulthood, and old age; and finally, mankind has four fingers on each hand, four toes on each foot and the thumbs and the great toes taken together form four. Since the Great

Spirit caused everything to be in fours, mankind should do everything possible in fours.

The Circle

by Tyon

The Oglala believe the circle to be sacred because the Great Spirit caused everything in nature to be round except stone. Stone is the implement of destruction. The sun and the sky, the earth and the moon, are round like a shield, though the sky is deep like a bowl. Everything that breathes is round like the body of a man. Everything that grows from the ground is round like the stem of a plant. Since the Great Spirit has caused everything to be round mankind should look upon the circle as sacred, for it is the symbol of all things in nature except stone. It is also the symbol of the circle that marks the edge of the world and therefore of the four winds that travel there. Consequently it is also the symbol of the year. The day, the night, and the moon go in a circle above the sky. Therefore the circle is a symbol of these divisions of time and hence the symbol of all time.

For these reasons the Oglala make their *tipis* circular, their camp-circle circular, and sit in a circle in all ceremonies. The circle is also the symbol of the *tipi* and of shelter. If one makes a circle for an ornament and it is not divided in any way, it should be understood as the symbol of the world and of time. If, however, the circle be filled with red, it is the symbol of the sun; if filled with blue, it is the symbol of the sky. If the circle is divided into four parts, it is the symbol of the four winds; if it is divided into more than four parts, it is the symbol of a vision of some kind. If a half circle is filled with red it represents the day; filled with black, the night; filled with yellow, a moon or month. On the other hand, if a half circle is filled with many colors, it symbolizes the rainbow.

One may paint or otherwise represent a circle on his *tipi* or his shield or his robe. The mouth of a pipe should always be moved in a circle before the pipe is formally smoked.

Invocation

by Sword

Before a shaman can perform a ceremony in which mysterious beings or things have a part, he should fill and light a pipe and say:

"Friend of *Wakinyan,* I pass the pipe to you first. Circling I pass to you who dwell with the father. Circling pass to beginning day. Circling pass to the beautiful one. Circling I complete the four quarters and the time. I pass the pipe to the father with the sky. I smoke with the Great Spirit. Let us have a blue day."

The pipe is used because the smoke from the pipe, smoked in communion, has the potency of the feminine god who mediates between godkind and mankind, and propitiates the godkind. When a shaman offers the pipe to a god, the god smokes it and is propitiated. In this invocation, when the shaman has filled and lighted the pipe, he should point the mouth toward the west and say, "Friend of *Wakinyan,* I pass the pipe to you first." Thus he offers the pipe to the west wind, for the west wind dwells in the lodge of *Wakinyan* and is his friend. The pipe should be offered to the west wind first, because the birthright of precedence of the oldest was taken from the firstborn, the north wind, and given to the second born, the west wind, and the gods are very jealous of the order of their precedence.

When he has made this offering the shaman should move the pipe toward the right hand, the mouthpiece pointing toward the horizon, until it points toward the north. Then he should say: "Circling, I pass to you who dwells with the grandfather." Thus he offers the pipe to the north wind, for because of an offense against the feminine god, the Great Spirit condemned the north wind to dwell forever with his grandfather, who is Wazi, the wizard. Then the shaman should move the pipe in the same manner, until the mouthpiece points toward the east and say: "Circling, pass to beginning day." This is an offering to the east wind, for his lodge is where the day begins and he may be addressed as the "beginning day.'' Then the shaman should move the pipe in the same manner until the mouthpiece points toward the south, and say: "Circling, pass to the beautiful one.'' This is an offering to the south wind, for the "beautiful one" is the feminine god who is the companion of the south wind and dwells in his lodge, which is under the sun at midday. It pleases the south wind to be addressed through his companion rather than directly.

The four winds are the *akicita* or messengers of the gods and in all ceremonies they have precedence over all other gods and for this reason should be the first addressed.

When the offering has been made to the south wind the shaman should move the pipe in the same manner until the mouthpiece again points toward the west, and say: "Circling, I complete the four quarters and the time.'' He should do this because the four winds are the four quarters of the circle and mankind knows not where they may be or whence they may come and the pipe should be offered directly toward them. The four quarters embrace all that are in the world and all that are in the sky. Therefore, by circling the pipe, the offering is made to all the gods. The circle is the symbol of time, for the day time, the night time, and the moon time are circles above the world, and the year time is a circle around the border of the world. Therefore the lighted pipe moved in a complete circle is an offering to all the times.

When the shaman has completed the four quarters and the time he should point the mouthpiece of the pipe toward the sky and say: "I pass the pipe to the father with the sky.'' This is an offering to the wind, for when the four winds left the lodge of their father, the wind, he went from it, and dwells in the sky. He controls the seasons and the weather, and he should be propitiated when good weather is desired.

Then the shaman should smoke the pipe and while doing so, should say: "I smoke with the Great Spirit. Let us have a blue day.''

14

Monotheism Among American Indians

Paul Radin

I

To most men monotheism is intimately bound up with the Hebrew scriptures and with those religions manifestly built upon its foundation—Judaism, Christianity and Mohammedanism. Because of the definite association with these three great historic faiths of the last three thousand years, and of the integral part it plays in those civilizations which, rightly or wrongly, we regard in many ways as representing the highest cultural expression to which man

From Paul Radin, "Monotheism Among Primitive Peoples," Special Publications of the Bollingen Foundation, no. 4 (1954). Radin (1883–1959) remains one of the foremost students of American Indian religion, especially that of the Winnebago of Wisconsin. The present essay was originally published in 1924; later, in his *Primitive Religion* (New York: Viking, 1937) and elsewhere, Radin took the position that "pure monotheism" was much rarer than he had originally thought, but David Bidney, in a critical review of Radin's work, gives much support to the position presented here ("Paul Radin and the Problem of Primitive Monotheism," in *Culture in History,* ed. Stanley Diamond (New York: Columbia University Press, 1960), pp. 363–379).

has hitherto attained, monotheism has come to have a very specific meaning and has been given a special evaluation. To the average man it signifies the belief in an uncreated, Supreme Deity, wholly beneficent, omnipotent, omniscient and omnipresent: it demands the complete exclusion of all other gods. The world in its most minute details is regarded as His work, as having been created out of nothing in response to His wish. To presuppose the existence of anything prior to Him is to deny His most salient attribute. He it is who intervenes in the affairs of man, and any assumption that He can act through the intermediation of other deities is idolatry by implication, even though he has expressly given these deities their forms, their attributes and their powers. It is never pure monotheism.

It is perhaps only natural that with so sharp and clear-cut a definition of the Deity there should have arisen the feeling that such a monotheism represents the highest attainable type of religious expression. Nations without it, however high their contributions to the world's progress in other directions may be, are looked upon unconsciously as inferior. Yet it would be unfair to state that it was merely this vague and unconscious estimate that lay at the basis of man's evaluation of the significance of monotheism. A cursory glance at the history of religious thought of the so-called primitive peoples or at the religious evolution of civilized nations before the advent of Christianity—the Jews alone excepted—did seem to indicate the existence of a number of distinct phases through which religion had progressively passed. The earliest stage, it seemed, was to be found among primitive peoples. There we find a religion characterized by a faith in innumerable, often indefinite, spirits, a belief in the general animation of nature: animism in short. All the great historical religions show, it is now generally admitted, definite indications of having passed through such a period.

This seemed to be followed by a second and much later stage in which the worship of definite, mainly anthropomorphic deities prevailed; the polytheism of the ancient Egyptians, Babylonians, Greeks and Romans. We encounter a distinct and possibly special phase in the religion of the ancient Persians where, as is well known, two great principles existed—the principle of Good and the principle of Evil. Ultimately we reach the last period, monotheism, and from this there has been no noticeable relapse. This was in brief what the history of all religions seemed to indicate.

It is the prevalent view today that where animism or polytheism prevails monotheism is excluded, and where monotheism prevails animism and polytheism are in the main absent; that as we pass from animism to polytheism, from dualism to monotheism, we are proceeding from a belief in a multiplicity of spirits devoid of special attributes, to a belief first in two deities and then to a belief in a single god—a god endowed with the highest ethical attributes. The evolution of religion thus manifests, it would seem, a definite tendency toward an integration of our mental and emotional life, a tendency toward the development of an exalted and positive ethical ideal. Both, it can be claimed, imply progress, one in the realm of the intellect and the other in that of morality. It is not astonishing therefore that even to many non-religious individuals pure monotheism should consequently connote the highest form of religious experience. And yet it is perhaps not amiss to point out that in a development such as that just outlined we are basing our evolution on factors that, in large measure, are essentially non-religious.

Be this as it may, certainly no one would seriously deny that it is the intellectual and ethical estimate of pure monotheism that has coloured the attitude of most people toward non-monotheistic and non-ethical faiths, and no fact could perhaps have demonstrated this so clearly as the reception accorded to the famous book written by that most courageous of thinkers, Andrew Lang. In 1898, he published ''The Making of Religion,'' in which he claimed that the evolutionary school in ethnology was hopelessly wrong in one of its fundamental assumptions, that namely a belief in a Supreme Deity did not now and never had existed among so-called primitive tribes. He contended that ethnologists, misled by certain preconceptions, had misinterpreted those indications pointing in such a direction, crediting to Christian influences those definite instances where the facts could not possibly be denied. But he went much farther. He contended that the fairly elevated conception of a Supreme Deity found among such simple tribes as the aborigines of Australia could only be understood by assuming that the traces of monotheism there encountered, represented a definite degeneration of an older and purer faith partially contaminated to-day by animistic beliefs. In other words, monotheism had preceded animism and a purer faith had secondarily been contaminated by the superstitious accretions of a later degenerate time. As was the case in so many of Lang's theories or intuitions, if you wish, he was only partially right.

It might have been surmised that such a theory would have been hailed with delight by the layman. Yet this was not the case. The layman indeed seemed to feel a certain resentment at having mere "savages" anticipate a supposedly exalted religious faith. That the professional ethnologist and ethnological theorist should have scouted the idea is natural enough, considering the ascendancy of the evolutionary theory at the time. To a certain extent, too, the specific instances selected by Lang and his manner of argumentation were partly responsible for the unfavourable reception of his thesis. We all know how his delight and skill in controversy often led him to defend uncritically selected facts and inherently weak positions. Yet it was not this, of course, that influenced the attitude of professional ethnologists. To have admitted among primitive peoples the existence of monotheism in any form would have been equivalent to abandoning their whole doctrine of evolutionary stages. And this they were not prepared to do, nor did the facts at the time definitely warrant it. No one, for instance, would have contended that the vast majority of the members of those tribes among whom the belief in a Supreme Deity had been found shared this belief, except perhaps in the vaguest degree, and it seemed apparent that even the few to whom it was in appearance an active faith found no difficulty in worshipping other deities as well. It might in fact have been said that actual worship was the precise thing the Supreme Deity did not receive. So attenuated and functionless a concept, known to a selected few in each community, could assuredly, the critics insisted, be best explained as due to Christian influence.

Twenty-five years have elapsed since Lang wrote his book and his intuitive insight has been abundantly corroborated. The ethnologists were quite wrong. Accurate data obtained by trained specialists have replaced his rather vague examples. That many primitive peoples have a belief in a Supreme Creator no one to-day seriously denies. For the notion however as held by Lang, that it represents a degeneration from a higher and purer faith, there is not the slightest justification; nor is there any adequate reason for believing that the specific forms which it has assumed, the "contaminations" to which it has been subjected, or the inconsistencies in which it has been involved, have ever been different.

It was one of Lang's great merits that he recognized some of the salient features of this belief in a Supreme Deity of the aborigines. Such a deity had no cults; prayers were only infrequently directed to him and he rarely intervened directly in the affairs of mankind. As we shall see, these statements are only partially true and, at best, hold for only the first of the two general groups into which creative deities can be divided. The second group embraces those whom Lang regarded as contaminated with later animistic accretions, where the Supreme Deity is represented as only partially a creator, and where he has become fused with mythological heroes—with the sun or the moon, with animals, or with anthropomorphic and, occasionally, indefinite spirits. The main character with which he became most frequently amalgamated was one who is the dominant actor in the mythologies of practically all primitive peoples. He is known in ethnological literature as the Transformer, Culture-hero, Trickster. The first term owes its origin to the fact that it is his rôle to transform the world into its present shape and to bestow upon mankind all the various elements of culture. We thus have two concepts: the Supreme Deity, Creator of all things, beneficent and ethical, unapproachable directly and taking but little interest in the world after he has created it; and the Transformer, the establisher of the present order of things, utterly non-ethical, only incidentally and inconsistently beneficent, approachable, and directly intervening in a very human way in the affairs of the world.

These two figures represent two contrasting and antithetic modes of thought; two completely opposed temperaments continually in conflict. All that has been called contamination and degeneration is but the projection of the image of the Transformer upon that of a Supreme Creator and vice versa. Indeed, it is only thus that certain inconsistencies in the portrayal of either can be understood. If, as we shall see, it is true that the Transformer has introduced certain human-heroic, occasionally but extremely rarely, even gross features into the otherwise elevated concept of the supreme deity, it is equally true that wherever the belief in a supreme deity has prevailed he has in large measure been purged of his nonmoral character and become invested with many of the attributes of a purposive and benevolent creator. But I am anticipating. It will be best to give a number of concrete examples, first, of a creator who in varying degree partakes of the attributes of a Transformer and Culture-hero; [1] and secondly, of a creator quite freed from such accretions.

II

Among the Crow Indians of Montana [2] the Sun is the Supreme Deity, but he has in the minds of many become so definitely merged with the Transformer, in this particular instance the Coyote, that the two cannot be kept apart. Long ago, so the myth runs, there was no earth, only water. The only creatures in the world were the ducks and old man (Sun, Coyote). He came down to meet the ducks and said to them, "My brothers, there is earth below us. It is not good for us to be alone." He thereupon makes them dive and one of them reappears with some mud in its webbed feet. Out of this he creates the earth and when he has made it he exclaims, "Now that we have made the earth there are others who wish to be animate." Immediately a wolf is heard howling in the east. In this manner everything in the world is created.

Not a very exalted type of creator you will justly exclaim. But he is a creator none the less in two essential respects: first, in that practically nothing exists until he creates it; and secondly, in that all his creative acts are the results of his expressed will and that they are beneficient. Let me point out one other fact—the new ethical re-evaluation of the Sun-Coyote. In the cycle connected with him as a Transformer he possesses hardly one redeeming feature. He is obscene, a fool, a coward and utterly lacking in self-control. Yet the moment he becomes associated with the creative deity all this disappears.

Let us take another example. Among the Thompson River Indians of British Columbia [3] the concept of a creator is still vague, but the creator himself is definitely dissociated from the Coyote. "Having finished his work on earth and having put all things to rights, the time came that the Coyote should meet the Old Man. . . . When he met him he did not know that he was the 'Great Chief' or 'Mystery,' because he did not appear to be different from any other old man. The Coyote thought, 'This old man does not know who I am. I will astonish him. He knows nothing of my great powers.' . . . After saluting each other the Old Man derided Coyote as a person possessed of small powers: the latter consequently felt annoyed and began to boast of the many wonders he had performed. . . . 'If you are he (Coyote) and so powerful as you say, remove that river and make it run yonder.' This the Coyote did. 'Bring it back.' The Coyote did so. . . . 'Place that high mountain on the plain.' The Coyote did so. 'Replace it where it was'; but this the Coyote could not do because the Old Man, being the superior in magic of the two, willed otherwise. The Old Man then asked Coyote why he could not replace it and the latter answered, 'I don't know. I suppose you are greater than I in magic, and make my efforts fruitless.' The Old Man then made the mountain go back to its place. . . ."

After declaring himself as the Great Chief, the Old Man addresses Coyote as follows: "Now you have been a long time on earth; and since the world, mostly through your instrumentality, has been put right, you have nothing more to do. Soon I am going to leave the earth. You will not return again until I myself do so. You shall then accompany me and we will change things in the world, and bring back the dead to the land of the living. . . ."

Often enough we are told very little about the creation of the world itself and we first meet the creator in a fully-formed world of his own. His task then becomes that of creating the present universe. This is the case, for instance, with an interesting figure of the Wintun Indians of Northern California [4] called Olelbis, "he who dwells on high." "The first that we know of Olelbis," the natives claim, "is that he was in Olepanti. Whether he lived in another place is not known, but in the beginning he was in Olepanti, the highest place. He was there before there was anyone here on earth and two old women were always with him." What interests us in Olelbis is that, although presumably only a creator of the universe in a very partial sense and although he subsequently creates the world in which we live, human beings, etc., and behaves very much as a normal culture-hero, he possesses no traces whatsoever of the attributes generally associated with such an individual. He is a highly ethical, beneficent deity concerned only with the welfare of mankind.

As we pointed out previously all these creators have some of the features of the Transformer, and yet it seems obvious that they cannot be explained as gradual developments from the latter. They are manifestly quite independent and if consequently we find a Supreme Deity with the attributes of a culture-hero, this is to be regarded as secondary, as an accretion which I cannot help feeling represents an attempt to bring him nearer to man. It failed, we may surmise, because of the strength of other religious currents and because of the absence of a cult in his honour.

In the second class of supreme deities, that group where we find only a faint admixture of the attributes of the Transformer, all doubt as to the deity's creative rôle and complete lack of intimate relation with mankind is removed. Intermediate divinities carry out his commands and it is to them that man must pray. These two new factors have led to a strengthening of his former traits. His character becomes correspondingly ennobled and to his ethical attributes are added omnipotence and omniscience. Yet as he becomes further removed from men, though reverence and awe may increase, he becomes of less interest to the ordinary individual, for the latter is naturally concerned only with those deities associated with his daily needs, i.e. with the minor gods. The Supreme Being thus develops into what has been admirably described as an otiose deity, one resting on his laurels after the creation of the world and leaving it entirely to its own devices.

Such an otiose deity is found, for instance, among the Wichita of Texas.[5] "In the times of the beginning there was no sun, no stars nor anything else as it is now. Time passed on. *Man-never-known-on-earth* was the only man that existed, and he it was who created all things. When the earth was created it was composed of land and water, but they were not yet separated. The land was floating on the water and darkness was everywhere. After the earth was formed, *Man-never-known-on-earth* made a woman whose name was *Bright-shining-woman*. After the man and woman were made they dreamed that things were made for them and when they awoke they had the things of which they had dreamed. Thus they received everything they needed. . . . Still they were in darkness not knowing what was better than darkness."

Here we have most emphatically an otiose deity. Apart from the creation of the earth and man he bestows, so to speak, only the potentiality of things. It is this first man who causes the sun and moon to appear and who creates day and night, but only in obedience to an impulse, be it remembered, which *Man-never-known-on-earth* has implanted within him. "The man that creates things is about to improve our condition," he is informed later on. "Villages shall spring up and more people will exist, and you will have power to teach the people how to do things before unknown to them." Throughout the story of creation this divine impulse is expressed by a voice directing the activities of the hero.

At times fortunately the creation is described at greater length. Thus among the Uitoto of Colombia,[6] South America, we find the following poetic account: "In the beginning there was nothing but mere appearance, nothing really existed. It was a phantasm, an illusion that our father touched; something mysterious it was that he grasped. Nothing existed. Through the agency of a dream our father, He-who-is-appearance-only, Nainema, pressed the phantasm to his breast and then was sunk in thought.

"Not even a tree existed that might have supported this phantasm and only through his breath did Nainema hold this illusion attached to the thread of a dream. He tried to discover what was at the bottom of it, but he found nothing. 'I have attached that which was non-existent' he said. There was nothing.

"Then our father tried again and investigated the bottom of

this something and his fingers sought the empty phantasm. He tied the emptiness to the dream-thread and pressed the magical glue-substance upon it. Thus by means of his dream did he hold it like the fluff of raw cotton.

"He seized the bottom of the phantasm and stamped upon it repeatedly, allowing himself finally to rest upon the earth of which he had dreamt.

"The earth-phantasm was now his. Then he spat out saliva repeatedly so that the forests might arise. He lay upon the earth and set the covering of heaven above it. He drew from the earth the blue and white heavens and placed them above."

The creation of all the various animals and plants then follows. We hear no more of him thereafter.

What are we to make of this wonderful bit of imagery? Surely there can be little doubt but that it represents an attempt to solve the riddle of creation by postulating something that existed before the beginning, and our primitive philosopher and theologian has quite logically assumed that the appearance of things preceded their actual existence. In the evolution of reality, according to him, three stages may be said to exist: nothing, the appearance of reality, reality. It is an admirable solution of the much vexed question of how a creator can create something out of nothing. There are other solutions conceivable and one of them is found among these very people, namely the creation of the world out of the one thing that existed, the body of the creator himself.

But the speculation of the Uitoto monotheist has gone much farther than this. In one myth we are told that "When in the beginning of things nothing existed, our father created words and gave us these words from the Juka-tree. Nofugeri and our ancestors brought these words to the earth. After he had brought these words to the earth in consequence of a dream, our ancestors gave us the words that our father had created."

In another instance the formulation is even more specific: "In the beginning the word gave origin to our father."

These are, of course, all interpretations of the religious man. The non-religious man, the realist, has had comparatively little influence upon the figure of the creator except in one important respect, namely in the strenuous efforts he has made to equate him with the ancestor of man, for the Uitoto, in a sense, are ancestor-worshippers.

Not far from the above-mentioned tribe we find the Kagaba,[7] among whom we encounter a female Supreme Deity and a profession of faith that should satisfy even the most exacting monotheist.

"The mother of our songs, the mother of all our seed, bore us in the beginning of things and so she is the mother of all types of men, the mother of all nations. She is the mother of the thunder, the mother of the streams, the mother of trees and of all things. She is the mother of the world and of the older brothers, the stone-people. She is the mother of the fruits of the earth and of all things. She is the mother of our younger brothers, the French and the strangers. She is the mother of our dance paraphernalia, of all our temples and she is the only mother we possess. She alone is the mother of the fire and the Sun and the Milky Way. . . . She is the mother of the rain and the only mother we possess. And she has left us a token in all the temples . . . a token in the form of songs and dances."

She has no cult, and no prayers are really directed to her, but when the fields are sown and the priests chant their incantations the Kagaba say: "And then we think of the one and only mother of the growing things, of the mother of all things." One prayer was recorded: "Our mother of the growing fields, our mother of the streams, will have pity upon us. For to whom do we belong? Whose seeds are we? To our mother alone do we belong."

Here we have pure pantheism and the recorder of the above data may perhaps be quite right when he insists that we can hardly expect an origin myth, for the All-Mother is obviously nature personified. I am not quite so convinced of this, but it is a fact that no origin myth has been recorded.

If there are traces, however faint they may be, of a direct intervention of the All-Mother of the Kagaba in the ordinary affairs of man, there are absolutely none in the cases now to be cited, the Tirawa of the Pawnee [8] of Oklahoma and the Earthmaker of the Winnebago [9] of Wisconsin.

In the Pawnee pantheon Tirawa reigned supreme. To him the

The face of Tirawa. These are the lines painted on the face of a child in a blessing ceremony, with the arch across the forehead and down each cheek, and the center line down the ridge of the nose. The arch is the sky, the home of Tirawa, and the center line is his breath, descending from the zenith, by way of the nose, to the heart of the child. From the 22nd Annual Report of the Bureau of American Ethnology, Part 2, p. 233.

lesser gods, both of the heavens and of the earth, as well as the people themselves acknowledged authority. Tirawa rules from his position beyond the clouds and both has created and governs the universe by means of commands executed by lesser gods who are subject to him.[10]

The two temperaments which we see clashing incessantly in the interpretation of the Supreme Diety, that of the permanently devout man and the idealist, and that of the intermittently devout, the practical man, the realist, are transparently reflected among the Pawnee. The supremacy of Tirawa is never questioned by the latter, but something of his rôle as creator of all things is taken from him. The sun, moon and the stars are not mentioned as specifically formed by him. They are merely given their proper places and functions, i.e. Tirawa, somewhat like the Culture-heroes, transforms things. The following is assuredly the account of the realist: "In the beginning was Tirawahut (the Universe-and-Everything-Inside); and chief in Tirawahut was Tirawa, the all-powerful, and his spouse was Atira (Vault-of-the-sky). Around them sat the gods in council. Then Tirawa told them where they should stand. And at this time the heavens did not touch the earth.

"Tirawa spoke to the gods, and said: 'Each of you gods I am to station in the heavens; and each of you shall receive certain powers from me, for I am about to create people who shall be like myself. They shall be under my care. I will give them your land to live upon, and with your assistance they shall be cared for. You, sun, shall stand in the east. You shall give light and warmth to all beings and to earth.' 'You, moon, shall stand in the west to give light when darkness comes.' 'You, evening star, shall stand in the west. You shall be known as Mother of all things; for through you all things shall be created.' '' [11]

It is the same realist who in the following litany converts him merely into the most potent of gods:

I
We heed as unto thee we call!
Oh send to us thy potent aid!
Help us, oh, holy place above!

II
We heed as unto thee we call;
Oh send to us thy potent aid!
Help us, Hotoru, giver of breath! [12]

And it is unquestionably the idealist who speaks in the following. It is a final profession of faith.

I
I know not if the voice of man can reach the sky;
I know not if the mighty one will hear as I pray;
I know not if the gifts I ask will all granted be;
I know not if the word of old we truly can hear;
I know not what will come to pass in our future days;
I hope that only good will come, my children, to you.

II
I now know that the voice of man can reach to the sky;
I now know that the mighty one has heard as I prayed;
I now know that the gifts I asked have all granted been;
I now know that the word of old we truly have heard;
I now know that Tirawa hearkens unto man's prayer;
I know that only good has come, my children, to you.[13]

There is no doubt whatsoever in the minds of the Pawnee that Tirawa reigns supreme and that the minor gods are his ministers only. In one of their prayers he is invoked in the following manner:

Father, unto thee we cry!
Father thou of gods and men;
Father thou of all we hear;
Father thou of all we see—
Father unto thee we cry! [14]

His unapproachability and the realization that only through his ministers, the lesser gods, can man be brought into relation with him is forcibly brought out in such an invocation as this:

Father, thou above, father of the gods,
They who can come near and touch us,
Do thou bid them bring us help.
Help we need. Father hear us! [15]

In the account of origins given by the Uitoto we saw the problem of the creation of the world out of nothing solved in a very ingenious manner. But no attempt was there made to create the creator. Yet this is precisely what the Winnebago of Wisconsin [16] essayed.

"What it was our father lay on when he came to consciousness we do not know. He moved his right arm and then his left arm, his right leg and then his left leg. He began to think of what he should do and finally he began to cry and tears began to flow from his eyes and fall down below him. After awhile he looked down below him and saw something bright. The bright objects were his tears that had flowed below and formed the present waters. . . . Earthmaker began to think again. He thought: 'It is thus. If I wish anything it will become as I wish, just as my tears have become seas.' Thus he thought. So he wished for light and it became light. Then he thought: 'It is as I supposed; the things that I have wished for have come into existence as I desired.' Then he again thought and wished for the earth and this earth came into existence. Earthmaker looked on the earth and he liked it but it was not quiet. . . . (After the earth had become quiet) he thought again of how things came into existence just as he desired. Then he first began to talk. He said, 'As things are just as I wish them I shall make one being like myself.' So he took a piece of earth and made it like himself. Then he talked to what he had created but it did not answer. He looked upon it and he saw that it had no mind or thought. So he looked upon it again and saw that it had no tongue. Then he made it a tongue. Then he talked to it again but it did not answer. So he looked upon it again and saw that it had no soul. So he made it a soul. He talked to it again and it very nearly said something. But it did not make itself intelligible. So Earthmaker breathed into its mouth and talked to it and it answered.''

Here we have a theory not so different after all from that of the Uitoto. The creator is represented as being born and coming into consciousness. Water is formed from his tears. But this does not take place as the result of a conscious wish. It is only after he has recognized the water and inferred that it had originated from his tears that he realizes his powers and begins to create at first gropingly and then confidently and intelligently.

Earthmaker, like the Tirawa of the Pawnee, never holds direct communion with men. He acts only through his intermediaries, the deities and the Culture-heroes he has created. At times, however, a daring realist will attempt to establish such a direct communion. I know of one instance where a man argued that if Earthmaker had created all the deities from whom we derive our powers, and if it is Earthmaker who bestowed them upon the deities, then he himself must possess even greater powers. Why not then supplicate Earthmaker directly; see him face to face, as one does the spirits? The man gives up everything—happiness, the goods of the world, lastly his own child, and finally he hears a voice from above saying: ''My son, for your sake I shall come to earth.'' The man turns in the direction of the voice, perceives a ray of light extending from the heavens to his camp and a voice again speaking: ''Only thus can you see me my son. What you ask of me, to see me face to face, I cannot grant.'' [17] So not even the realist can alter him profoundly; he is a deity unapproachable and invisible.

In one of the cults, practically a feast to all the gods and a plea for victory in war, a further attempt has been made to convert him into a god of the general type:

''Hearken, Earthmaker, our father, I am about to offer you tobacco. My ancestor concentrated his thoughts upon you. The blessings you bestowed upon him . . . those I ask of you directly (i.e. and not through the customary intermediation of other spirits). Also that I may have no troubles in life."

Or we get an even more definite attempt at transformation into a cult-deity:

"Hearken, Father who dwells above, all things you have created. Yet if we were to offer you some tobacco you would thankfully accept it you said. I am about to offer you a handful of tobacco and a buckskin for moccasins and a white-haired animal to be cooked so that you may have a holy feast. . . . If you accept them, the first thing I ask of you will be the honour of killing an enemy in full sight of the people, of leading war-paths. . . ." [18]

Yet if there is one thing upon which practically every Winnebago would agree it is that Earthmaker is under no conditions ever associated with war. What we have here is not merely an attempt to make him a cult-deity but an example of swaggering so very common among primitive people.

The most difficult of all the concepts of the Supreme Deity to understand is that found among the Dakota.[19] A very remarkable account was secured from them which purported to be the secret instructions for a priest (shaman). In this priestly doctrine it is definitely asserted that the Great Mystery, the Supernatural Being called Wakan Tanka, cannot be comprehended by mankind. Wakan Tanka behaves like a definite individuality, may be pleased or displeased, propitiated or placated and its aid may be secured by appropriate sacrifice. This Great Mystery communicates with mankind through various individuals and in various ways. The chosen medium is the shaman. The following are the doctrines which only the shamans know, according to Mr. Walker, the recorder of these facts:

> Wakan Tanka is one, yet it is many who are
> Wakan Tanka Waste, the Benevolent Gods:
> Wakan Tanka Sica, the Malevolent Gods.[20]

The Benevolent Gods are of two kinds, the Gods and the Gods' Kindred, the former divided into the Superior and the Associate

Gods, the latter into the Subordinate Gods and the God-like. Each of these four classes consists of four individuals, the individuals of the Superior Gods being the Sun, Sky, Earth, Rock; of the Associate Gods, Moon, Wind, the Feminine, the Winged God; of the Subordinate, the Buffalo, Bear, Four Winds, Whirlwind; of the god-like, the spirit, ghost, spirit-like, the imparted Supernatural Potency.

We now come to the most remarkable part of this mystic theology. Wakan Tanka, the Great Mystery, has four essences to be regarded as one—the Chief God, the Great Spirit, the Creator and the Executive. The Chief God has four individuals (Sun, Moon, Buffalo, Spirit) that are as one; the Great Spirit, four individuals (Sky, Wind, Bear, Ghost) that are as one; the Creator-god, four individuals (Earth Feminine, Four-Winds, Spirit-like) that are as one, and lastly, the Executive God, four individuals (Rock, Winged, Whirlwind, Potency) that are as one. This mysticism is carried through in every detail. So, for example, all these individualities, apart from the four winds, had no beginning, though some came before others and some bear the relation of parent and offspring. The Dakota informant added, "This is Akan (mysterious), for no one of mankind can comprehend it. They will have no end." Another informant in answer to a direct statement that he had named eight deities and yet claimed that they were but one, replied, "Yes. The sun and moon are the same, the sky and the wind are the same, the Rock and the Winged one are the same, the Earth and the Beautiful woman are the same. These eight are only one. The shamans know how this is but the people do not know. It is a mystery." This same man stated that he frequently prayed to Wakan Tanka and that if the prayer was about things of great importance it was carried to the Sun; if about health or strength, to the Sky; if about implements, to the Rock; if about food or clothing and such things, to the Earth.

Clearly this is explicit monotheism avowedly mystical. The deities as intermediaries have disappeared; they are merely aspects of the Great Mystery. "When Wakan Tanka wishes one of mankind to do something he makes his wishes known either in a vision or through a shaman," one of Mr. Walker's informants stated. This same individual was quite definite as to the oneness of Wakan Tanka: "The shamans address him as Tobtobkin, which in their language means four times four. He is like sixteen different persons; but each person is *kan* (mysterious). Therefore they are all the same as one." [21]

Such is the creed of the priests. No pretence is made that it holds for the people. Among them the sixteen aspects of godhead are sixteen distinct deities, although the shamanistic terminology has penetrated to them too. In a myth about the wind it is stated, Wi (the Sun) was chosen because he was Wakan Tanka and his wife Moon and the Sky and the Rock were all chosen for the same reason. Yet apparently they all appeared as distinct deities. Nor, for that matter, need we suppose that all the shamans, in spite of their creed, were not sometimes more polytheistic than monotheistic. It seems a rather suspicious circumstance that one of the shamans in answer to certain interrogations stated: "Rock is the oldest. He is the grandfather of all things. Earth is the next oldest. She is the grandmother of all things. Sky comes next. He gives life and motion to all things. Then follows the Sun. *He is above all things and above all Wakan Tanka.*"

But the inconsistencies are really unimportant. The significant fact remains that such a mystical Supreme Essence was postulated and actually became the official creed of all shamans.

This last example has introduced us to certain mystical elements, and although it may be somewhat beside the point, I cannot refrain from giving another instance of a very special nature in which mysticism is carried still one step farther.

Among the Winnebago Indians [22] an interesting religious revival has recently taken place based largely on a religion borrowed from their southern neighbours and which included certain marked Christian features. The older Winnebago concept of Earthmaker, as set forth previously, has in this new faith been equated with the Christian Deity. Yet the main element in this new syncretism has, however, nothing to do with Christianity. It is the worship of the peyote (a small cactus found in northern Mexico), which when eaten, either in the natural state or in a concoction brewed from it, produces certain narcotic effects. It was after partaking of the peyote rather copiously that a certain individual developed the following theology which he dictated to me in Winnebago: [23]

"Then again I prayed to Earthmaker. . . . As I prayed I was aware of something above me and there he was! Earthmaker to whom I was praying, he it was. That which is called the soul, that is it, that is what one calls Earthmaker. Now this is what I felt and saw. All of us sitting there, we had all together one spirit and I was their spirit or soul. Whatever they thought of I immediately knew. I did not have to speak to them and get an answer to know what their thoughts had been. Then I thought of a certain place far away, and immediately I was there; I was my thought. . . . All those that heed Earthmaker must be thus, I thought. I would not need any more food, for was I not my spirit? Nor would I have any more use of my body. . . . My corporeal affairs are over."

III

We have now briefly enumerated some of the main types of monotheism to be encountered among primitive peoples. But monotheism itself presents a number of phases. A recent classification of its history divides it into three stages; into monolatry, i.e. a belief in a Supreme Being but the persistence of the worship of other deities at the same time; implicit monotheism, i.e. a belief in a Supreme Deity yet no definite denial of the existence of other gods, and lastly explicit monotheism, a belief in a Supreme Deity and a denial of the existence of other gods.[24] If this were true, it might at first glance follow that we would have to deny the existence among any primitive peoples of anything except monolatry. But it might be asked, is it really the mere fact of the worship of other gods or spirits or Culture-heroes that constitutes the fundamental difference between explicit monotheism and monolatry? What of those cases where lesser gods have been created by a Supreme Deity; where all their powers have been derived from him; where they are merely his intercessors? Are we to interpret every act of worship not directly addressed to a Supreme Deity but to his divinely appointed intermediaries as contrary to the spirit of mon-

otheism? I am afraid that we should then soon find ourselves confronted with great difficulties. I cannot enter into the theological
aspects of this question here. For us it is the historical aspects of
this question that are of prime importance, and to some of these we
must now turn. How, it may be asked, are we to imagine the intermediary rôle of certain deities and Culture-heroes to have developed and what relation does the Supreme Being bear to the other
deities?

Everyone acquainted with the religion and mythology of primitive peoples is well aware of the fact that the same deities and Culture-heroes who figure as the ministers of a Supreme Deity are also
known in an entirely different connection where no such relation is
involved. The Winnebago, for instance, have four Culture-heroes
and in many versions of their exploits there is not the slightest indication of their having been created by Earthmaker. The account
of their creation by him seems obviously secondary. The same is
true in regard to a deity who is regarded as the chief of the evil
spirits. In many Winnebago myths, in fact in all those not concerned with the problem of the origin of man, it is explicitly stated
that the chief of the evil spirits is equal in power and importance to
the great, good spirit. In one of the ritualistic origin myths, on the
other hand, he is explained away as the Deity's first inadequate attempt at creation. Having been cast aside as unsatisfactory, he imi-
tates Earthmaker but only succeeds in creating evil. Many more
myths of this type could be adduced all pointing in the same direction and all tending to demonstrate that the religious system-
atization is secondary. The intermediary rôle occupied by many
deities and Culture-heroes is clearly the reflection of this unifying
influence of the concept of a Supreme Creator.

The second of our problems is more difficult. Can we not
indeed satisfactorily explain the concept of a Supreme Deity by
regarding him as representing the successive transformations of
some particular deity or of some individual spirit? May he not, for
instance, represent the triumph of the god of some particular cult?
Evolutionists have generally answered this question in the affirma-
tive. They would insist in fact that the Winnebago are an excellent
case in point. First we have a belief in a number of deities all of

equal importance; one then becomes identified with the chief of the evil spirits, and the other with the chief of the good spirits. Gradually but never completely the latter then displaces the former. Such an interpretation is quite reasonable. Yet one factor, it seems to me, has always been forgotten in such an analysis. Why should these transformations all take place synchronously or, if you will, why should they occur in the simplest as well as in the more complex civilizations; and why should they always be connected with the elaborations of religious cults? Why in fact should the unification of religious concepts always go hand in hand with the marked development of a high ethical ideal? Why, for example, should a coarse, selfish, stupid figure in mythology suddenly become an ethical, intelligent and benevolent being when associated with a creator?

The ethical re-evaluation of the Transformer of the myths has never been adequately stressed. A far more fundamental question is involved here, namely how to account for the tendency toward unification in religious beliefs. For this a number of explanations have at different times been advanced. The most important are those which represent it as a reflection of certain forms of social organization, the influence, for instance, of a markedly centralized government or of highly elaborate and unified cults. But it can easily be shown that no correlation whatsoever exists between the existence of a belief in an ethical Supreme Creator and such integrated social units. Some tribes with such a unified social and ceremonial organization possess it, many, indeed the vast majority, do not. But even if we were to grant that such social units had had a perceptible influence upon the wider adoption of a belief of this kind, and I am inclined to regard this as likely, we are no nearer to a real solution.

IV

If, as most ethnologists and unbiased students would now admit, the possibility of interpreting monotheism as part of a general intellectual and ethical progress must be abandoned and if social causations hardly touch the fundamental problem involved, only two alternatives remain open to us. We may either regard such

a belief as innate in the theological sense or as the expression of a
certain temperament. The first lies quite outside my province. To
explain what I mean by the second and how it affects our problem I
must permit myself a slight digression.

It is a matter of common experience that in any randomly
selected group of individuals we may expect to find, on the whole,
the same distribution of temperament and ability. Such a view, I
know, has certain terrors because of national and class prejudices,
but I do not think it can be really seriously questioned. Certainly
not for temperament. But, you might ask, is this true for primitive
peoples? Is not their mentality, is not their whole emotional nature
utterly different from our own? Most laymen, all sociologists and
many ethnological theorists are of that opinion. Nothing in reality is
wider from the mark. Perhaps I need hardly insist upon this after
the examples of logical and speculative thinking I have given you.
Primitive people, as a matter of fact, are quite as logical as ourselves and have perhaps an even truer sense of reality. There is not
the slightest indication of the existence of any fundamental difference in their emotional nature as compared with ours. I think we
may, in fact, confidently assume that the same distribution of ability and temperament holds for them that holds for us. Indeed I think
there is ample reason for believing, granted that chance mating has
existed since man's first appearance on earth, that the distribution
of ability and temperament never has been appreciably different.
What has differed is the size of populations with its corollary of a
larger proportion of men of a certain type of ability and temperament. We must bear this in mind in estimating the culture of primitive peoples. At the discovery of America, for instance, it is
extremely doubtful whether there were more than 1,250,000
individuals north of the Rio Grande.

If therefore we are right in assuming the same more or less
fixed distribution of ability and temperament in every group of approximately the same size, it would follow that no type has ever
been totally absent. I feel quite convinced that the idealist and the
materialist, the dreamer and the realist, the introspective and the
non-introspective man have always been with us. And the same
would hold for the different grades of religious temperament, the

devoutly religious, the intermittently, the indifferently religious man. If individuals with specific temperaments, for instance the religious-aesthetic, have always existed we should expect to find them expressing themselves in much the same way at all times. And this, it seems to me, is exactly what we do find. The pagan polytheistic religions are replete with instances of men—poets, philosophers, priests—who have given utterance to definitely monotheistic beliefs. It is the characteristic of such individuals, I contend, always to picture the world as a unified whole, always to postulate some First Cause. No evolution from animism to monotheism was ever necessary in their case. What was required were individuals of a certain psychological type. Alongside of them and vastly in the majority have always been found others with a temperament fundamentally distinct, to whom the world has never appeared as a unified whole and who have never evinced any marked curiosity as to its origin.

Such too is the situation among primitive peoples. If anything the opposition of the two types is much clearer. All the monotheists, it is my claim, have sprung from the ranks of the eminently religious individuals. It is in the ritualistic version of the Winnebago Origin Myth for example, that Earthmaker is depicted as a Supreme Deity who definitely creates the other deities and the Culture-heroes; it is in the ritualistic version of the Culture-hero cycle again that a non-moral, buffoon-like hero, whose acts are only incidentally beneficial to mankind, is transformed into an ethical, intelligent, beneficent creator. No other explanation for the characteristics of the Supreme Deities, as I have attempted to sketch them, is indeed conceivable except upon the assumption that they reflect a definite type of temperament, examples of which we know actually exist in every primitive group. Such people are admittedly few in number, for the overwhelming mass belong to the indifferently religious group, are materialists, realists, to whom a god, be he Supreme Deity or not, is simply to be regarded as a source of power. If men of this type accept such a god, he is immediately equated with the more concrete deities who enter into direct relations with man and as a result contamination ensues. It is thus that that particular type of Creator arose, where a marked admixture of attributes belonging to the Culture-hero and Transformer was manifest.

On such an hypothesis a really satisfactory explanation of the existence and of the dominant traits of the monotheism among primitive peoples can be given. Monotheism would then have to be taken as fundamentally an intellectual-religious expression of a very special type of temperament and emotion. Hence the absence of cults, for instance, the unapproachability of the Supreme Being, his vagueness of outline and his essential lack of function. Whatever dynamic force he possessed for the community is that with which the realists invested him. In so doing they frequently converted him into a cult-deity, into a creator of gods; made him but one among many. This is merely monolatry if you wish, but this in no way detracts from the possibility that the faith of the religious man himself may have been different, may have been essentially explicit monotheism. Yet, even if we should not care to press this claim, the existence of monolatry and implicit monotheism must constitute a definite challenge to the views still current as to the development of the concept of a Supreme Creator.

The view still held both by the ethnological theorist and the student of comparative religion is frankly evolutionary. Only recently in a remarkably lucid address by the late Dr. Buchanan Gray three stages in the development of Hebrew monotheism are assumed; the earliest extending perhaps even beyond the Exile, in which the Jews were divided into two groups one constituting apparently the large majority, worshipping Jahveh and other deities at the same time, and the other worshipping only Jahveh but yet not denying the efficacy of other gods for the people. The second is represented by the belief of the prophets of the third century and after, where Jahveh is thought of as controlling the destinies of all nations but where, at the same time, it is not definitely asserted that no other gods exist. The last stage, that of Deutero-Isaiah, gives us the definite formulation that there is no God but one. Dr. Gray goes on to say, "The existence of this third type of belief in Israel cannot be definitely traced back beyond the sixth century. Implicit monotheism might, according to the judgment passed on the age and meaning of certain passages, be traced perhaps somewhat earlier than the eighth century: but wherever and so soon as we find the first type of belief, monotheism, whether implicit or explicit, is excluded.'' [25]

This is quite definitely in line with the orthodox evolutionary theory. The cardinal error is and always has been the assumption that every element in culture must have had an evolution and one generally comparable to that which exists in the animal world. But it is precisely in its application to culture, to thought and to temperament that the evolutionary theory even in its heyday proved so unsatisfactory and even harmful. It requires no long preparatory stages for an individual with inborn artistic abilities to draw figures both correctly and with a remarkable feeling for line; and there is no reason whatsoever for supposing that certain concepts require a long period to evolve. What, concretely speaking, did Dr. Gray imagine had happened in Israel between the first and the third stages of monotheism? Apparently an increase in intelligence and in the capacity for abstract thought. This is but the old unconscious assumption that progress must make equal strides along the whole line. The general acceptance of explicit monotheism at one stage (if indeed there ever has been or could be such a general acceptance), and its apparent absence in the two earlier stages is taken to mean that it did not exist before. The existence of two varying attitudes toward God at one and the same time, as in the previously cited case of Hebrew monolatry, is regarded as somehow implying that explicit monotheism was absent. Dr. Gray himself partially realized the force of this criticism, for he says further on: ''We may admit the possibility in the abstract that even before the eighth century there may have been individual Hebrew monotheists of whom no trace has survived; but the religion of the people as a whole—of the teachers, prophets, priests, as well as the mass of the people—was not monotheistic.'' [26] To Dr. Gray the existence of such a monotheist was a bare possibility because at bottom he could not think of explicit or implicit monotheism except as the result of a gradual evolution and, I surmise, because he would have seen no way in which to explain it if it had actually been found.

Another theologian and historian of religion, the very stimulating Archbishop of Upsala, Dr. Söderblom,[27] is also definitely evo-

lutionistic in his interpretation. Instead of simply beginning with
animism or pre-animism, however, he begins with three factors:
Animism, the belief in supernatural power, i.e. *mana,* and the
belief in Culture-hero creators (*Urheber*). He does not deny the existence of the All-Father or Creator concept but assumes it as something shadowy and vague among primitive peoples and in his opinion utterly distinct from real monotheism in any form. He, like so
many people, can explain the marked resemblances of so many
Supreme Creators with the Culture-heroes in but one way, namely
that the latter have largely contributed toward the formation of the
former. To explain the third, i.e. the mystical aspect, he has re-
course to the *Mana* concept. This in itself is exceedingly suggestive
especially if we take the belief in Culture-heroes and the *Mana* concept as being in the nature of psychological tendencies, but unfortu-
nately Dr. Söderblom does not confine himself to this aspect of the
question but predicates an evolutionary development for both concepts. For, like the most orthodox of evolutionists, he cannot bring
himself to believe that the mentality of primitive people is not essentially different in kind from our own. He has been led astray, if
I may say so, by the data he selected. He practically bases his analysis on the somewhat antiquated instances found in Lang, i.e. on
the ridiculously inadequate and unsatisfactory material from Australia and the vague statements found in early accounts of the American Indians. But the real criticism of his position is that just indicated, that to him explicit and implicit monotheism must represent
the last phases of a long and gradual development.

Explicit monotheism, it is true, is rare among primitive peoples, but it is possibly not quite so uncommon as the literal reading
of the facts might seem to indicate. Knowing the tremendous part
symbolism plays in the interpretation of religious phenomena, particularly the Godhead in our own civilizations, what right have we
to assume that it played an inferior rôle in avowedly similar temperaments among primitive peoples especially when it is universally
admitted that symbolism permeates every aspect of primitive man's
culture? What the facts really are it is admittedly difficult to ascer-
tain, but from my own experience I am inclined to assume that a
limited number of explicit monotheists are to be found in every

primitive tribe that has at all developed the concept of a Supreme Creator. And if this is true we can safely assume that they existed in Israel even at a time when the mass of the people were monolatrists.

The problem, in short, that confronts us is not as has always been erroneously assumed, the origin of monotheism. That is one which I should say even antedates Neanderthal man. The historical problem connected with monotheism, implicit and explicit, is as I see it, not how monotheism arose but what made it the prevailing and exclusive official religion of a particular people. This we must assume to have been largely in the nature of an historical accident. The Jews and Mohammedans, the adherents of the purest form of monotheism known today, are certainly not innately gifted in this regard. It is true that the factors concerned in the complete credal triumph of monotheism in Judaism, Christianity and Mohammedanism have never been satisfactorily explained, but they are emphatically of an individual historical and psychological nature. For myself, I am inclined to believe that the spread of monotheism is far more definitely a reflection of certain facts of a general sociological order than has hitherto been recognized. Certainly it has obviously not been the triumph of the unifying principle over the disruptive, of abstract over concrete thought. Yet, on the other hand, there must be something subtly appealing in monotheism, for wherever it is found a definite influence is seen to be exercised over the thought of those who are stubborn polytheists and animists. Nowhere indeed has it ever been completely submerged once it has made its appearance, no matter how great the mass of foreign accretions piled upon it.

I am afraid that the thesis I have advanced will seem to many exaggerated, quite contrary to all the ideas customarily associated with primitive peoples. Most of us have been brought up in the tenets of orthodox ethnology, and this was largely an enthusiastic and quite uncritical attempt to apply the Darwinian theory of evolution to the facts of social experience. Many ethnologists, sociologists and psychologists still persist in this endeavour. No progress will ever be achieved, however, until scholars rid themselves, once and for all, of the curious notion that everything possesses an evolutionary history; until they realize that certain ideas and certain concepts are as ultimate for man as a social being as specific physiological reactions are for him as a biological entity. Both doubtless have a history; but in the one case its roots lie in pre-social man and in the other in the lower organisms. It must be explicitly recognized that in temperament and in capacity for logical and symbolical thought, there is no difference between civilized and primitive man. A difference exists—and one that profoundly colours primitive man's mental and possibly his emotional life; but that is to be explained by the nature of the knowledge the latter possessed, by the limited distribution of individuals of certain specific temperaments and abilities and all that this implied in cultural elaboration. In no way, however, does this affect the question of the existence among primitive people of monotheism in all its different varieties. Such a belief, I cannot too often repeat, is dependent not upon the extent of knowledge nor upon the elaboration of a certain type of knowledge, but solely upon the existence of a special kind of temperament. When once this has been grasped, much of the amazement and incredulity one inevitably experiences at the clear-cut monotheism of so many primitive peoples will vanish and we shall recognize it for what it is—the purposive functioning of an inherent type of thought and emotion.

Notes

1. For an excellent discussion of the conditions found in aboriginal Australia, cf. the famous work of W. Schmidt, *Der Ursprung der Gottesidee,* 1912.

2. R. H. Lowie, *Myths and Traditions of the Crow Indians,* pp. 14 ff., in Anthropological Papers of the American Museum of Natural History, vol. XXV, part I, New York 1918.

3. J. Teit, *Traditions of the Thompson River Indians of British Columbia,* p. 48, in Memoirs of the American Folklore Society 6, Boston 1898.

4. J. Curtin, *Creation Myths of Primitive America,* London 1899, pp. 3 ff.

5. G. A. Dorsey, *The Mythology of the Wichita,* Washington 1904, pp. 25 ff.

6. K. T. Preuss, *Religion und Mythologie der Uitoto,* Göttingen 1921, vol. i, pp. 166–168. Cf. also K. T. Preuss, *Die höchste Gottheit bei den Kulturarmen Völkern,* in *Psychologische Forschung,* vol. ii, pp. 173–186.

7. *Ibid., Psychologische Forschung,* vol. ii, pp. 167–173.

8. G. A. Dorsey, *Traditions of the Skidi Pawnee,* Memoirs of the American

Folklore Society 8, Boston 1904, and A. C. Fletcher, *The Hako, a Pawnee Ceremony* in Twenty-second Annual Report, Bureau of American Ethnology, Washington 1911.

9. P. Radin, *The Winnebago Indians* in Thirty seventh Annual Report, Bureau of American Ethnology, Washington 1923, pp. 277–316.

10. G. A. Dorsey, *Traditions of the Skidi Pawnee*, pp. xviii–xix.

11. *Ibid.*, pp. 3–4.

12. A. C. Fletcher, *ibid.*, p. 286.

13. *Ibid.*, pp. 343 ff.

14. *Ibid.*, p. 314.

15. *Ibid.*, p. 314.

16. P. Radin, *ibid.*, pp. 212–213.

17. *Ibid.*, pp. 291–293.

18. *Ibid.*, pp. 447, 455.

19. J. R. Walker, *The Sun Dance and other Ceremonies of the Teton Dakota*, in Anthropological Papers of the American Museum of Natural History, vol. xvi, part I, 1917.

20. *Ibid.*, pp. 78–92.

21. *Ibid.*, pp. 152–159. [Reprinted here in chapter 13—eds.]

22. P. Radin, "The Peyote Cult of the Winnebago Indians" in *Journal of Religious Psychology*, 1914, pp. 1–22.

23. P. Radin, *The Autobiography of a Winnebago Indian* in University of California Publications in American Archæology and Ethnology, vol. xvi, Berkeley 1920, pp. 441–442.

24. C. Buchanan Gray, *Hebrew Monotheism* (Oxford Society of Historical Theology, Abstract of Proceedings for the Year 1922–23).

25. *Ibid.*

26. *Ibid.*, 8–13.

27. N. Söderblom, *Das Werden des Gottesglaubens* (German translation 1916).

15

An American Indian View of Death

Dennis Tedlock

I

In the summer of 1966 I made a short visit to Zuñi, in western New Mexico, after an absence of several months. First I called on a friend who lived some miles outside the town of Zuñi itself. He told me early in the conservation that "something tragic" had happened in Daniel's family down at Zuñi. He didn't know any details, but it was some sort of accident. Daniel's grandson, the eldest son of his daughter Ann, was dead.

That would be Otho, I thought. I remembered that he had been a member of the junior high basketball team; his mother and Lewis, his stepfather, always went to the home games to see him play. He did a large share of the work around the house. Once, while Lewis was preparing figurines for a family sacrifice, Otho had told me, "The Zuñis are different from any other people in the world."

I went on down to Zuñi to see Ann and Lewis. Ann looked worn and her hair was in disarray; we shook hands gently and I looked slightly away from her and unintentionally chose as my greeting *ko' ton lakyatikyanaawe,* which, like *ko'na ton tewanan aateyaye,* means "How have you been?" but covers a shorter period of time. Ann answered with an almost whispered *k'ettsa-*

248

nisshe, "Happy," and then started weeping and turned and went into the next room for a while. When she came out she sat at the opposite end of the room and said nothing until she had regained her composure.

Lewis was in better spirits than Ann and was quite cordial from the start. After we exchanged a few opening remarks he introduced the subject of the accident. As he went through the details Ann listened but remained quiet. He showed me the rifle that had fired the shot that killed Otho and said he wanted to "get rid of it," to sell it or something. He demonstrated with the rifle how the thing had happened: Otho had mistakenly thought the sight at the muzzle was out of line with the one at the stock; he had stood the gun on the ground with the barrel pointing at his head and had hit at the sight. The safety slipped and the shot fired; the bullet entered the front of his chin but did not emerge, going straight up into his head. "We just didn't know what to do when they brought him here looking like that," Lewis said, and added that more than once Otho had warned his own younger brother about the dangers of the rifle and hadn't even let him use it; "But here he had to go up there with his short road and get himself killed." Tom (Otho's mother's brother) had seen him trying to straighten the sight and had warned him of the danger, but he didn't listen. As for the sight, it turned out that there had been nothing wrong with it at all.

Lewis thought Otho's death made sense in terms of the way Otho had been acting lately. Spending the summer up on Daniel's farm, Otho had been learning new skills much too fast: "He had never driven a tractor before, but here he knew things about it I didn't know," Lewis said. Otho had cultivated Daniel's whole cornfield with the tractor; he weeded Rose's (his grandmother's) whole garden by hand. "I guess he was in a hurry because he was going to lose his life," Lewis said. He added, "It looks bad for Daniel," and "Daniel is a mess," because Daniel, whenever he needed something done, always asked Otho. He said that Daniel and Tom knew much more than he did about the accident and would tell me all about it when I went up to the farm.

Ann brought me a commercial color photograph of Otho and said, "This is his last picture." I brought in a stack of pictures of the family they hadn't seen yet, choosing not to show them any that happened to include Otho, but when they brought out the pictures I had given them in the past, they went through all of them, making no comment whenever Otho appeared. One of the older pictures, taken by Lewis with my camera, included Ann, Daniel, and myself; in it, Ann had a peculiar expression. On seeing this picture, she confessed that she had deliberately made a face at Lewis when he took it; she now demonstrated that face, a wide-eyed look with jutting chin and tilted head, and laughed a little. But she was still quiet most of the time. At her instructions Lewis gave me something to eat, though it was long past lunch time.

I arrived at the farm in late afternoon. Rose and her youngest daughter came out of the house to greet me, smiling, and Rose shouted to Daniel, who was down hoeing in the cornfield. He came up and greeted me as a kinsman. We had talked only a short while when he introduced the subject of the accident. He said that before the farming season Otho had broken one of his mother's windows with a stray baseball. Otho had been so concerned about this that Daniel decided to give him the money to buy some new glass. Otho measured the window, bought the glass, and installed it, all on his own. Partly because of his gratitude toward Daniel, he later said that he wanted to spend his summer up on the farm, helping out with things. Daniel emphasized to me several times that he did not "coax" or press Otho to come up to the farm. Otho had been learning a good deal about silversmithing lately and had been helping his mother at it, and Daniel didn't want to interfere with that.

Otho did come up to the farm and did a great deal of work. But just lately, Daniel had noticed, he had been teasing and joking around with his grandmother, Rose. This is something grandsons do with their maternal grandmothers, but Otho had never done it before. In hindsight, Daniel saw this as an indication of the coming accident and regretted not having said anything about it beforehand. Also, Otho had been learning the use of the tractor with unusual speed. Daniel knows of a young man at Zuñi who died after dreaming that his deceased maternal grandmother served him a good meal at Kachina Village (the home of the dead), and he now wonders whether Otho didn't have an ominous dream before the accident. If he did, he didn't tell anyone about it.

Daniel linked Otho's death with other unhappy events on the farm. "Something's not right," he said, and, "My distributor's not plugged in right." First came his own accident, the previous fall, in which he had almost been killed when his team ran away with his wagon. Some time later, his son Tom was knocked down by a horse and still has a large scar on his upper lip. And now the death of Otho: Daniel was away from the farm when Tom and Otho had their accidents; he said he was now afraid to leave the place for fear something more might happen.

In his detailed account of Otho's death, Daniel said that Tom, who had been hunting with Otho, had gone to a neighbor's for help at the time of the accident since Daniel himself was away. Daniel later saw the tracks Tom made on his way for help: he had walked, not run. The neighbor had lent Tom a tractor, teaching him enough about its operation so that he could pull a trailer to where Otho was lying to bring in his body. Tom had a lot of trouble with the tractor but somehow managed. He was on his way down to the farmhouse with the body when Daniel got back from Zuñi. At the house Daniel was told there had been an accident, but he didn't know Otho had already "passed away" until Tom arrived with the body. "Then I got scared," Daniel said. Otho had been hunting and still had a couple of black flickers (Lewis' woodpeckers) stuffed under his belt.

During the four days since the accident Daniel had gone up to a nearby ranch and down the valley to the sheepdipping place, though not out of the general area of the farm. He said he didn't feel much like staying around the house. While we talked about all this, a neighbor, an elderly woman who had been away at the time of the accident and had just returned, stopped in to see Rose and to find out what had happened. The women talked in the kitchen; when the talk came around to Otho, Rose and her daughter wailed for a few minutes, just as Ann had when she first saw me.

Daniel grew restless and suggested we take a walk down to the gardens; we did this at dusk. These were the gardens Otho had weeded. As we walked back to the house, one of Daniel's grandsons, who had been out sheepherding, came running with the news that a ram had died. This made Daniel mad and he swore in English. It was getting dark as we rode with tractor and trailer over a hill to the sheep corral, not very far from the site of the accident. Tom was there with the ram. We loaded it into the trailer and Tom and I rode back with it. Tom shook my hand; on the way he started to talk about the accident. He said that Otho had been after a sparrow hawk; he had missed a couple of shots and decided there must be something wrong with his rifle sight. He stood the rifle on its butt and pounded at the sight with the pocket knife I had once given Tom; Tom warned him not to do this but he only laughed.

Tom said he wasn't looking when the gun went off. He held Otho "until he was cold." He told Otho, "You shouldn't have done that," and shook him, "but his eyes just rolled around." Tom said to me, "My conscience is hurting me," and, "I was going to kill a deer for you, but then that accident happened." He had decided to do no hunting for two years. He said that Otho had been working too hard: "Whenever we had a little time he said, 'Let's go cultivate that corn,' and we did."

There had been no empty shell in Otho's gun, Tom said; they had looked all over for the shell but couldn't find it. He suggested that "somebody must have taken it."

It was almost dark when we got back to the house. For dinner we had a stew of potatoes and jerked mutton, a sauce of red chili, fresh vegetables from Rose's garden (radishes, new onions, and coriander), tea made from coreopsis (a wildflower), coffee, and watermelon. After dinner Rose told us about the dream she had had the night before: she saw a line of Mixed Kachinas (masked dancers), and Otho, she knew, was the one in the middle, holding a bundle of figurine sacrifices. The kachinas left, and as they did so the last one in line gave the *ik'ok'u* call, a high-pitched whine like the call of a deer.

Sometime after the accident, Daniel told me, Rose had heard a radio playing when there wasn't any radio turned on. Otho had had a transistor radio, said Tom, but "he took that with him." Daniel said Rose was "acting this way" because of the death and because "that's the way the Indian is," but that she would soon be all right. Last night had been the last of the four nights of mourning for Otho, Daniel said; this morning, the door of the house had been left open so that "the soul could go out." He said that Rose had been thinking of Otho each day, because, when the rest of the family came in at the end of the day, he didn't come in with them.

That night in bed I had a chance to think about all this. It was natural enough to have a passing thought that Tom might have accidentally shot Otho and then, in terror, had made up a story, but I would never have seriously entertained such an idea except for the fact that no empty shell was found. I spoke of this to no one. With the ambiguity of Zuñi feelings about a death like this, I thought, it really doesn't matter all that much who fired the shot. The fact is that there has been an accidental death and that everyone connected feels guilty in some degree, most of all Tom because Tom was actually present at the event. No one in the family questioned Tom's story directly though they may have had thoughts like mine. Whatever the problem of the missing shell, the fact remains that Tom is an experienced and careful hunter and that the location of Otho's wound makes sense in terms of Tom's story.

The next morning I drove Daniel down to Zuñi for some errands; among other things, he wanted to pay a call on Otho's mother. She spoke to him in a serious and even sharp tone, saying that his insistence on continued involvement in Zuñi politics, including his outspoken criticism of others in public meetings, had been costly to the family. She had long told others that she wanted Daniel to resign his position in the tribal government and that he was a *peyek lhana,* "loud mouth"; now she was saying all of this to his face. He looked at the floor and she started weeping. He defended himself evenly and then changed the subject.

The second evening, after dinner, Daniel told me of the curious circumstances that followed the death, some months previous, of the star convert of a protestant mission at Zuñi, a man in late middle age who was widely respected at Zuñi despite his Christian activities. He had died on the long ride to a church hospital; Daniel thought he might have been saved had his wife taken him to the public hospital near Zuñi. After his death his wife said that he would be going to heaven, but that in order for him to do so his body would have to be brought directly to the mission church and not to his home, and that his relatives would have to refrain from crying. There was a lot of criticism of her around Zuñi. Daniel thought her plan absurd, since "even white people" bring a body home, and the relatives all cry, just as the Zuñis do. In any case, the body was taken directly to the church. Instead of having her husband buried in the cemetery in front of the ruin of the seventeenth-century Spanish mission, where Zuñis must be buried if they are to go to Kachina Village when they die, she had him buried in the new cemetery south of town. After the funeral she dreamed that she saw her husband at the church clad only in newspaper. She then asked that the body be removed from the new cemetery and reburied in the proper place. No one would help her do this because, as Daniel put it, "Nobody's got a right to dig up a person who's already been buried." She also expressed the wish that her sons be initiated into the Kachina Society, something that had never been done because the family was so intent on being Christian. But, according to Daniel, her boys are now adults, too old to be initiated, and that is where the matter must rest.

My visit ended the next day. Tom started hunting again within less than a year. Otho's picture still hangs on the wall of his mother's house, and she is the only person who still talks about him much. Neither she nor anyone else ever mentions him by his Zuñi or his English name; she always refers to him as "the one who died."

II

Nothing could be more difficult than making sense out of the sudden, "accidental" death of a young person like Otho. In the process of trying to do this, Lewis, Ann, Daniel, and Tom raised a whole range of possibilities. First, there was their own guilt. At the simplest level, if Otho had stayed home for the summer instead of going to the farm, the accident would never have happened, and to the extent that Daniel was the cause of Otho's going, he was to blame for Otho's death. And then, if Tom had been more forceful in warning Otho when he pointed the gun at himself, again the accident would never have happened. Tom even succeeded in bringing me into the total web of cause and effect when he mentioned that it had been my pocket knife with which Otho had hit the gun.

At a subtler level, everyone had failed to pay attention to what were later seen as portents of Otho's death. The most compelling omens, missing in Otho's case, are unexpected visions. As a boy Daniel once heard a crying sound at night; he went out with a torch and discovered that the sound came from a shinbone sticking out of a bank of earth. Within a few years, everyone in his immediate family had died. On another occasion he saw sparks shooting out of some brush where there was no fire; some time later he learned that his aunt had died. Another time, he and Rose and Tom had seen a boy they knew headed for the door of a house, but they discovered moments later the boy was nowhere in sight yet the door of that house had been locked from the outside the whole time; not long after that, the boy died.

More common than these waking omens are the ones that come in dreams. If one dreams of losing a tooth, or of being served a meal by a deceased relative (most often a maternal grandmother), it is a warning that "you will die, or someone in your family will die." The dreamer can be "cured" by being placed under the protection of a medicine society. No one will ever know whether Otho had such a dream, but Daniel seemed to be tracing an equivalent omen in Otho's sudden change of behavior toward his grandmother, as if joking with a living grandmother were like having a meal with a deceased one, both of them being intimate acts with either a woman who is getting old or one who is already dead. With more foresight, or with a clearer omen, Daniel might have brought Otho under the protection of the medicine society of which he himself is a member.

The most obvious portent of Otho's death was his precocity, his "hurry": he learned things too fast, he brought long tasks to an efficient completion, and perhaps someone could have resisted this. Instead, Daniel came to rely on Otho whenever he wanted something done. Years later, Daniel called my attention to the farm buildings of a neighbor who had recently died: there were his wagon shed newly built, his house freshly plastered, and his storage cellar topped with new masonry; everything looked tidy and finished. The comparison with his own house, surrounded by clutter and unfinished projects, was implicit: a house of the living next to a house of the dead.

At the broadest level of responsibility, Daniel saw the accident in the context of the recent life of his whole family: "Something's not right." The senior man in a family, more than any other person, must see to it that he and his kin are in the proper relationship to the cosmos. This is *tewusu*, "religion." In everyday terms, it means taking a piece of bread and a bit of meat at a meal and throwing them into the fire, saying, "Grandfatherly people, eat!" This is the only way the dead get anything to eat; in return, they grant *haloowilinne*, "good fortune." Anyone may give them food, but the older people have the main responsibility. At each solstice there are other sacrifices: figurines made of willow, string, feathers, and paint are brought to life by the breath of the maker. Everyone in the family gives these figurines to the dead in general; males give them to the Sun Father and, if they have been initiated into the Kachina Society, to the kachinas; women give them to the Moon Mother. The actual making of the figurines is strictly the responsibility of the men, who must take the whole family into account. A man like Daniel, because he is a member of a medicine society, must also make figurines at each full moon, including one for the dead of his society; he makes these monthly figurines only for himself, but their sacrifice brings blessings to his whole family. Both the monthly and the solstice sacrifices are followed by a four-day abstention from sexual relations; the winter solstice sacrifice is followed by an abstention from meat and from business dealings as well.

In addition to these individual religious acts, a man should participate in the masked dances of the Kachina Society at least once a year, and any man or woman who is a member of one of the Zuñi medicine societies should put in an appearance at the winter solstice meeting of that society. Such participation, together with the private sacrifice of food and figurines, represents only a minimum effort to keep a good footing in the cosmos. Whoever forgets to give food to the dead is out of joint with the dead; whoever forgets the figurine sacrifice is out of joint with the Sun Father or the Moon Mother; whoever goes for a whole year without masking himself as a kachina is out of joint with the kachinas; and whoever fails to bring his or her personal token of membership to the solstice meeting of a medicine society has lost the protection of the beasts of prey. If a person does remember to do these things but does them incorrectly or with a lack of *tsemaa k'okshi,* "good thoughts, all on one side," it is the same as if he had not done them. In putting himself out of joint he ruins his *haloowilinne,* the good fortune that comes from giving thought to cosmic (as opposed to merely human) matters. When Daniel said, "My distributor's not plugged in right," he was coining a metaphor that described not only his bad connection with the cosmos but the multi-faceted quality of the proper connection.

The clearest sign of the loss of *haloowilinne* is accidental injury, either to oneself or to a relative. Daniel saw his own accident with a wagon, his son Tom's accident with a horse, and his grandson Otho's fatal accident with a gun (all of which had occurred within less than a year) as expressions of a single state of disharmony for which he himself might be responsible. But at the same time, when he observed that the two accidents other than his own had happened while he was away, he was in effect suggesting that his *haloowilinne* was still intact and that his only mistake had been in leaving others without its protection.

Beyond the failure of relatives to do whatever might have prevented a death, there is the possibility that ill will on the part of some outsider might have been at work. Some people, never one's own kin, are *aahalhikwi,* "witches," men and women who get sick at heart when someone has better fortune than they do, or when someone insults or even merely slights them. A witch will wish and plot the death of a person who makes him feel sick, or if that person is too strong, he will hurt him indirectly by attacking someone close to him. Ordinarily it is illness rather than an accident that befalls the victim, but Tom was loosely suggesting some sort of witchcraft in Otho's death when he said that "somebody" must have taken the empty shell. No one made much of his idea, but it was true that a well-known witch had been seen in the area of the farm on several occasions, driving around on the back roads. Otho's own mother, for her part, broadly related witchcraft to the family fortunes when she attacked Daniel for his outspoken participation in politics. Her point was that some of the people he offended might be witches.

In addition to the neglect of relatives and the malice of witches, there is still a third possibility: that the deceased intended his own death. Zuñis think of this possibility in much broader terms than those of the English concept "suicide," since they do not bother with the difference between "conscious" and "unconscious" motivation. The most common case of intending one's own death is that of a person who mourns too much and too long over a lost loved one, usually a spouse; when Daniel's neighbor died (the one who completed so much construction and repair), the widow died within a couple of months. Another possible case of intending one's own death is to have an accident of one's own making.

A storyteller once called my attention to such a case in the tale of "The Boy and the Deer." [1] A boy who was abandoned by his mother and raised by deer was finally discovered and captured by hunters. After his reunion with his mother, he borrowed his grandfather's bow and quiver and went out each day, wandering around. On the fourth night his mother asked him to get the center blades of the broadleaf yucca for her; she needed the fibers to finish the basket she was weaving.

> The next morning, when he had eaten
> he put the quiver on and went out.
> He went out on Big Mountain and looked around
>   until he found a large yucca
> with very long blades.
>
> "Well, this must be the kind you talked about." It
>   was the center blades she wanted.
> He put down his bow and his quiver, got hold of the
>   center blades, and began to pull.
> (*with strain*) He pulled

it came loose suddenly
and he pulled it straight into his heart.
(*softly*) There he died.

He died and they waited for him but he didn't come.

The description here is that of an accident, but the narrator's exegesis was as follows:

Probably he had it in his mind to kill himself, that's the way I felt
when I was telling it. All that time he was with his deer folks,
and all that time he had it on his mind. He never did grow up
with his family, but with those deer, in the open air, and probably he didn't like it in the house.

The narrator did not see any need to be crystal clear about whether the boy "planned" his own death or whether he simply had something on his mind and let the accident happen.

Otho's case bears a chilling resemblance to that of the boy in the story. No one suggested what might have been on Otho's mind, but in any case he had the outward symptom of restlessness, like that other boy, and had chosen to spend his time away from home. His accident seems no less improbable than the one in the story. He pointed the gun at himself despite his previous lectures to his own brother about its dangers, and he kept pointing it when Tom told him not to. On top of that, it turned out that the sight, which he hammered with the pocket knife, had had nothing wrong with it in the first place.

There is one further possible key to Otho's death, and that lies in his *onanne*, "road." At birth the Sun Father sets the proper span for every person's life, giving long roads to some and short roads to others; as Lewis suggested, Otho may have had a short one. When a person has truly come to the end of his appointed road, nothing can be done about it. But there is the possibility of premature death: one may meet with an obstacle on one's road, and this, as Daniel has said, must be "brushed off," swept aside, if one is to continue on that road. Such an obstacle may require the help of one of the medicine societies called *ona yaanakya tikyaawe*, "Societies for the Completion of the Road.'' The obstacle could take the form of dangerous dreams, susceptibility to accidents, or internal illness caused by witches. If Otho's death was the result of some such problem, it was premature and could have been avoided by the proper diagnosis. But there is also the matter of Otho's speed along his road: his precocity or ''hurry'' may have meant that he was near the end anyway and was trying to get everything done, but it may also have meant that he was traveling his road too fast and arriving at the appointed end of it too soon.

Though it may be that some people truly have short roads to begin with, there is only one kind of death that is easily acceptable as a timely arrival at the end. That is when a very old person goes to sleep and fails to awaken. Such an end is not regarded as ''dying'' at all, in the ordinary sense; it is rather said that the person has awakened not here but in the afterworld.[2] Less fortunate souls must linger around their homes for four days after death and then set off for the afterworld at a walking pace.

III

If a person does not die at home, he is brought home, just as Otho was taken from the farm down to his mother's house in the town of Zuñi. Word is sent to all the relatives and close associates of the deceased, including anyone who may have sponsored him in joining a religious organization. The mourners begin to arrive while the body is being prepared. They say prayers and sprinkle cornmeal over the body. Some people weep, the women loudly and the men quietly, but others, even though they may have been close to the deceased, do not.

The body is laid out with the head to the east, the one way the living should not lie when they sleep. Two or three close male relatives measure the body with a length of rope and go out to dig the grave. Meanwhile the close female relatives bathe the body with suds made from the bulb of the yucca plant and rub cornmeal on it, never completely exposing it. Next they dress the body in fine new clothes—not work clothes, but not ceremonial clothes either—and ornament it with silver and turquoise jewelry. Each garment is gashed so that its spirit will be free to accompany the spirit of the deceased. To these "civilian" clothes, the religious associates of the dead person will add whatever is appropriate; for a deceased officer of the Kachina Society, a white embroidered kilt such as kachina impersonators wear; for a medicine society member, a black loin cloth; for a Rainmaker Priest or a Bow (War) Priest, a cloud cap of fluffy white cotton.[3] These same associates paint the face as it would be painted for participation in a ceremony; for a Rainmaker Priest, that would mean a black chin, a black line passing over the upper lip, and corn pollen over the upper part of the face.

Meanwhile, if there is a surviving spouse, he or she must be kept away from fire and be bathed in cold water, first the hair and then the whole body. The spouse will remain aloof and quiet, keeping away from fire and eating no meat or salt, until four nights have passed.

When the preparation of the body has been finished it is wrapped in blankets. The blankets are laced shut all the way up to the face, which is left open until the gravediggers return. The mourners sprinkle cornmeal on the face, or on the breast if the face has been painted. As the blanket is closed over the face, the weeping grows louder. No one accompanies the gravediggers when they carry the body to the cemetery.

During the Spanish period the Zuñis were compelled to bury their dead in front of a Franciscan mission. The mission was abandoned in 1821 but the graveyard has remained a sacred place for all Zuñis; to be buried elsewhere would mean separation from one's own. The body is placed in the grave with the head to the east. Before it is covered the lacings on the blanket are cut so as not to entrap the dead person; for the same reason, if there is a coffin, a hole must be drilled in it. The grave is seldom marked in any way.

According to Daniel, a person who serves as a gravedigger must be *ottsi,* "manly": if he were to feel pity while in the graveyard and say something like, "Oh, my poor child," or let a tear fall on the ground, he would get sick because the dead person would want him. After the burial he must wash off any dirt that might have gotten on his legs and wash off his shoes as well, holding them over burning pine resin to drive away the spirits of the dead. Some men place cotton in their ears and nostrils before entering the graveyard so as to keep out any particle of dust.

While the burial is taking place, the mourners at the home of the dead person throw large quantities of food into the fire. Until four nights have passed, this and all other food sacrifices made by the mourners are meant not for the dead in general, as would normally be the case, but for this one dead person.

The kin of the deceased break or otherwise damage all of his intimate possessions; whatever was not placed in the blankets with the body is either burned or held for separate burial. In Otho's case the possessions included a transistor radio; whatever may have been done with it, "he took that with him," as Tom put it. If the possessions included the feathered-wrapped ear of corn that is the personal token of membership in a medicine society, it is taken by the society and dismantled, the feathers to be included in a sacrifice to the deceased.

The immediate family of the dead person must make a figurine sacrifice as soon as possible. If the burial takes place early enough in the day, they do this before sunset on that same day; otherwise, they will wait till the next morning. They go out west of town, by the bank of the river. There they bury the remaining possessions of the deceased; if he owned his own mask for kachina impersonation, as Otho did, they bury that in a separate hole. Then they dig another hole closer to the river and set up their figurines in it, praying over them. In addition to the figurines they would normally give to the dead in general, there are on this occasion others for their own dead relative. A day later, when the breath of these sacrifices has gone to the dead, someone will come back to fill up the hole they stand in.

The *pinanne*, "spirit" (literally "wind"), of the dead person, which in life was lodged in the breath and ultimately in the heart, remains among the living until four nights have passed. It may make itself known in various ways. After Daniel's neighbor had died, one of Daniel's sons killed a deer, and, remembering that the dead man himself was a fine hunter, he cast the deer's liver into a fire as a sacrifice; at that moment, the screen door of the dead man's house swung open and then shut again. At night the spirit of the dead person will make scratching sounds around the house if no door or window is left open for it to pass in and out at will. In its loneliness, the spirit will want to take someone with it, especially a surviving child òr spouse, and it may make an unwelcome appearance in a dream. Such was the case with the deceased protestant convert Daniel spoke of, who appeared to his wife clad in the newspapers which were his only burial clothes.

For four mornings a surviving spouse must go out to the east to pray and to sacrifice cornmeal. Black cornmeal is held in the left hand, passed around the head four times, and cast away; this "makes the road dark" so as to prevent dream visits by the spirit. The black cornmeal is followed by the more usual sacrifice of white cornmeal, which is held in the right hand. The survivior may also make a special series of two or four figurine sacrifices, four days apart. The following is the prayer to acccompany such a sacrifice: [4]

> *Face east, holding two sets of figurines, saying:*
> On THIS day · my ELders · who WON the holy waters · toDAY · what's YOURS is here · the HOly double I created · the HOly double in my hand · I STAND in your roads · I GIVE you this holy double
> *Here, plant the set of figurines for the dead in general.*
> May you HOLD our holy double · may you OFfer me ALL your good wishes
> *Here, sprinkle white cornmeal.*
> Likewise · YOU whom I called ——— [*for a husband say "father," for a wife "mother"*] · YES indeed in daylight · we lived · our minds entwined · you WON the holy waters · what's YOURS · I OFfer now to you · the HOly double I created · to clasp · to SHARE my holy double
> *Here, plant the set of figurines for the spouse.*
> You have no REAson to take ANYone aWAY · WherEVer the ladders descend · the PRIEST of Corn has children · some are BOYS · some are GIRLS · their ROADS still face ahead · and SOMEone a person of knowledge perhaps · for some REAson · with FOUL heart · with WEApons · unDID your strength · may

THIS be the ONly one you catch in your thoughts · may you
OFfer us your GOOD wishes · may we be SAFE on the GOOD
pollen way · may our ROADS be fulfilled
Here, sprinkle white cornmeal.

The "holy double" is of course the figurine sacrifice, which is in
effect a self-sacrifice.[5] "Good wishes" is a translation of
haloowilinne, the good fortune that comes, in this case, from the
proper relationship between the living and the dead. Above all, the
dead person must not take away a surviving spouse or child or anyone else who has not come to the end of his appointed road, unless
it be the "person of knowledge," or witch, who caused the death.

On the fourth morning after death, the door is left open so that
the spirit can leave the house for good. The people at the farm did
this for Otho even though Otho's home was down at Zuñi. If a
spirit should linger beyond this time, making noises at night, it may
be driven out by filling the house with incense of pine resin.

If the death was premature, and especially if the deceased intended his own death, the spirit travels only as far as Wind Place
(Spirit Place), a ruin about a mile west of town. There it must wait
until it reaches the end of the road that was intended for it by the
Sun Father, only then to join the other dead.

A surviving spouse who remarries too soon invites the reap-
pearance of the dead person. The visit might come in a dream, but
if it were to happen in the wakeful state the deceased would come
as a walking, wailing corpse.

IV

One thing the dead can never do is to return among the living
as living human beings. This permanency of death is a peculiarly
human problem; other forms of life are free from it because they
live in a different kind of time. They do "die," but death does not
have the same meaning for them because they are simply reincarnated: a deer becomes a deer at death, a bear becomes a bear, and so
on; their lives are like the seasons, or like the lives of perennial

plants. In Zuñi religious terminology they are *ky'apin aaho''i*, "raw (or soft) people," whereas human beings are *akn aaho''i*, "ripe (or cooked) people." Humans are also called *tek'ohannan aaho''i*, "people of the light," because their Sun Father summoned them from the darkness of the underworld to live in his light. Emergence into the light was the first in a whole series of unique historical events that separated these "ripening" people from the raw (or natural) world and its cyclical time. In at least some of its features, an individual life-span is a reenactment of these same humanizing events, beginning with a formal presentation of the newborn infant to the Sun Father. Death, or "the end of the light," undoes the effects of both human and personal history, eventually returning the person to the raw world. The course this undoing takes depends on what the person did during his life. As one of Daniel's sons put it, "the more you learn here, the better it'll be for you over there."

A boy first learns something that will prepare him for death when he is initiated into the Kachina Society. This occurs in two stages, the first around the time he is five to nine years old and the second when he is ten to fourteen. Beginning with the second initiation he learns the masked impersonation of the *kokkookwe*, "kachina people," the dead Zuñis who live at Kachina Village, beneath a lake at a two days' walk to the west.[6] Not only does he learn to dance and sing like these dead, but he may even join one of the quadrennial pilgrimages to the shore of the lake itself. When he dies, and when his spirit has left his home, he will arrive at Kachina Village after two days, unless he is one of those who must linger at Wind Place. If he had a mask of his own in life, rather than borrowing the masks of others, he will be able to join the constant dancing of the dead. Rose foresaw this for her grandson Otho when she dreamed, on the night before his spirit departed, that she saw him in the middle of a line of masked dancers.

Occasionally women are initiated into the Kachina Society in order to cure them of having been badly frightened by kachinas. Otherwise a woman goes to Kachina Village when she dies by virtue of having been married to a member of the society, rejoining her first husband. This is a reversal of the situation in life, where a man leaves home to go and live with his wife and her family. The widow Daniel spoke of, who had her converted husband buried in the wrong graveyard and left him with no way to get to Kachina Village (even if he had wanted to) will have no place to go when she herself dies. Whatever may become of her and her husband, they will not be among Zuñis, and neither will their sons, who are now too old to join the Kachina Society.

The people of Kachina Village depend on the living for their whole existence; they have no other source for food and clothing than the *pinanne* or "spirit" of the sacrifices made to them (the clothing is the feathers, paints, and string of the figurines). Moreover, being spirits themselves, kachinas cannot give birth to kachinas: their numbers are increased only by the deaths of the once living. For their part, the kachinas give the living the kind of good fortune that is particularly theirs to give: *ky'ashima,* all kinds of life-giving moisture. The kachinas bring fecundity not only to the crops but to human beings themselves, to domestic animals, and even to cottage industries such as today's silversmithing. They also give sheer pleasure: kachina impersonators and their songs are *tso'ya* "beautiful" (literally, "multicolored"), so much so that it is almost as if they wished to attract the living to the world of the dead.[7] Indeed, if someone dies while dancers are present in the town, it is said that the kachinas took that person with them.

The kachinas who owned their own masks in life may return among the living in spirit form, entering the masks of the living dancers. Anyone at Kachina Village may return among the living as a cloud, most happily in a whole group of rainclouds, but a person who seldom participated in dances in life or who never went to see the dances will be alone in the sky, a "lying" cloud that gives no rain. When the living pilgrims to Kachina Village come back to Zuñi walking in the rain, there is weeping all over the village because they have truly brought the dead back with them.

The people of Kachina Village, when they are not traveling back to Zuñi in cloud or spirit form, are in some ways very much like the "ripe" people they once were. They are human in general form, they wear clothes, and they still eat cooked food, or at least the spirit of cooked food. Like the living, they even have witches

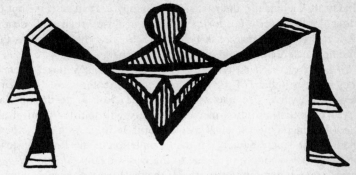

A cloud with downy feathers, painted on pottery. Here is a Zuñi woman's comment on this design: "A prayer that a person may come back after death with the rain and thunder. We put the head in the clouds to show that it is a person. The clouds are the dead." From Ruth Bunzel, *The Pueblo Potter* (Dover, 1972), pp. 110, 113.

among them. But in other respects they have moved one step back towards the raw world. Most of them cannot speak; instead they have cries something like the cries of animals, especially the cry of the deer. When they sing their songs have words, but they always sing in unison rather than as individuals. Instead of having individual identities, with one-of-a-kind faces and personalities, they are *types* of people: deliberate and dignified, clumsy and always out of step, idiotic and childlike, kindly and simple, ugly and dirty, handsome and showy, quick-tempered and violent, exasperated and lazy, or eternally afflicted by some nervous tick. They are sketches of real people, made in broad strokes. The living know them, when they are impersonated, not by *personal* names but by the names of their *masks:* the clumsy type is called *Hehe'a,* the quick-tempered type is called *Salimopiya,* and so on.[8] While a living man has his *Hehe'a* mask on, he is *Hehe'a* and cannot be addressed by his personal name. Once he has died and gone to Kachina Village, the living will never again address him by his own name. The women of Kachina Village share in this same loss of identity.

There is danger in any reassertion of individual identity among the living on the part of a person who is dead. To see clouds or to dream of kachinas in their masks is a happy portent of rain, but to recognize the face of a lost relative is a close brush with death. Rose's dream fell exactly in between: she knew that Otho was the middle dancer, but he did have his mask on.

Some of the dead go elsewhere than Kachina Village, even if they were members of the Kachina Society, or the wives of members, while alive. Anyone who once came close to death and was saved by initiation into a medicine society will join the dead of all the other medicine societies of the world at *Shipaapuli'ma,* where there is one single Society for the Completion of the Road. Instead of being at the bottom of a lake to the west of Zuñi, *Shipaapuli'ma* is high on a mountain to the east. If the dead person not only joined a medicine society but learned how to impersonate the beasts of prey, he or she will be able to do the same among the dead, and to return in spirit to the living impersonators. The eastern dead may visit Kachina Village, but that is not their primary interest.

The people of Kachina Village and of *Shipaapuli'ma* are still susceptible to death, and it is still the human kind of death in that it is a change of one's very being. In fact, they must die three more times before their humanness is completely unravelled and they enter the completely raw world. There are two views as to where they find themselves when they have died for the fourth and final time. Either they are all the way back at the hole where their own ultimate ancestors first emerged from the earth at the beginning of historical time, which is even farther west than Kachina Village, or they have descended, death by death, to the lowest of the four underworlds, which is where the ancestors lived before their emergence. Either way, they are returned to the conditions that existed before the institution of the Kachina Society and the medicine societies among the Zuñis, before the Zuñis themselves were separated from other peoples, before the first human death took place, and even before the Sun Father first gave the human predecessors self-awareness by calling them into his light. At this point, the four-times-dead leave the spiritual life and are reincarnated as raw people, never again to live the lives of ripe people.

The human predecessors who came up through the underworlds were "moss people" with tails, webbed feet and hands, and covered with slime; in other words, they were something like salamanders. People who have died four times do not revert to such a state but rather become the kinds of raw beings for which they had an affinity in life: those who were members of a medicine society might become a mountain lion, bear, badger, wolf, eagle, mole, rattlesnake, or red ant; those who were witches might become a coyote, owl, or bullsnake; those who were members of the Kachina Society might become deer.[9] Otho may ultimately become a deer, and that is what did happen to the boy who stabbed himself with the yucca in the story of "The Boy and the Deer."

The course of death is much simpler for children who never learned anything that would prepare them for it. Such children, especially before they become dependent on cooked food, are still relatively raw, and it only takes a single death to carry them into the purely raw world. They become something not unlike the ancient moss people, changing into turtles, watersnakes, and frogs.

The only way a living person can escape eventual return to the endless reincarnation cycle of the raw world is to become one of the *Uwanam Aashiwani,* "Rainmaker Priests." One does not ask to do such a thing; the priests watch for a young man or woman of the right temperament and they do the asking. Once asked, a person will try to say no, because it is such a serious thing. Even some of those who accept will eventually resign. The priests have spouses and families, like other people, but they devote much of their lives to fasting and prayer. They should never kill other living beings, and they even avoid stepping on ants. They do not even contaminate themselves with the death of plants: like anyone else, they sow their own cornfields, but the people do the harvesting for them. When they pray, they pray not only for themselves and their families, but for all the Zuñis, and not only for Zuñis, but for all human beings, and not only for humans, but for all the beings of the earth, "even every dirty bug." [10] When they go into retreat in summer, entering rooms that are four rooms removed from any outside door, their spirits leave their bodies and travel all over the earth to divine the future. Like the Kachina Society, they help to bring the summer rain, but theirs is the kind of rain that wets not only the fields of the Zuñis but the whole earth.

At the beginning, in the fourth underworld, the Rainmaker Priests lived on the shores of the ocean that surrounds the earth; they joined the other underworld people in their upward and then eastward migration toward the light, helping to find the way to Zuñi, the middle of the earth, with their divinatory powers. At death their spirits return to the shores of the ocean, where they rejoin all the previous priests. These are the ultimate makers of the earth's rains. Their successors among the living invoke them by their *individual names,* going as far back as the names are known.[11] They are at one and the same time the most distant and the most intimate of the dead.

Formerly there was another and quite opposite way of escaping eventual reincarnation, and that was to become one of the Bow (or War) Priests, the protectors of the Rainmaker Priests and of the people. Whereas the Rainmaker Priests neither kill nor even quarrel, the Bow Priests took upon themselves not only the bodily but the spiritual risks of battle, bringing the spirits of slain Apaches and Navajos back to Zuñi. They converted these spirits into bringers of rain and went into retreat to purify themselves.[12] When they were at war, their *haloowilinne* came from the twin warrior sons of the Sun Father and from the beasts of prey, but when they were at home they prayed to the spirit Bow Priests that protect the dead Rainmaker Priests, and that is what they became when they died. They are the ultimate makers of lightning.

In prayers the living Zuñis ask that good fortune shall come *ishalhmatte,* "forever," but there are those who wonder about the death of the world itself. At the beginning the earth itself was raw, or soft, and the fathers and grandfathers of Daniel's generation began to wonder whether it was getting too ripe, too hard. He says that they prophesied a famine, and that the famine is already here but has been hidden by the apparent bounty of the supermarket. At the end, his elders said, our tools and utensils and everything we have made will rise against us; the stars will fall and we will all be boiled by a hot rain.

Notes

1. This tale is translated in full in Dennis Tedlock, *Finding the Center: Narrative Poetry of the Zuni Indians* (New York: The Dial Press, 1972), pp. 3–32. The passage quoted here should be read aloud with a short pause between each line and a longer pause for the strophe breaks.

2. Matilda Coxe Stevenson, *The Zuñi Indians,* Annual Report of the Bureau of American Ethnology 23 (1904), pp. 309, 567.

3. These are the burial clothes described by Ruth L. Bunzel, *Introduction to Zuñi Ceremonialism,* Annual Report of the Bureau of American Ethnology 47 (1932), pp. 482–83. Much of the balance of my description of funeral and burial procedures is based on Stevenson, pp. 305–17.

4. This is my translation of the Zuñi text given in Ruth L. Bunzel, *Zuñi Ritual Poetry,* Annual Report of the Bureau of American Ethnology 47 (1932), pp. 633–34, lines 1–42. It would be intoned rapidly, with pausing only at the major breaks and for breath, and with stress on the capitalized words and syllables.

5. As Barbara Tedlock has shown in "Prayer Stick Sacrifice at Zuni" (unpublished manuscript in the library of the Department of Anthropology, Wesleyan University), the figurines are a surrogate for the self and therefore a "sacrifice" in the strictest sense, rather than a mere "offering." They are even brought to life by the breath of the maker and referred to as living beings; they are, as it were, a man-made substitute for domestic animal sacrifice.

6. "Kachina," which has found its way into American English, is the Hopi word for these beings.

7. This interpretation of the relationship between the kachinas and the living is developed in Barbara Tedlock, *Kachina Dance Songs in Zuni Society: The Role of Esthetics in Social Integration* (unpublished M.A. thesis in anthropology, Wesleyan University), pp. 71–74.

8. For a lengthy roster of Zuñi kachinas and their characteristics, see Ruth L. Bunzel, *Zuñi Katcinas,* Annual Report of the Bureau of American Ethnology 47 (1932), pp. 905–1086.

9. Dennis Tedlock, "Zuni Religion and World View," in *Handbook of North American Indians,* ed. Alfonso Ortiz (Washington: Smithsonian Institution, in press), vol. 9, chap. 49.

10. Bunzel, *Zuñi Ritual Poetry,* pp. 666–667; Tedlock, *Finding the Center,* pp. 32, 142, 152. During World War II, the male rainmakers received draft deferments as clergy.

11. Bunzel, *Zuñi Ritual Poetry,* p. 656.

12. Stevenson, pp. 579–85.

Index

Aborigines (Australian), 221–222, 223
Acoma Pueblo, 110, 112–113, 115
Ajo Mountain, 46
Akchin, Ariz., 46, 64, 73
Akicita (four winds), 208, 216, 218
Albuquerque, N.M., 182
Algonkian Indians, xviii, 146–147, 169
Algonquian Indians, 101
Allegory, 191
Andawlerhsemhlorhs pistæi (attendant), 5
Anegam, Ariz., 44, 45–46, 48, 55–56, 73
Animism, 123, 220, 221, 222, 223, 241, 244, 245
Anthropomorphism, 186–187, 202, 220, 223
  in Ojibwa ontology, 153–158, 167
Anza, Juan Bautista de, 42
Apache Indians, 73, 105, 107, 111, 113, 270
Arapaho Indians, 76, 77, 78, 79, 80–81, 82, 83, 87, 94, 107
  Ghost dance doctrine of, 88, 92, 95
Arhkawdzem-Tsetsauts (attendant), 5
Arizona, 88, 114
Assiniboine Indians, 107, 111
Atira (deity), 230

Ätíso'kanak (characters in myths), 150, 156, 157, 163, 164, 165, 167
Australia, 221, 244
Aztec Indians, 53

Babylonians, 220
Bandelier, Adolph, 112, 114
Bannock Indians, 87, 94
Baraga, Bishop R. R., 145
Barbeau, Marius, 3–12
Beaver Indians, xiv, xvii, xix, 193–204
  cosmic structure of, 193–198, 203
  shamanism of, 201–204
  vision quest of, 198–201, 203
Berens, Chief, 148, 173
Berens River, 170
Bible, 100
Bidney, David, 151
Birchstick (person), 159–160, 162, 164
Bird, Larry, xxi
Black Elk (holy man), xiv, xv, xvi, xix, 20–41, 106, 108, 115–116
Black Mountain, 55–56
Black Short Nose, 79–80
Blake, William, xx
Bloodstoppers and Bearwalkers (Dorson), 161
Blubber, 13
Blyth, R. H., 115
Bow (War) Priest, 261, 270

"Boy and the Deer, The" (tale), 258–259, 269
British Columbia, 225
Brown, Joseph Epes, xxii, 20–41
Bu pingeh (dance plazas), 184
Bureau of Indian Affairs, 115
Burial rites, 260–264

Caddo Indians, 88, 95
Cahuilla Indians, 107
California, xiv, 85, 107, 108, 112, 113, 114, 225
Cantonment, Okla., 92
Captain Dick, 85
Carlisle, Pa., 79, 80, 94
Castaneda, Carlos, xiii, 192
Charms, of medicine man, 6, 10, 12
Chayani (shaman), 112
Cheyenne Indians, 76, 77, 79, 81, 86, 92, 94, 108, 111
Ghost dance doctrine of, 88, 91, 92
Chimayó, N.M., 183
Christianity, xx, 76, 82, 83, 169, 219, 220, 221, 222, 236, 245, 253–254
Peyote rite and, 96, 97, 99
Chükü clowns, 113
Cigarettes, 67–68, 97
Circle, sacredness of, 216
Clowns, sacred, xvii, 105–118
actions of, 106
in creation stories, 109–111
as medicine men, 112–113
mystical liberation of, 108
sexual displays of, 113–115
symbolism used by, 109
terror in, 107–108
Cochiti Pueblo, 112, 114
Cohonino Indians, 87
Cold clowns (*Kwirana*), 180
Colombia, 227
Comanche Indians, 96, 100
Ghost dance doctrine of, 95
Concise Oxford Dictionary, 151
Conjilon Peak, N.M., 182
Contraceptives, xi
Copulation, 115
Corn meal, 45, 46, 47, 63–64, 65, 72, 109, 260, 264
Crazy Dance, 114
Crazy Horse (chief), 21
Cree Indians, 111
Creek Indians, 114

Crow Indians, 99, 114
Ghost dance doctrine of, 92
monotheism among, 224–225
"Crying for a vision" ritual, 20–41
purification lodge, 23–31, 35
songs in, 29, 30, 40
use of pipe in, 21–33, 35, 36, 38, 39
Culture and Experience (Hallowell), 162
Curing, *see* Seeing and curing
Cushing, Frank Hamilton, 112

Dakota Indians, monotheism among, 234–235
see also Lakota Indians; Oglala Sioux; Sioux Indians
Dance plazas (*bu pingeh*), 184
Darwinian theory, 245
David, King, 82
Death, xv, 248–271
ambiguity of feelings about, 248–254
burial rites, 260–264
dreams of, 250–251, 255, 265
existence after, 264–270
making sense of, 254–260
Delaware Indians, 88
Deloria, Vine, xxii
Delphian oracle, 83
Dictionary (Baraga), 145
Dictionary of Psychology (Warren), 143, 151
Dildos, 114
Dog, of Takánakapsâluk, 16
Dorson, Richard M., 161, 163
Dreams, 6, 200–201, 264
of death, 250–251, 255, 265
in Ojibwa ontology, 154, 156, 164–168, 171, 172, 173
Drugs, xiv–xv, 103–104
Drums, 6, 67, 97, 98, 193
Duck, John, 149

Earthmaker (deity), xvii–xviii, 232–234, 236–237, 238, 241
Edson, Casper, 79, 82
Egyptians, ancient, 220
Eliade, Mircea, xiii, 192
Empiricism, xx, 100
English language, 115, 124, 130, 136, 137, 140, 252, 254
Eschatology, 96
Eskimos, xi, xv, xvii, 13–19, 106–107
Ethics, 96, 101

Ethnogeography of the Tewa (Harrington), 186–187
Euclidean geometry, 122
Evolution, xiii, 220–224, 238–239, 245
Explicit monotheism, 237, 243, 244–245

Famine, 14, 18, 270
Fasting, xv, xvi, 5, 34
Finger (shaman), 208–213
Fletcher, Alice C., 169
Flint, in mythology, 148, 153, 154
Foods, from Indians, xi
Fort Bidwell, Calif., 85
Four Winds, 208, 216, 218
  in mythology, 153, 154
Fours, concept of, 215–216
Fox Indians, 114
Fox language, 101
Freud, Sigmund, 197
Freudianism, 196–197

Gaming sticks, 78
Gautama Buddha, 83
Genitals, 114
Ghost dance doctrine, xv, xviii, 75–95
  moral code in, 83–84
  mythology of, 83
  names of, 95
  official statements of, 80–82
  ritual of, 82–83
  tribal differences in, 84–95
"Ghost shirt," 93–94
Gitemraldaw (chief), 6
Gitenmaks, B.C., 4
Gitksan Indians, xiv, xviii, 11
Gitsegyukla, B.C., 7
Gnosticism, 100
Gray, Dr. Buchanan, 242–243
Great Chief (deity), 225
Great Hare (*Misábos*), 153
Great Turtle (*Míkinäk*), 159
Greeks, ancient, 220
Greenberg, Joseph H., 146, 147
Gukswawtu (shaman), 9
Gulf of California, 42

Haida Indians, 107
Halaaits, see Medicine men
Hallowell, A. Irving, 141–178
Harrington, J. P., 186
Hazy Mountain, N.M., 181
Hebrews, 219, 242, 243
Heidegger, Martin, xiii

Hesi Ceremony, 108
Hewitt, J. N. B., 169
Heyoka clown, 105–106
Hidatsa Indians, 191
Hopi Indians, xiii, xiv, 112, 113, 115, 121–129, 181
  concept of space, 121–123, 127–129
  cosmic forms of time, 123–127
Horned Water Serpent dance, 113

Iglulingmiut Eskimo, 19
Implicit monotheism, 237, 242–243, 244
Incense, 97, 264
Inipi lodge, 23–31, 35
Invocation, by a shaman, 217–218
Iroquois Indians, xviii, xix, 107, 113, 169
Isarrataitsoq (deity), 17
Isleta Pueblo, 110
Israel, 245

Jemez Pueblo, 114
Jesus Christ, xv, xx, 83, 86, 99, 100, 102
Jewelry, 261
Jicarilla Apache, 111, 113
Jimsonweed, xiv
Jones, William, 169
Judaism, 219, 220, 242, 243, 245

Kachina (deities), 181, 252, 257, 265
Kachina Society, 256, 261, 266–267, 268, 269
Kachina Village (home of the dead), 250–251, 254, 266–268
Kagaba Indians, 229
Kaldirhgyet (attendant), 5
K'apyo shure clowns, 110
Kashia Pomo Indians, xvii
Kceraw'inerh (medicine man), 4
Keres Pueblos, xxi
Kino, Eusebio Francisco, 42
Kiowa Indians, 83, 96
  Ghost dance doctrine of, 88, 95
Kitwanga, B.C., 11
Klutchie (shaman), 139–140
Komarik, Ariz., 45, 48, 73
Koshari clown, 110, 111, 112–113
K'ossa (warm clowns), 180
Koyemshi clowns, 113, 114
Kwakiutl Indians, xix–xx, 107, 114, 191

Kwiraina clowns, 110
Kwirana (cold clowns), 180

La Madera, N.M., 183
Lakota Indians, 205, 207, 209, 211, 212, 213, 214, 215
  see also Dakota Indians; Oglala Sioux; Sioux Indians
Lame Deer, xiii, xv, 106
Lamenting, 20–41
  purification lodge, 23–31, 35
  songs in, 29, 30, 40
  use of pipe in, 21–33, 35, 36, 38, 39
Lang, Andrew, 221–223, 244
Language
  Hopi metaphysics and, 121–129
  and Ojibwa ontology, 144–149, 151, 153
  reflection of Wintu thought in, 130–140
  of shamans, 208, 213
  see also names of languages
Latin language, 115
Lee, Captain J. M., 85
Left Hand (chief), 78
Lévi-Strauss, Claude, xii, 190, 191, 192
Lévy-Bruhl, Lucien, xii
Linton, Ralph, 139
Logan, Beeman, xii, xiii, xxi
Lophophora williamsi (peyote cactus), xiv, 96, 236–237
Lord's Prayer, 11
Lovejoy, Arthur O., 151
Lumholtz, Carl, 42

Ma Tsu, 115
Mackenzie Basin, xix
McLaughlin, James, 89
Maidu Indians, 108, 112
Making of Religion, The (Lang), 221–223
Malemuit Eskimo, 107
Mana concept, 99, 244
Manitu concept, xviii, 169
Marett, R. R., 169
Masked dancers (Mixed Kachinas), 252
Masturbation, 114
Ma'ura (deity, "Earthmaker"), xvii–xviii, 232–234, 236–237, 238, 241
Medicine bundle, xviii, 201
Medicine men, xii, 3–12, 76, 78, 89, 105, 180, 205, 215

charms of, 6, 10, 12
fasting to become, 5
sacred clowns as, 112–113
songs of, 7–10
Medicine societies, xix, 259–260, 262, 268
  see also Midewiwin
Menomini language, 101
Menstruation, 19, 45, 65, 139, 196, 197, 198
Mental telepathy, 101
Messiah Letters, 80–82
Metaphysics
  Hopi, 121–129
  of Oglala Sioux, 205–218
  ontology of Ojibwa Indians, 141–178
Mexico, 96
Midewiwin (society), xix, xxii, 147, 148, 149
Midnight Water Song (Peyote rite), 97
Midwinter Ceremony, 113
Míkínäk (Great Turtle), 159
Misábos (Great Hare), 153
Miscarriage, 18–19
Miwok Indians, 113
Mixed Kachinas (masked dancers), 252
Mohammedanism, 219, 245
Mohave Indians, 87
Monolatry, 237, 242, 243
Monotheism, 219–247
  evolution theory of, 220–224, 238–239
  as inherent thought and emotion, 239–246
  main types of, 224–237
  meaning, 220
  relationships of deities in, 237–239
Montana, 224
Montezuma Canyon, Utah, xx, xxi
Mooney, James, 75–95
Moral code, of Ghost dance doctrine, 83–84
Morgan, T. J., 80
Mormons, 94
Morning Water Song (Peyote rite), 97, 98
Mount Grant, Nev., 78
Mule Dance, 114
Mythology, 163, 197, 199, 201, 204, 223, 224, 228, 238, 239
  compared with science, 191
  of Ghost dance doctrine, 83

Ojibwa, 148, 149–154, 156–159,
    164–165
  of Tewa Indians, 179

Nahua language, 53
Nainema (deity), 227–229
Narhnorh (spirit), 5
National Formulary, xi
Native American Church, xiv, xv,
    96, 98, 104
Nature, Indian relationship to, xii,
    140
Navajo Indians, xix, xx–xxi, 87,
    107, 108, 109, 111, 270
Neanderthal man, 245
Nevada, 79, 86
New Mexico, 108
New Testament, 99
Neweekwe clowns, 112
Newton, Sir Isaac, xx
Newtonian concepts, xx, 122
Niskyaw-romral'awstlegye'ns
    (chief's wife), 6

Obsidian-covered Mountain, N.M.,
    181
Occult, 123
Oglala Sioux, 205–218
Ojibwa Indians, xiv, xvi, xviii, xix,
    xxii, 111, 141–178
  mythology, 148, 149–154, 156–
    159, 164–165
Oklahoma, 77, 88, 94, 96, 229
Olelbis (deity), 225–226
Omens, of death, 255
One-Star (shaman), 214–215
Ontology, Ojibwa, 141–178
  anthropomorphism in, 153–158,
    167
  dreams in, 154, 156, 164–168,
    171, 172, 173
  introduction to, 141–145
  and linguistic cognitive orienta-
    tion, 145–149, 151, 153
  metamorphosis in, 158–164,
    166–167
  "persons" of mythology and,
    149–153
  psychological unity of, 168–173
Oral contraceptives, xi
Orenda concept, xviii, 169
Ortiz, Alfonso, xx, 179–189
Otiose deities, 226–227

Paganism, 241

Paiute Indians, 78, 87, 94
  Ghost dance doctrine of, 84–87,
    95
Pantheism, 229
Papago Indians, xiv–xv, xvi, xviii,
    42–74
Parish, Essie, xvii
Parsons, E. C., 184
Pawnee Indians, xvii
  monotheism among, 229–232
Pehei'pe clown, 112
Penis, 114, 115
Persians, ancient, 220
Peyote cactus (*Lophophora wil-
    liamsi*), xiv, 96, 236–237
Peyote rite, xiv, xv, xx, 96–104,
    236–237
  arrangement of tipi for, 97
  healing effects of, 103
  heightened sensibility in, 101–
    102
  lesson of, 99–101
  mystical experience in, 102–103
  sacrament in, 98, 104
  songs of, 97–98, 101–102
  vision in, 102
  warnings about, 103–104
*Pharmacopeia of the United States
    of America,* xi
Phister, Lieutenant N. P., 85
Physics, 123
Pima Indians, 42, 43
Pinacate, Sonora, 46
Pine Ridge, S.D., 90, 91
Pinési (Thunder Bird), 154–158
Piñon nuts, 78–79
Pipe, 173, 207, 211, 212
  circular moving of, 216, 217–
    218
  in Ghost dance doctrine, 92
  in lamenting ritual, 21–33, 35,
    36, 38, 39
  in shaman invocation, 217–218
Pisinimo, Ariz., 45, 65, 73
Pit River Indians, 87
Pneuma (supernatural force), 99
Polytheism, 221, 236, 241
Ponca Indians, 114
Porcupine (religious leader), 86
Poshayaank'i (deity), xvii
Pottery, 267
Prayer, 97, 111, 140, 223, 229,
    231–232, 237, 263–264
Prayer sticks, 45–46, 48, 55, 63,
    64, 67
Premature death, 259, 269

Preparation, The (speech), 49–53
Price, Rev. Mr., 11
Protestant missionaries, 115
Psychological unity, of Ojibwa ontology, 168–173
Puberty, 166, 171, 173, 198–199
Pueblo Indians, xix, 109, 110–111, 114, 179, 183, 184
see also names of Pueblo tribes
Purification
in Ghost dance, 82
in salt pilgrimage, 43, 44, 66–73
by sweat-bath, xv, 89
Purification lodge, 23–31, 35

Quijotoa, Ariz., 46
Quitting Song (Peyote rite), 97

Radin, Paul, xiii, 141–178, 219–247
Rainmaker Priests (*Uwanam Aashiwani*), 261, 269–270
Rasmussen, Knud, 13–19
Rattles, 9
Red Ant ceremony, 109
Red Leaf camp, S.D., 91
Red River, 92
Redfield, Robert, 142
Reid, Susan, 191
Relativity, 122, 123
"Religion of the North American Indians" (Radin), 169
Religious persecution, 115
Ridington, Robin, 190–204
Ridington, Tonia, 190–204
Road, The (concept), xxii, xxiii, 39–40, 97, 259–260
Roadman (Peyote rite), 97
Rocherdéboulé, B.C., 4
Roman Catholic church, 97, 261
Romans, ancient, 220
Rosebud agency, S.D., 90

Sacrament
Peyote as, 98, 104
tobacco as, xi–xii
Sacred Pipe, The (Brown), xxii
Sahagún, Bernardino de, 53
Salt pilgrimage, xv, xviii, 42–74
the journey, 46–63
preparation for, 43–46
purification in, 43, 44, 66–73
sea power and, 63–66
songs of, xvi, 69–72
speeches for, 47, 48–54, 55–63, 68–69

Salty Badger, Sonora, 64
San Ildefonso Pueblo, 183
San Juan Pueblo, 181, 183, 184
San Miguel, Ariz., 46, 64
Sandia Crest, N.M., 182
Santa Clara Pueblo, 183
Santa Rosa, Ariz., 44, 45–46, 47, 48, 53, 55–56, 60, 64, 68
Saskatchewan River, 92
Saul, King, 82
Scatalogical rites, 112
Science, compared with mythology, 191
Scott, Captain H. L., 87
Scratching stick, 63, 66, 73
songs, 69–72
Scriptures, Hebrew, 219
Sea, power of, 63–66
Sea Spirit, xvii, 13–19
Seeing and curing, 3–118
"crying for a vision" ritual, 20–41
Ghost dance doctrine, xv, xviii, 75–95
by medicine men, xii, 3–12, 76, 78, 89, 105, 112–113, 180, 205, 215
Peyote rite, xiv, xv, xx, 96–104, 236–237
sacred clowns, xvii, 105–118
by shaman, xiii, xiv, xv, xviii–xix, xxii, 13–19, 65, 66, 72, 108–109, 112, 139–140, 192, 193–198, 201–204, 208, 209, 210, 212, 213, 214, 234, 235
"Self and Its Behavioral Environment, The" (Hallowell), 142
Seneca Indians, xii
Seri Indians, 64
Seven Arrows (Storm), xxii
Sexual displays, 113–115
Sexual relations, 114, 256
Sha'lako (ceremony), 114
Shamans and shamanism, xiii, xiv, xv, xviii–xix, xxii, 65, 66, 67, 72, 108–109, 112, 139–140, 208, 209, 210, 212, 213, 214, 234, 235
of Beaver Indians, 201–204
cosmic structure, 192, 193–198, 203
invocation for, 217–218
journey to the Sea Spirit, 13–19
songs of, 15, 201–203
and totemic symbols, 193–198, 201, 202, 204

Sharp Mountain, 46, 54
Shimmering Mountain, N.M., 181
Shipaapuli'ma (home of medicine societies), 268
Short Bull (religious leader), 91–92
Shoshoni Indians, 94
  Ghost dance doctrine of, 88, 95
Sicun, concept of, 213–215
Sign language, 76
Silversmithing, 250, 266
Sioux Indians, xiii, xiv, xv, xvii, xviii, 76, 105, 106, 108, 169
  Ghost dance doctrine of, 89–95
  see also Dakota Indians; Lakota Indians; Oglala Sioux
Sioux language, 101
Sipofene (primordial home), 179
Sitting Bull, 88, 89
Skan, concept of, 208–213
Slotkin, J. S., xx, 96–104
"Societies for the Completion of the Road" (medicine societies), 259–260, 268
Society of the Mystic Animals, xix
Söderblom, Archbishop N., 243–244
Songs, xvi, 5, 66, 214, 215
  in lamenting, 29, 30, 40
  of medicine men, 7–10
  of Peyote rite, 97–98, 101–102
  of salt pilgrims, xvi, 69–72
  of shamans, 15, 201–203
Sorcerers, 160, 162, 163, 164, 166, 170
  see also Witches and witchcraft
Space, Hopi view of, 121–123, 127–129
Speaking in tongues, 101
Speeches, for salt pilgrimage, 47, 48–54, 55–63, 68–69
Spotted Eagle (*Wanbli Galeshka*), 21, 26, 30, 33, 37
Standing Rock agency, 89
Starting Song (Peyote rite), 97, 98
Starvation, 14, 18, 270
Stephen, Alexander, 114, 115
Steward, Julian, 114
Stone Man Mountain, N.M., 182
Storm, Hyemeyohsts, xxii
Sun, in mythology, 151–152, 153
Sun-Coyote (deity), 224–225
Sun dance, 76, 208
Sun Father (deity), 265, 268, 270
Swanassu, see Medicine men
Sweat-bath, 89

Sword (shaman), 205–208, 213–214, 217–218

Takánakapsâluk (Sea Spirit), xvii, 13–19
  powers of, 13–14
Talayesva, Don, xiv
Technology, Indian, xi
Tedlock, Barbara, 105–118
Tedlock, Dennis, 248–271
Temlarham, B.C., 4
Tens, Isaac, xv, xvii, xviii, 3–12
Tens, Mary, 11
Tens, Philip, 11
Tewa Pueblos, xiv, 114
  world view of, 179–189
Tewa World, The (Ortiz), 188
Texas, 96, 227
Thompson, Stith, 159
Thompson River Indians, 225
Thunder Bird (*pinési*), 154–158
Time
  Hopi view of, 123–127
  Zuñi view of, 264–265
Tirawa (deity), xvii, 229–232, 233
Tlalocs (rain gods), 53
Tobacco, xiii, xv, 23, 25, 26, 27, 49, 113, 169–170, 233, 234
  sacramental meaning of, xi–xii
Tortillas, 45
Totemism and shamanism, 190–204
Touch, healing by, 87
Trance, 3–4, 88, 93, 140
Truchas Peak, N.M., 182
Tsigwee (medicine man), 8
Turtle Mountain, N.M., 181
Tyon (shaman), 215–216

Uitoto Indians, 227–229, 232, 233
Unalit Eskimo, 107
Underhill, Ruth, 42–74
Universe, Hopi view of, 121–129
Ute Indians, 94
Uwanam Aashiwani (Rainmaker Priests), 261, 269–270

Velarde, Luis, 42
Visions, 9
  of Beaver Indians, 198–201, 203
  in Peyote rite, 102
  see also Lamenting; Seeing and curing
Vitalistic beliefs, 123
Vulva, 115

Wábano ceremony, 149
Wakan, concept of, xviii, 169, 205–207
Wakan-Tanka (deity), xvii, 21, 22, 24, 25, 26, 28–29, 30–31, 32, 34, 35, 36, 38, 39, 40, 207, 208, 210–211, 234–236
Walapai Indians, 87–88
Walker, J. R., 205–218, 234, 235
Walker Lake, Nev., 86
Wanbli Galeshka (Spotted Eagle), 21, 26, 30, 33, 37
War Department, U.S., 85
Waralsawal (attendant), 5
Warm clowns (*k'ossa*), 180
Washington, D.C., 79, 80
Washo Indians, 87
Water drum, 98
Waterbird (Peyote rite), xv, 97, 102
Weaning, 198–199
Weltanschauung (description of universe), 122
White Buffalo, 94
Whorf, Benjamin Lee, 121–129, 143
Wichasha wakan (holy man), 20–21, 206
Wichita Indians, 88, 226–227
Winnebago Indians, xvii–xviii, xix, 101, 169
    monotheism among, 229, 232–234, 236–237, 238, 241
Winnebago language, 101–102, 237
Winship, George P., 184
Wintu (Wintun) Indians, xiv, 108, 225–226
Wintu language, 130–140
    categories of, 131
    concept of self and, 134
    expressing relationships in, 137–138

expression of number in, 131–133
external form in word formation, 136–137
verbs in, 134–136
view of reality in, 139–140
Wisconsin, xix, 229, 232
Witches and witchcraft, 257–258, 264, 266–267
    see also Sorcerers
Wolf clan, 5
World, Indian view of, 119–271
    of death, xv, 248–271
    Hopi metaphysics, 121–129
    monotheism in, 219–247
    Oglala metaphysics, 205–218
    Ojibwa ontology and behavior, 141–178
    shamanism and totemism, 190–204
    of the Tewa, 179–189
    Wintu thought, 130–140
Wounded Knee, battle of, 78, 93
Wovoka (religious leader), 75, 77, 79, 82, 86, 94
Wyoming, 77, 88, 94

Yagesatï (deity), xvii, 193, 194, 196, 197, 198, 202
Yellow Legs (chief), 148
Yellow vomit (disease), 72–73
Yomepa ceremony, 112
Yuki Indians, 114
Yukon Indians, 107
Yuma Indians, 64

Zen Buddhism, 115
Zia Pueblo, 110–111
Zuñi Pueblo, xiv, xv, xvii, xviii, xxii, 108, 109, 112, 113, 114
    view of death, 248–271

DENNIS TEDLOCK was raised in New Mexico, where he was a pupil of the Cochiti artist Joe Herrera and took a B.A. at the University of New Mexico. After study among the Navajo, Koasati, and Zuni, he received a Ph.D. in anthropology from Tulane in 1968. He has taught at Berkeley, Wesleyan, The New School, and Yale, and currently holds a University Professorship at Boston University. His first book was *Finding the Center: Narrative Poetry of the Zuni Indians* (Dial).

BARBARA TEDLOCK was raised in Washington, D.C., where she studied painting at the Corcoran Gallery and drama at the Arena Stage. Later she took her B.A. at the University of California at Berkeley and studied painting at the Art Students League in New York. In 1973 she received an M.A. in anthropology from Wesleyan for her work on Zuni music. Currently she is studying for the Ph.D. in anthropology at the State University of New York at Albany.